Detroit Burning

ALSO BY TOBIN T. BUHK

American Hangman: A Biography of Amos Lunt, the Executioner of San Quentin (McFarland, 2022)

The Lonely Hearts Killers: The Bloody Passions of Martha Beck and Raymond Fernandez (Exposit, 2020)

Pardonable Matricide: Robert Irving Latimer, from Michigan's "Most Dangerous Inmate" to Free Man (Exposit, 2019)

Detroit Burning
The Race Riots of 1863

TOBIN T. BUHK

Exposit

Jefferson, North Carolina

ISBN (print) 978-1-4766-9216-6
ISBN (ebook) 978-1-4766-5201-6

LIBRARY OF CONGRESS AND BRITISH LIBRARY
CATALOGUING DATA ARE AVAILABLE

© 2024 Tobin T. Buhk. All rights reserved

No part of this book may be reproduced or transmitted in any form or by any means, electronic or mechanical, including photocopying or recording, or by any information storage and retrieval system, without permission in writing from the publisher.

Front cover image: Birds-eye view showing about three miles square of the central portion of the city of Detroit, Michigan, 1800s (Library of Congress); other elements © Shutterstock

Printed in the United States of America

Exposit is an imprint of McFarland & Company, Inc., Publishers

Exposit

Box 611, Jefferson, North Carolina 28640
www.expositbooks.com

Table of Contents

Acknowledgments — vii
Preface: The Great Riot — 1
Introduction — 3
Major Figures in the Detroit Riot of 1863 — 8
Timeline — 11

Part 1—Kindling (February 27, 1863) — 13
  1. The Past as Prologue (1833–1863) — 15
  2. Behind Closed Doors: Law and Order in Detroit, c. 1863 — 36

Part 2—Torch (Monday, March 2–Friday, March 6, 1863) — 59
  3. "The Faulkner Outrage" (Monday, March 2–Wednesday, March 4, 1863) — 61
  4. The Case for the Prosecution (Thursday, March 5, 1863) — 75
  5. The Case for the Defense (Friday, March 6, 1863) — 84

Part 3—Inferno (Friday, March 6, 1863) — 91
  6. Blaze (Friday Afternoon, March 6, 1863) — 95
  7. Wildfire (Friday Afternoon, March 6, 1863) — 102
  8. Detroit Is Burning (Friday Night, March 6, 1863) — 113

Part 4—Ashes (Saturday, March 7–May 1863) — 125
  9. Cinders (Saturday, March 7, 1863) — 127
  10. Sermons (Sunday, March 8, 1863) — 145
  11. Inquest (Saturday, March 7–Tuesday, March 24, 1863) — 150

12. Witnesses (Monday, March 9–Tuesday, March 24, 1863)	160
13. Black, White, and Sepia (March 1863)	167
14. Whitewash: The Trials of the Rioters (April–May 1863)	176

Part 5—Rebuilding — 187

15. Residual Effects and Legacy	189
16. Lessons: The Children's Crusade	204
Epilogue	219
Appendix 1: "The Riot"	225
Appendix 2: Kids in the Big House, Juveniles in the Detroit House of Correction	228
Appendix 3: The Rev. Sylvan S. Hunting's Sermon of March 15, 1863	233
Appendix 4: Questions for Study and Contemplation	236
Chapter Notes	237
Bibliography	259
Index	261

Acknowledgments

The author would like to thank the staffs of the Burton Historical Collection, the Archives of Michigan, and the Library of Michigan for their gracious assistance in locating source material.

Reaching so far back in history and shining a flashlight into the deepest and darkest recesses is a challenging proposition, one not without the risk of an occasional error of fact. While every effort has been made to avoid them, any such errors are the author's and the author's alone.

Preface:
The Great Riot

By March 1863, the conflict that many assumed would last weeks had lasted almost three years. Several epic battles left cornfields littered with bodies. More than 23,000 fell during the Battle of Shiloh the previous April; 22,000 during the Second Battle of Bull Run in August 1862; 23,000 less than a month later at Antietam; and almost 18,000 at Fredericksburg in December 1862.

Just about everyone in Michigan knew someone who fell during these bloody clashes. During the conflict, Michigan would outfit dozens of regiments, many suffering high casualty rates. The 1st Michigan Infantry, for example, lost more than a third of its number to death, disease, or wounds. White limestone headstones and one-legged soldiers hobbling around the streets of Detroit presented powerful reminders of the war's toll.

Anti-war angst went beyond the loss of loved ones. Just a river away from Canada, Detroit became a waypoint for draft-dodgers and deserters, and some Detroiters sympathized with the Knights of the Golden Circle, a secret organization devoted to creating a pro-slavery state. The city's Copperheads—Democrats who favored a peace treaty with the Confederacy—added to these anti-war voices. They clashed with the city's Republicans who tended to see the war as a necessary evil in settling the longstanding arguments over slavery and states' rights.

Rumors of a new draft bill, which had circulated in Detroit throughout February, became fact when news of the Conscription Act hit the streets on March 5, 1863. The law angered war-weary and anti-war Detroiters, whose hostility became tangible on the afternoon of March 6, 1863, when William Faulkner left city hall.[1]

• • • •

"I deem your crime the very worst of which a human being can be guilty, and one for which there can hardly be sufficient punishment, and do, therefore, give you the full sentence of the law: to remain in the State Prison, at Jackson, during the remainder of your natural life."[2]

With these words, Wayne County recorder's court judge Benjamin Franklin Hawkins Witherell brought the gavel down on the case of the *People v. William Faulkner*, sending the now-convicted rapist to the state prison. The "remainder" of Faulkner's "natural life" would amount to mere minutes if the mob surrounding the courthouse managed to nab him before the sheriff's deputies could deliver him to the fortress-like county jail complex.

On Friday afternoon, March 6, 1863, William Faulkner emerged from the courthouse as the perpetrator of the "Faulkner Outrage" and the most hated man in Detroit. As soon as the crowd saw his silhouette materialize in the doorway, they surged forward, formed an arc around him and the deputies chosen to march him to the county jail, and began to assail him with insults.

Afraid that the crowd would attempt to usurp Witherell's authority and take the prisoner to a nearby tree for a little frontier justice, Acting Sheriff Francis X. Cicotte called in the troops. The provost guard arrived a few minutes later, and the trio of sheriff's deputies—John Esser, John Fenn, and James Hepburn—pushed Faulkner through the crowd and began the march north.

When Faulkner stepped out of the courtroom that afternoon, he stepped into history as the catalyst for the great riot of 1863. Although he couldn't have realized it at the time, he had become a pawn in a much larger conflict involving a complex combination of political and social factors.

Introduction

The cinematography of the Civil War, as told through the lens of high school history textbooks, Hollywood epics, television documentaries, and revisionist historians, too often relies on wide-angle and panning shots which can result in a simplified view of a complex series of unfortunate events. From this distance, the actors are reduced to silhouettes. The camera is too far away to really see real people. The blemishes, scars, moles, and wrinkles of historical personages are obscured by the directors, the make-up artists, and the stagehands of history. The devices of Hollywood magic, when applied to historical events, often lead to a misleading vision of history. This is particularly true of everyday folks, who often end up depicted as extras, as animatic yet indistinct dots in the background. This has been the case with the real participants in the Detroit riot.

The Detroit riot of 1863 was a single frame in the epic story of Civil War–era America. Often relegated to a mere blurb in social histories, the event is often described as a draft riot. If true, then it was only one of several that occurred in northern cities in 1863 and not by a long shot the biggest or the worst (that dubious distinction belongs to the riots that tore New York apart at the seams in July 1863). Once again, the story is simplified when viewed from a distance: working-class white Detroiters, forced by the new draft law (or Conscription Act) to fight to free slaves, reacted by attacking the city's Black population.

Bringing the camera closer, using a series of close-up shots on the people involved, reveals a much more complex interplay of social and political factors underlying the event. The draft law was a factor but only one of several and probably not the most significant one. Writers who have examined the riot often overlook the fact that Wayne County had already reached its quota of soldiers, so none of the rioters were in jeopardy of conscription.

Much of what follows is the result of an attempt to bring the camera closer, to capture the event with a series of close-ups that reveal how and why Detroit nearly self-immolated on Friday, March 6, 1863; to identity, if possible, the responsible parties; and to single out the heroes and the villains.

The result is history without the cheesecloth or makeup. It isn't pretty. In fact, one might say it's ugly. Very, very ugly.

Why focus on something so revolting? Turning a blind eye to the past is to ignore the lessons that it can teach and possibly become the victim of a repeated event. This is a story from the past but an object lesson for the future.

And why focus the camera on the Detroit riot? It is a vital scene in the history of the city and in a broader context the history of Michigan, but at the same time, this single frame represents a microcosm of the political and social landscape of the United States at the apex of one of the country's defining moments.

Bringing the camera closer to events that occurred more than 150 years ago is easier said than done. The treatment of the riot in early Detroit histories is mostly anecdotal. Even Clarence Burton's multivolume biography of Detroit devotes less than a page to this watershed moment in the history of the metropolis.

A Thrilling Narrative, published in 1863, is the lone contemporary work other than newspapers to cover the riot. The 24-page pamphlet is really more of a compilation of voices than a history; it contains a patchwork of testimony taken from coroner's inquests and excerpts of newspaper reports (exclusively from the *Advertiser and Tribune*; the *Detroit Free Press* is not represented) along with some editorials and a few interviews with eyewitnesses. These interviews, not published anywhere else, make it a unique resource. This work of unknown authorship serves as a sort of Ur–*Hamlet* for historians and sociologists investigating race relations of this era.

The pamphlet features "THE RIOT," a poem by Benjamin Cutler Clark, Sr. The 17 stanzas encapsulate the social and political factors behind the tragic event from the perspective of a contemporary writer. Penned by an African American, it also captures the viewpoint of a marginalized community whose voices were often heard only through the filter of newspaper editors. The poem is featured throughout this work to represent those unheard voices.

The city's two major newspapers, the *Advertiser and Tribune* and the *Free Press*, provide invaluable insight into Civil War–era Detroit, but the modern concept of journalistic ethics did not exist at the time. Their feuding editors fought duels not with sabers or pistols but with words, which led to news that was anything but unbiased. Nonetheless, this is a key facet of the story.

When it came to news of the riot, the *Free Press* would become the voice most often heard outside of Detroit. *Advertiser and Tribune* editors explained why the rival paper became the preeminent source on the riot. "The reason why the *Free Press* account of the riot was more extensively copied than that of the *Advertiser and Tribune*, is simply that the *Free Press* exchange list is chiefly made up of its morning edition, whilst the *Advertiser and Tribune* list is from the afternoon edition, principally, and the *Free Press* containing ostensibly a later account [of the riot] was used."[1] Since the riot took place after the afternoon edition of the *Advertiser and Tribune* went to press and its "exchange list" primarily consisted of its afternoon edition, the *Free Press* account became the most widely "copied" or re-reported.

In addition, of the two newspapers, the *Free Press* has been by far the more utilized by historians, in part because it covered the riot and aftermath more extensively than the rival paper and in part because the pages of the *Free Press* from the Civil War era are easier to access. Issues from 1863 have been digitized, which makes keyword searches possible, and are available in multiple places, whereas *Advertiser and Tribune* issues from the same year remain tucked away in rolls of microfilm. Without the availability of keyword searches, finding relevant *Advertiser and Tribune* articles involves a time-consuming process of threading the microfilm reader with a brittle strand of film and combing through columns of text. As a result, researchers and students of history too often see only part of the story: the part filtered through the Democratic *Free Press*. The Republican viewpoint remains buried in archives.

A big part of the story—one that has been overlooked or possibly even ignored by historians—can be found in a cardboard box in the Archives of Michigan in Lansing. About the size of a copy-paper box, it contains the trial records of Detroit's recorder's court from the year 1863.

Each file is enclosed in an outer wrapper noting the date, docket number, and name of the case. The trial records sometimes contain nothing more than the indictment, but sometimes they also include trial testimony scribed in the shaky hand of the court clerk. The black ink has faded to brown, and the paper is brittle, flaking, and the color of Dijon mustard, but nevertheless these documents have aged well and don't look a day over 160.

They contain the largely unwritten, untold story of law and order in Detroit, including who may have done what during the riot. Many of these case files contain eyewitness testimony that has not been heard since the clerk recorded it.

These untold stories include the tragic sagas of teenaged prostitutes, chicken thieves, murderers, and arsonists. To peruse the files is to walk the mean streets of Detroit in 1863. They contain a nearly-complete picture of crime in the metropolis from that year.

They should also include the story of one very infamous individual whose "outrage" provided the spark that ignited Detroit's Third Ward, except his story is mysteriously absent from the collection. Case files 431 and 432, *The People v. William Faulkner*, are missing. And cross-referencing each file with the corresponding entries in the recorder's court docket indicate that they are the only two missing from the entire year. A visual inspection of each file from 1863 failed to turn up the lost documents, so they were not accidentally tucked into the wrong wrapper, either.

They're simply gone, so any testimony recorded during the trial is lost to history.

As a result, the story of the "Faulkner Outrage" exists only in highly-biased newspaper coverage, which means that only a part of Faulkner's story is told. The missing part involves allegations of a conspiracy to railroad an innocent man and an unfair trial that led to an unjust verdict. Both the judge and prosecutor later criticized the trial as a miscarriage of justice, but any evidence in the trial record has apparently gone into the memory hole. It is possible that the files were pulled when the governor later reviewed the case; it is equally possible that someone involved with the case took the files as a memento of a watershed moment in Detroit history; it is also conceivable that a sticky-fingered researcher took them

Introduction 7

home at some point. For many years--long before they were handed over to the State Archives—these records were kept in an unsecured room on the sixth floor of the court building and accessible to anyone.

In any event, they're gone. If they exist, they likely contain something that indicates why Judge Witherell condemned the trial over which he presided. Perhaps someday these missing files will emerge from the historical ether.

• • • •

Before delving into the world of Detroit circa 1863, a brief note about language. This work draws from the voices of people whose experiences have been preserved in diaries, letters, trial transcripts, and newspaper articles. These voices are presented without alteration, modification, expurgation, or exaggeration. Their word choice is unaltered, and many of their expressions would be considered highly offensive and inappropriate today. The author neither condones nor promotes such language and presents it only as part of the historical record.

Word choice is a vital element of the story, particularly in determining the bias of a particular newspaper account. Since the *Free Press* stood accused (by the *Advertiser and Tribune*) of fomenting racial unrest with its highly-inflammatory reporting in the weeks and months leading up to the riot, a close examination of the words used by their journalists becomes necessary.

In 1863, several descriptors were used to describe African Americans: "black," "colored," "darky," "negro," "nigger," "Son of Ham," and others.

Yet these words were not used interchangeably, particularly in the *Free Press*. While both the *Advertiser and Tribune* and the *Free Press* used "black," "colored" and "negro" as generic and seemingly inoffensive terms to describe people of color, *Free Press* writers also employed the terms "darky" and "nigger" (and a few others) when they wanted to ridicule the city's Black population. Because these terms tend to show up only in reports that belittle, mock, ridicule, and deride, it is evident that some journalists of the era weaponized the "n-word" and used it to attack rather than to categorize or describe.

As offensive as all of this language may be to modern readers, it is an important part of this story. This is history without the makeup.

Major Figures in the Detroit Riot of 1863

A note about birthdays: Not until 1867 did the State of Michigan require cities and towns to compile lists of births, deaths, and marriages, leaving church baptismal records as the primary source for information about births predating 1867. Court records, military service records, and newspaper obituaries can be used to pinpoint birthdates, but obituaries can be hit or miss depending on whether the deceased was a prominent personage.

Tracking down birthdates of the alleged rioters posed particular problems. Many immigrated from European countries, and contemporary newspapers as well as court clerks tended to anglicize German surnames, which often resulted in spelling variances. Newspaper reports seldom cited specific ages, instead using descriptive terms such as "young boy." In some instances, recorder's court trial records provide approximate ages, but this is the exception rather than the rule. As a result of these factors, finding exact ages became a real feat of historical detective work and in most cases involved cross-referencing entries in the 1850, 1860 and 1870 federal censuses.

The Law

William Champ, 45, fire marshal
John Logan Chipman, 33, defense attorney
Francis X. Cicotte, 51, Wayne County undersheriff
Peter Fralick, 53, Wayne County sheriff
David M. Freeman, 44, Wayne County deputy sheriff and Third Ward constable

Major Figures in the Detroit Riot of 1863

James Knox Gavin, 29, Wayne County prosecuting attorney
Minot T. Lane, 55, justice of the peace and police court judge
Dennis K. Sullivan, 32, Wayne County deputy sheriff and 7th Ward constable
Benjamin Franklin Hawkins Witherell, 66, recorder's court judge

The Principals in the Faulkner Case

William (Thomas) Faulkner, 42, alleged perpetrator of "the Faulkner Outrage"
Mary Brown, 10, alleged victim of William Faulkner
Ellen Hoover, 11, alleged victim of William Faulkner
Rosa Brown, 38, aunt and adopted mother of Mary Brown

The Soldier

John Van Stan, 38, 2nd lieutenant, 14th Regiment Michigan Infantry

The Rioters

Robert Carey, 14, accused of smashing windows as the mob moved down Beaubien Street
William Carlow, 21, accused of looting and burning Benjamin Singleton's residence
Francis Carr, 19, accused of looting during the riot
Edward Crosby, age unknown, shot in the face during the assault on Whitney Reynolds' house
William Crosby, age unknown, accused of smashing furniture
John H. Davis, age unknown, identified as the rioter who threw stones at Lewis Pierce
Peter Doran, 14, eyewitnesses who saw Davis throwing rocks at Faulkner's escort
Antoine Downer, age unknown, seen assaulting Joshua Boyd and Louis Houston
Timothy Drummond, 19, identified as one of Joshua Boyd's and Louis Houston's assailants
Cornelius Dwyer, 16, threw stones at Faulkner and later seen smashing windows on Beaubien

Brian (Bernard) Groghan, age unknown, accused of disrupting fire service during the riot

Charles Hall, 22, accused of looting and burning Benjamin Singleton's residence

Jerry Hanifan, age unknown, seen throwing rocks at the Whitney Reynolds residence

Michael Hider (Heider), 17, accused of looting during the riot

John "Conrad" Kalb, age unknown, accused of attacking Joshua Boyd

Alexandre Lefevre, 19–20, accused of disrupting fire engines during the riot

Andrew Manning, age unknown, identified as one of the assailants at Whitney Reynolds' house

John Miller, 15–16, according to an eyewitness, chased down and beat an unidentified Black boy

William Naylor (Nailor), 17, charged with destroying the "dwelling house" of Benjamin Singleton

James Robinson, 17, heard to yell, "Hurry, and bring in the coals"

Cyrus Sleker, age unknown, seen throwing stones at Whitney Reynolds' house

Peter Smith, 15–16, accused of inciting the mob with statements like "Let's give them hell"

Third Ward Residents / Eyewitnesses

Louisa Bonn, 20, Whitney Reynolds' daughter

Parker Bonn, 28, Louisa's husband

Joshua Boyd, age unknown, employee of Whitney Reynolds

Thomas Buckner, age unknown, Third Ward resident

Ephraim "the Prophet" Clark, 63, sexton of the AME Church

Marcus Dale, 31, employee of Whitney Reynolds

Louis Houston, age unknown, employee of Whitney Reynolds

Solomon Houston, age unknown, employee of Whitney Reynolds

Lewis Pierce, age unknown, occupant of Whitney Reynolds' house on March 6, 1863

Sarah Reynolds, 43, wife of Whitney Reynolds

Whitney Reynolds, 47, owner of the cooper shop at 132 Beaubien

Timeline

Wednesday, March 4, 1863	William Faulkner arraigned in recorder's court. He pleads "not guilty."
Thursday, March 5, 1863	Trial of William Faulkner commences, with J. Knox Gavin for the people, J. Logan Chipman for the defense (concludes March 6).
Friday, March 6, 1863	"The Great Riot" (see the beginning of Part 3, "Inferno," for a detailed breakdown of events).
Saturday, March 7, 1863	Fearing for Faulkner's safety, authorities put him on a train for Jackson in the early hours of the morning.
	Coroner's inquest into death of Charles Langer commences (concludes Monday, March 16).
Tuesday, March 10, 1863	Joshua Boyd dies at St. Mary's Hospital.
Wednesday, March 11, 1863	Coroner's inquest into the death of Joshua Boyd commences.
Friday, March 13, 1863	Coroner's inquest into the death of Charles Langer concludes at soldiers' barracks.
Monday, March 23–Tuesday, March 24, 1863	Examination of 21 rioters occurs in police court; Bernard Groghan escapes.
Wednesday, April 1, 1863	Fire Marshal Champ releases his report detailing damage caused during the riot.
Thursday, April 9, 1863	Francis Carr and Michael Hider plead guilty to larceny; Judge Witherell sentences them to six months each in the House of Correction.
Monday, April 13–Thursday, April 17, 1863	Trials of Hall, Naylor, Crosby, and Davis for "Beginning to destroy and pull down a dwelling house" take place in recorder's court.
Wednesday, April 16, 1863	Trial of John "Conrad" Kalb for assault with intent to kill takes place in recorder's court.
Wednesday, April 29, 1863	Bernard Groghan writes a letter to the *Free Press*.

Timeline

Thursday, May 21, 1863	Justice Lane sentences Mary Brown and Ellen Hoover to 90 days in the Detroit House of Correction for larceny.
Tuesday, May 26–Saturday, May 30, 1863	Fourteen defendants, including Crosby, Naylor, and Hall, tried for "riot" in recorder's court.
Saturday, May 30, 1863	Judge Witherell sentences Carr and Hider to six months in the Detroit House of Correction for theft during the riot.
Tuesday, February 28, 1865	The Metropolitan Police Act passes in the Michigan state legislature.
Monday, May 15, 1865	The first group of officers from the newly-established Detroit Police Department begin active duty.
Thursday, December 30, 1869	William Faulkner granted a pardon by Governor Henry P. Baldwin. He returns to Detroit and settles in the Third Ward, where he opens a vegetable stand.

PART 1

Kindling
(February 27, 1863)

1

The Past as Prologue (1833–1863)

> 'Twas in Detroit city, the State of Michigan,
> Where mob law reigned rampant, disgraceful to man,
> In killing and beating both women and men,
> And sacking and burning beyond human ken.
> —From "The Riot" by Benjamin Cutler Clark, Sr.

Racial unrest was not a new phenomenon in Detroit in 1863.

In an 1870 article about the Faulkner case, a *Detroit Evening Post* writer characterized the city as a "powder magazine only needing a spark to produce an explosion."[1] William Faulkner provided that spark, but how did the streets of the Third Ward become lined with gunpowder in the first place? Prying up the cobblestones of pre–Civil War Detroit reveals an underlayment of disquietude rooted in deep-seeded racial attitudes stretching back to a time before Michigan became a state.[2] These attitudes are perhaps best illustrated by a few of the many entries in Detroit's lengthy chronology of racial unrest in the three decades leading up to the Civil War.

The first major incident took place in 1833, when sheriff's deputies arrested a Black couple who had escaped from slavery and planned to send them back to Kentucky.

In 1830, Thornton Blackburn and a fellow slave named Rutha escaped slavery in Louisville, Kentucky, and made their way north. They married and settled in Detroit, where they lived for three years in freedom until their former owner Thomas Coquilliard discovered their location. Coquilliard hired a slave catcher, who contacted Detroit authorities and requested the return of the runaway slaves.

The Blackburns were arrested and brought to court. Deemed

runaway slaves, they were ordered to the county jail pending transportation south. Reportedly, Sheriff John M. Wilson and his deputy Lemuel Goodell stood to earn $50 each when they delivered the couple to the docks, where they would board the *Ohio*. When asked if he worried about an attempt to wrench the prisoners from his grip, Wilson supposedly held up a bullwhip and bragged that he "could scare every nigger that would be there with this."[3]

The situation inflamed the city's Black residents, many of whom had escaped slavery and had made their home in the City of the Straits. An angry mob formed outside the courthouse, trailed the procession to the steps of the jail, and massed outside the front door.

Friends of the couple had no intention of allowing them to be sent down the river. They hatched an ingenious escape for Rutha. Two friends—Tabitha Lightfoot and Caroline French—came to visit her and remained in her cell until nightfall. Mrs. French swapped clothes with Rutha and agreed to remain in the cell while Mrs. Lightfoot escorted her out of the building. Before anyone realized what had happened, Rutha Blackburn had reached the other side of the Detroit River.

When Lemuel Goodell discovered that his $50 had walked out of the jail in the clothes of Mrs. French, he marched to the Steamboat Hotel and confronted Madison Lightfoot, husband of Rutha's escort to Canada, and George French, husband of the woman now occupying Rutha's cell in the county jail.

French demanded his wife's immediate release, but by helping to spring Rutha Blackburn from the Wayne County jail, Mrs. French put herself in a precarious situation. Thomas Coquilliard wanted to bring Mrs. French back to Kentucky to take Rutha's place. He even planned to exhibit French as the infamous "hell-cat" from Michigan and conduct a public auction, but French avoided this horrific fate when she fled Detroit and joined Rutha across the river.

Meanwhile, Thornton Blackburn awaited deportation, but incensed citizens did not plan to let him go without a fight. Another angry mob formed outside the jail, where a carriage waited to take Blackburn to the steamship *Ohio* for his journey south.

Sensing a possible violent confrontation, Sheriff Wilson addressed the mob, but his words fell on deaf ears. Blackburn, who knew many in the crowd, suggested that he might have a better chance and asked

1. The Past as Prologue (1833–1863)

Wilson if he could speak. Wilson acquiesced, and Deputy Goodell escorted Blackburn to the jailhouse steps. From the top step, Blackburn dug into his right pants pocket and pulled out a pistol, which he leveled at the shocked deputy. "Stand back, god damn you, or I will blow you through!"

Goodell ducked into the jail and slammed the door behind him, leaving Wilson surrounded by angry rioters armed with clubs, fence pickets, and stones wrapped in handkerchiefs. The sheriff managed to draw his pistol and squeeze off several shots before one of the rioters felled him with a stone. Having sustained a skull fracture, Wilson crumpled to the ground and lay motionless while protestors hijacked the carriage, drove Blackburn into the woods outside the city limits, and then secreted him across the river to freedom.

The incident triggered fear of widespread violence, and authorities called in the troops. A cavalry company patrolled the streets and rounded up every Black person they encountered.

Wilson survived the head wound (he died about a year later), but word spread throughout Detroit that he had succumbed to his injury. "The announcement was made at every corner," wrote a *Detroit Daily Post* journalist in a retrospective piece about racial unrest in Detroit, "that 'the Niggers have risen and the sheriff is killed.' Every colored man and woman found in the streets was arrested and lodged in the jail, which was crowded to the door."

News of Wilson's premature demise drifted east. Promptly arrested in Ontario, Thornton and Rutha became the subjects of an extradition debate. Canadian authorities mulled the possibility of sending the pair back to Detroit, and therefore back to slavery in Kentucky, but eventually released them when it became clear that Wilson hadn't died from his wounds.

Thornton and Rutha Blackburn eventually settled in Toronto, where Thornton became a successful entrepreneur. The man who barely escaped being sent down the river established the first taxicab business in the city. He achieved the ultimate revenge when he traveled to Louisville and "stole" his mother from Thomas Coquilliard.[4]

In the immediate aftermath of the "Blackburn riot," several Black Detroiters were arrested and sentenced to work on a chain gang and pay a fine. George French joined his wife in Canada. Madison Lightfoot, who stood accused of knowing who gave the pistol to Thornton Blackburn, spent three days behind bars, and his wife was fined $25 as the supposed ringleader of the escape gambit.

Racial tensions remained high for over a year. The Black community was blamed for attempting to destroy the jail, and white business owners refused to hire Black workers. A general exodus ensued as Black Detroiters sought refuge across the river in Windsor.

Detroit averted a major catastrophe, but the Blackburn incident had a chilling effect on the city's Black community. The City by the Straits became less of a destination than a waypoint, the border to freedom pushed east by fugitive slave catchers. A few years after the Blackburn incident, leading citizens formed the Detroit Anti-Slavery Society, a group organized to promote the abolitionist viewpoint. The society spawned similar movements, such as the Colored Vigilance Committee of Detroit, which played a major role in moving fugitive slaves into Canada on the Underground Railroad. The Fugitive Slave Act of 1850 further increased traffic across the river.

Another small-scale riot involving a fugitive slave erupted a few years after the Blackburn case. In 1838, a slave named Henry escaped from St. Louis and ended up in Detroit, where a slave catcher spotted him six months later. Arrested and hauled into court, Henry admitted that he had run away but surprised court-goers by expressing a desire to return to his master in St. Louis. Angry protestors lined the streets between city hall and the county jail and pelted Henry's armed escorts with bricks and paving stones. The guards responded by rushing the crowd with bayonets. In the ensuing struggle, at least one protestor was bayonetted and the city marshal was shot. The crowd, which consisted of both Black and white protestors, managed to free Henry, but he refused to run away a second time. He was rearrested and sent back to St. Louis.

The Blackburn and Henry cases indicated that, despite the best efforts of anti-slavery advocates, Detroit fell short of being a sanctuary city. These incidents also suggested that some strong-minded Detroiters had no qualms about circumventing the law when they perceived an injustice. In the case of Thornton and Rutha Blackburn, this meant delivering the fugitives not to but from the slavecatchers, which almost assured an armed confrontation with city constables, the city marshal, and the county sheriff. Faulkner would likewise become the subject of a rescue attempt but one with a much different goal than safe passage to Canada.

Despite these dangers, some escaped slaves decided to make a home in Detroit. The city's Black population rose to just over 600 in 1850 and to just over 1,400 in 1860. A majority of Detroit's "Free Colored" population resided primarily in the Third, Fourth, Sixth, and Seventh wards.[5]

These four wards, however, fell short of the Elysian fields many hoped to find north of the Mason-Dixon line.

Other incidents of racial unrest involved brothels that catered to Black and white clientele. Many of these establishments were clustered along the eastern margin of the city in the Tenth Ward, which was dominated by German immigrants who may have viewed the presence of Blacks as an unwanted invasion of their territory.[6]

Sometime during the afternoon of July 4, 1855, a melee broke out at a "dance hall" run by a Black man named Charles Lawrence. An unnamed German was severely injured, which led to a violent protest the next day. A mob pelted the establishment with stones before setting it on fire. Several people were injured during the fray, including a little German girl who, according to a *Free Press* reporter, was "struck on the head by a brickbat thrown by a negro" and who later died from her wounds.[7] The word "amalgamation" does not appear in the press coverage although the repeated use of the word "colored" to describe the proprietor and his clientele suggest that race was a major factor in the riot.

Such outbreaks of violence would dot the front pages of the *Free Press* throughout the 1850s. In 1856, the paper reported on "The Breaking Up of a Negro Den," which occurred in an unspecific location when "several persons assembled around a tenement occupied as a negro house of ill-fame, and, after ejecting the inmates, did such injury to the building—an inferior one—as to render it untenable."[8]

The attempts to break up brothels evolved from spontaneous acts to more premeditated and audacious attacks. During the summer of 1857, a mob of forty to fifty destroyed four Tenth Ward brothels. They began with a dance hall located on Croghan Street just past the railroad tracks that formed the line between the Seventh and Tenth wards. With the dance hall in flames, they sacked an establishment run by Charles Lawrence, who endured a similar attack two years earlier.

The nameless, identity-less, amorphous whirlwind of humanity set on the "inmates," which led to a violent affray. Then, they moved south to Congress Street, where they attacked another bordello, destroying everything in the house. During the three-hour orgy of violence, the mob destroyed six brothels, burning three to the ground. None of the rioters, however, were arrested or even named in the papers, but the *Free Press* identified them as "mostly, if not all, Germans."[9]

Later that summer, another mob of seventy-five to a hundred assailed a Tenth Ward bordello at the corner of St. Aubin and Atwater streets and a stone's throw from the river's edge. The mob surrounded the house, showered it with bricks and stones, and demolished everything inside. The ripped apart beds and smashed chairs. Then, they moved west, crossing the railroad (Detroit & Milwaukee Railway) tracks into the Seventh Ward, where they besieged another bordello on Orleans Street between Franklin Street and Jefferson Avenue.[10]

Third time was not a charm for dance hall proprietor Charles Lawrence. During the summer of 1858, another large mob, whom the *Free Press* identified as "German inhabitants of the vicinity," organized to remove "disorderly houses" in their neck of the woods. According to the after-action report on page one of the June 4, 1858, edition, "they targeted establishments inhabited by a conglomeration of negro and white outcasts," which included Charles Lawrence and William Turner.

To prevent a general melee, a contingent of law enforcement officers led by John Van Stan raced to the scene to find "260 Germans" surrounding Turner's house. To mollify the crowd, they went into the brothel and attempted to arrest the "inmates." During the ensuing scuffle, several residents of the house fled. Those who remained resisted, so Van Stan and his crew of four officers enlisted a few "Germans" to help them make the arrests. When the deputies and their prisoners left, the crowd burned the structure to the ground.

Turner and his entourage ended up in police court, where a reporter described them in terms that belied his feelings: "They were as motley and degraded a set as one would desire to see by way of a novelty. The men were all negroes of the degraded class, dirty, filthy, and ragged…. The women were about half white, and, with one or two exceptions, more dirty and disgusting than their male companions. One of the white women was a good looking girl of handsome features and black eyes, whose husband was numbered among the negroes in custody.... It is extremely difficult to image how such women could endure the contact of the company in which they were found, but of the truth of the fact there could be no doubt."[11]

After a few more riots in 1859, Tenth Ward residents had managed to destroy many of the brothels clustered along the railroad tracks, but they would soon realize that cleansing the city of "disorderly houses" was like shoveling sand pitchfork. After paying fines and serving brief stints behind bars, the bordello owners and their "inmates" simply relocated to other wards. Business was simply too good, and it would become even more brisk when the war began.

These Tenth Ward disturbances contain a few common denominators that provide vital backstory to riot of March 6, 1863, and how newspaper reporters presented it to their readers: certain groups of Detroiters would revert to mob justice if they felt it necessary to remove a perceived "evil" from their neighborhoods; these groups were identified as primarily German immigrants residing on the city's east side; and they identified the "evil" as bordellos in which Blacks and whites comingled.

• • • •

Detroit was a growing metropolis at the outbreak of the Civil War in 1861. The opening of the St. Mary's Canal in 1855 increased the flow of iron and copper into the city, which led to a spike in manufacturing and an increased need for workers. In the decade from 1850 to 1860, the population more than doubled to more than 45,000, making Detroit the union's eighteenth largest city in 1860.[12] This influx included German and Irish immigrants who had moved west from New York, Boston, and other Eastern cities as well as escaped slaves who had taken the Underground Railroad north. Many of these working-class Detroiters lived in the eastern portions of the city, in the Third, Fourth, Seventh, and Tenth wards.

The Third Ward would become the epicenter of the 1863 riot.

On a map, the Third Ward resembled an obelisk. The Detroit River formed the base of the densely-populated trapezoid; the Detroit &

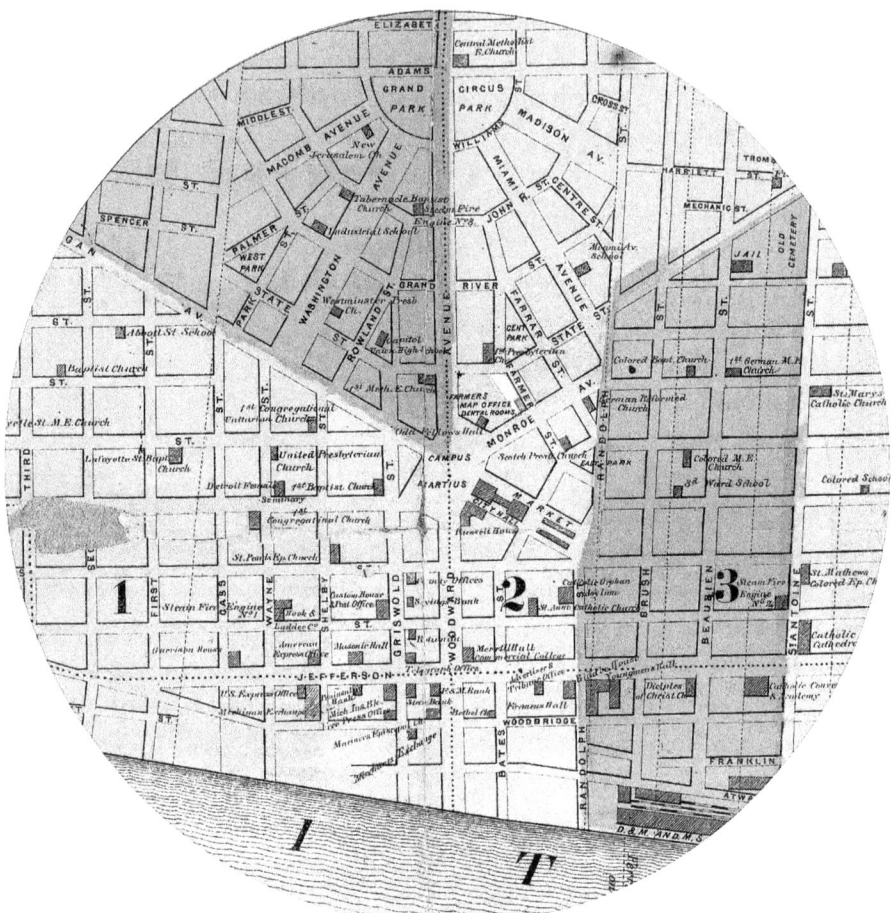

Detail from Silas Farmer's *Guide Map to the City of Detroit, 1863*. The edge of the circle represents a distance of half a mile from Campus Martius (New York Public Library).

Milwaukee Railway terminal, situated along the riverfront, meant a constant foot flow into the city, which gave rise to several bordellos on Atwater Street.

Randolph Street formed the Ward's western border. The city's markets sat just west of this line in the Second Ward, which made this one of the most trafficked areas in the city where merchants or "hucksters" from the Third Ward interacted with their customers.

The Wayne County jail stood at the northernmost point of the Third Ward. Situated on Beaubien between Gratiot and Clinton streets,

1. The Past as Prologue (1833–1863)

Bird's-eye view of the Wayne County jail complex. The sheriff's residence—the white façade in the foreground—stands in stark contrast to the stone cell blocks behind it. Just beyond the bricked-in yard is the city police court. Faulkner was hurried through an alley running behind the court building and into a back door of the jail complex (courtesy Burton Historical Collection, Detroit Public Library).

the jail complex also included a sheriff's residence and the city's police court. Running north to south, St. Antoine Street formed the Ward's eastern boundary and the dividing line between the Third and Fourth wards.

Inside this densely-populated trapezoid, Irish and German immigrants rubbed elbows with former slaves. The 1860 census provides a good snapshot of the diversity that characterized Detroit's Third Ward. Neighbors of Ephraim and Phoebe Clark, former slaves from Kentucky, included a livery stable operator from Ireland named Thomas Cox, a saloonkeeper from Germany named Henry Rush, and a "Jewish minister" from Germany named L. Adler.[13]

The Third Ward populace also included a number of indigents, many of them school-aged children, who lived threadbare, hand-

Detroit police court at the back of the county jail complex on the corner of Clinton and Paton streets. This image was taken sometime after 1870, when Paton Alley was renamed Paton Street by a June 16, 1870, city ordinance. The tall, forbidding brick wall (by this time painted white) behind the tiny courtroom is the yard of the Wayne County jail (courtesy Burton Historical Collection, Detroit Public Library).

to-mouth existences. At one time or another, many of these street toughs ended up in the county jail, which led to critical overcrowding until the opening of the Detroit House of Correction in 1861.

Desperation drove some of the girls, some as young as ten, into the oldest profession.

They joined a population of Third Ward sex workers who plied their trade in bedrooms or "cribs" atop saloons. Some, like thirteen-year-old Julia Davis, were lured by the promise of good money; others, like fourteen-year-old Sarah Higgins, were ensnared with narcotic-laced substances such as laudanum or alcohol (see Chapter 15).

A shadowy group of purveyors, such as the notorious madam Christine Thede, catered to a mixed group of clientele including sailors who brought iron ore from Upper Peninsula mines and soldiers garrisoned at Fort Wayne. Because the business was conducted in the shadows, and because many of the workers only remained for short periods of time, these characters become some of the most challenging to find in the historical record.

Catering to Black and white customers, however, virtually ensured posterity. These "amalgamation dens" were frequent targets of police raids, and because of a not-so-subtle political agenda, led to page-one articles in the *Free Press*. Take Mary Shepard, for example. She would have faded into historical obscurity if not for the fact that she did not discriminate among her paying clients. She became a press darling after police raided a brothel she operated out of a residence between Brush and Beaubien streets (see Chapter 15). These five minutes of infamy ensured the madam a degree of immortality; as the decades passed, her name passed from yellowed newspaper to rigid microfilm and today to jpg files.

The extent of prostitution in the Third Ward is perhaps most evident in the fact that one of the city's most infamous districts, Paton Alley (sometimes called "Paton's Alley"), was located a stone's throw away from the county jail between Beaubien and St. Antoine.

• • • •

In February 1863, Detroit had a split personality containing two separate yet related identities best represented by the city's primary news outlets: the *Advertiser and Tribune* and the *Free Press*. While Federal soldiers traded lead with rebels, editors and writers for the two newspapers waged a war with paper bullets.

The modern concept of journalistic integrity did not apply to mid–19th-century editors and reporters. They sensationalized and in some cases even fabricated news altogether. In 1862, for example, *Louisville Daily Journal* editor George Prentice created a bandit named Sue Mundy to confound and embarrass Union military leaders, who chased their tails trying to hunt down the fictional guerrilla in Kentucky.[14] Newspapermen also used their pages to promote political beliefs, which led to a war of words between the *Advertiser and Tribune* and the *Free Press*.

Paton Street, once the infamous Paton Alley, in a lantern slide taken sometime around 1870. The side of the police court can be seen in the left foreground. According to the March 7 *Free Press* account of the riot, Paton Alley was completely obliterated during the riot, possibly targeted because of "amalgamation dens." On Farmer's *Guide Map to the City of Detroit, 1863*, Paton Alley appears as an unnamed dotted line running vertically between the jail and the "Old Cemetery." On later maps, it appears as a named street (courtesy Burton Historical Collection, Detroit Public Library).

At the time, articles ran without bylines (editorials were sometimes signed "ed"), so determining who said what becomes a real feat of historical detective work. With a little legwork, however, it is possible to identify the men who yielded the épée pens in these dueling newspapers.

The *Advertiser and Tribune* was born with the merger of the *Daily Advertiser* and the *Tribune* in 1862. A board of directors led by Henry Barns and James E. Scripps managed the new conglomerate. In addition to Barns and Scripps, Detroit "historiographer" Silas Farmer

1. The Past as Prologue (1833–1863)

names seven individuals as "associated with 'The *Advertiser and Tribune*' either as proprietors or editors until 1877": Charles K. Backus, H.E. Baker, William M. Carleton, James F. Conover, Hiram Walker, Edward C. Walker, and Eber B. Ward.[15] All were ardent supporters of Abraham Lincoln and the Republican Party.

Early Detroit historians present conflicting information as to the editorial leadership of the newspaper in 1863. George Catlin names John E. Scripps as the editor, while Farmer describes Scripps as the business manager. According to Farmer, Henry Barns, the former editor of the *Tribune*, managed the editorial side of the business. A later news item names John F. Conover, also a former editor for the *Tribune*, as the sole "editorial writer" during the *Advertiser and Tribune*'s fifteen-year lifespan. It is logical to conclude that each of these three men had a hand in the content and tone of the paper's news.

A native of England, Scripps came to Detroit via Chicago in 1859. A few years later, he rose to the position of general manager of the *Daily Advertiser*. Farmer described Scripps as "inclined to liberality."[16]

Writing to correct an editorial that appeared in the *Advertiser and Tribune* in late March 1863, George C. Bates describes forty-eight-year-old Henry Barns as "one of the editors" and fingered him as the author of a piece that painted Bates as a freeloader who sponged off of a Republican senatorial candidate. The offending article was signed "*Advertiser & Tribune*." If indeed Barns authored this piece, then he likely authored some of the scathing editorials blaming the *Free Press* for fomenting the 1863 riot. A one-time postmaster, Barns played an active role in the city's Republican politics.[17]

Thirty-three-year-old James F. Conover came to Detroit a decade earlier as a lawyer, but he wandered into the newspaper business when he invested in the *Free Democrat*, which, oddly enough, was a Republican-leaning publication. After serving as secretary to Michigan Republican governor Kinsley S. Bingham, Conover returned to Detroit and with Bingham's help became one of the *Tribune*'s editors. When the *Tribune* later merged with the *Advertiser*, "he became sole editorial writer."[18] He and Barns disliked each other intensely, their feud stemming from a disagreement over the Senate candidacy of Zachariah Chandler. Barns eventually let Conover write a piece nominating Chandler, who went on to serve three terms in the U.S. Senate.

Another writer who played a prominent role in the production of the *Tribune* was Charles Kellogg Backus. A Princeton graduate, Backus came to Detroit in 1862 and took a position as reporter for the newly-merged *Advertiser and Tribune*. An 1894 *Free Press* article about Backus described his role: "From reporter he filled every place on the paper, among them legislative correspondent." The newspaper everyman was only nineteen years old in February 1863.[19]

These four men—Scripps, Barns, Conover, and Backus—created the *Advertiser and Tribune* in their own political and social image. They set the tone for news coverage in 1863 and did more than anyone else in blaming the rival paper for the riot.

Named the *Democratic Free Press and Daily Intelligencer* at its inception in 1831, the *Tribune*'s adversary went through several ownership changes in the years leading up to the war. In 1862, ownership passed to a triumvirate composed of Jacob Barns, C.H. Taylor, and Hiram Walker. Despite the black-and-white political differences between the two papers, two of the three *Free Press* owners had connections with *Advertiser and Tribune*: Barns was the brother of *Tribune* editor Henry Barns, and Hiram Walker owned an interest in both papers.

Editorial duties were the purview of William E. Quinby, who began as a legal reporter for the *Free Press* in 1860. According to an 1894 sketch of *Free Press* history, "By 1863 Mr. Quinby had become managing editor of the institution."[20] Quinby led a staff that included writer Henry Munson Utley, who later described Quinby as the paper's "city editor."[21]

These men were all avowed Democrats, which put them at odds with many of Lincoln's policies. They disagreed with his handling of the war and with the Emancipation Proclamation, which rebranded the war into a conflict over slavery rather than states' rights.

And they weren't sheepish about their beliefs. In a eulogy written about *Free Press* editor William E. Quinby in 1908, *Detroit Times* correspondent James Shermerhorn identified "commercial and impersonal journalism" as the cause of Quinby's death. "So when that strange creature of modernity—commercial and impersonal journalism—claimed his bride of the years [the *Free Press*]," Shermerhorn wrote, "his life went out, also."[22]

Shermerhorn insinuates that Quinby had a narcissistic bent and used the pages of the *Free Press* to promote his social and political beliefs. These beliefs came into full display after the riot, when the rival editors indicted *Free Press* personnel on several counts.

The world of journalism in Civil War–era Detroit was a small one, and even the bitterest of rivals sometimes crossed paths. On one such occasion in January 1863, *Free Press* impresario Jacob Barns made a prediction: within six months, a mob would reduce Detroit to ashes.

In the wake of the riot, the editors of the *Advertiser and Tribune*, a group that probably included Jacob Barns' brother Henry, blamed the *Free Press* for helping to make that prediction come true. "We have charged that the riot on Friday was a *Free Press* riot, and endeavored to show by what process it had educated the ignorant mob up to the necessary ferocity. Its process has been gradual but sure, permeating every department of the paper—news, local and editorial—displaying a hate and desperation that have provoked before now serious comment from sober-minded citizens."

According to a lengthy editorial in the *Advertiser and Tribune* of March 10, 1863, this "gradual but sure" process of educating "the ignorant mob up to the necessary ferocity" against Blacks intensified in the weeks leading up to the riot.[23]

This "education" involved several "lessons" designed to discourage racial equality, including the use of scare tactics. An editorial in the December 2, 1862, edition suggested that freed Blacks would siphon from a finite pool of resources to the detriment of the white community. "They who invite the negro, must maintain the negro … no cruelty can be greater than to give the blacks even freedom to starve, except the cruelty of forcing white men to starve in order to give the blacks freedom."

This theme would continue into the new year. In a January 1 piece, freed slaves were depicted as an economic burden. "The North cannot stagger on in this struggle under the crushing load of four millions of emancipated negroes, yet these are the conditions on which, under present auspice, peace must be attained or war carried on. Who hopes for success under them?"

A few days later, the *Free Press* postulated that the idea "niggers are 'American CITIZENS of African descent,' involves more serious consequences than any one has yet conceded to it." Full citizenship, the article noted, would make long-standing racial segregation of "American CITIZENS of African descent" as "illegal and indefensible" as racial segregation of "American citizens of Caucasian descent." Significantly, the writer put the word "CITIZEN" in all caps when referring to those of "African descent."

On January 14, 1863, the editors asked their readers, "Are we not only to waste our blood and treasure in the degrading task of emancipation but to supply every negro in the heart of the old States with what white men can not obtain—a comfortable property to live on?"

In February, the tone and language intensified. The February theme revolved around the idea that racial equality would lead to a shift in power away from the white majority.

In criticizing the notion of Black combat troops, the editors wrote, "The niggers themselves claim that they ought to have at least the line officers, Captains, &c., because under the law authorizing their being employed they are eligible for any position from that of Major General down; besides, as, under Mr. Lincoln's decision that they are 'American citizens of African descent,' they may hold the office of President, they naturally esteem themselves entitled to the small regimental offices."

"On the other hand," the editors continued, "the white volunteers say that if niggers are appointed officers they will be obliged to show them that military respect, such as presenting arms and touching caps, which the military demands."

The editorialist went on the suggest that white people would eventually be completely subjugated. "The niggers, however, contend that the white soldiers will be obliged to submit to this. They say that they have Zach Chandler, Abe Lincoln, and the law of the Republican Congress upon their side, and that they, as the naturally superior race, are destined to rule this continent—proving their superiority by quoting liberally from abolition authorities."

"Our opinion," the writer concluded, "is that the niggers will come out ahead. As the Government is now conducted entirely for their benefit, they may demand what they please."

The next salvo hit the pages on February 6, with the assertion that "the nigger bill which has passed the House of Representatives is very careful to permit the President to appoint black officers, Major and Brigadier Generals for instance. When it becomes a law we expect to see Fred. Douglas [sic] or some prominent barber buck, arrayed in all the glory of twin stars. Let the white volunteers prepare to touch their caps to black generals."

On February 8—three weeks before the riot—an editorial in the *Free Press* attacked the twin concepts of abolition and racial equality. The writer predicted that the attempt "to clothe negroes with political rights" would inevitably lead to a violent conflict: "all of the signs of the times indicate that the project of nigger citizenship will receive a baptism of blood which will appall the authors of it, and will cause the poor deluded negroes to curse them."[24]

If Detroiters would undergo a "baptism of blood," alleged the *Tribune* editors, then the *Free Press* editors would be the "authors" or high priests.

The indignant tone and harsh word choice reached a feverish pitch whenever the press reported on "amalgamation," which was considered a crime with the alleged perpetrators tried in police Court and those found guilty sentenced to short stints in the House of Correction.

A police raid on a brothel in which white and Black mixed—called "amalgamation dens" in the press—typically led to a page one item in the *Free Press*. Since the rival *Advertiser and Tribune* did not cover these stories in any depth, the *Free Press* articles become the primary window into how Detroiters viewed mixed-race relations. This raises an important albeit unanswerable question: did the tone and coverage of the *Free Press* articles reflect public sentiment in Detroit or just that of its editors?

It is logical to infer that the "amalgamation" articles mirrored the opinions and racial biases of more than a few Detroiters, but one thing is certain: raids of "amalgamation dens" received more extensive coverage than those of other brothels. In the struggle to enforce city ordinances against bordellos in the years leading up the riot, the law arrested several proprietors, including notorious red light notables such as Christine Thede, but these instances seldom led to anything more than a mere mention, whereas "amalgamation dens" usually led to lengthy articles of several column inches.

Several such instances occurred in 1860, most of them raids on establishments at Beaubien and Hastings streets in an area called "The Bush."

In January, a fight broke out on Hastings Street. The group scattered when the constables appeared, but they managed to collar a few of the prostitutes. The arrests led to a page one item about "AN AMALGAMATION ROW," and the writer named the nymphs du pavé as Kitty Briggs, Mag Burke, Ellen Griffin, Mary Walker and "some others of equal celebrity."

The writer emphasized the "amalgamation" angle: "On Saturday night they gathered in force, the males being all negroes, and the females all, or nearly all, white."

Morphing into editorial, he added, "This circumstance suggests a fact which is invariable in connection with amalgamation cases, viz.: that the whites are always females. There is no instance within the knowledge of those who are acquainted with such matters where a white man has descended so far as to amalgamate with a negress, either in these very common amalgamation dances, or in the connubial relation. There are, however, an abundance of white females in this city who live with and among the negroes entirely, and never associate with people of their own color. The fact would seem to show that the angelic portion of the human race is not only perfect in goodness, but unapproachable in depravity."[25]

This "invariable connection" reappeared a month later when a *Free Press* editor, again commenting on the raid of an "amalgamation den," wrote, "In all of these cases the males are negroes and the females white. There is not an instance on record where the contrary is known, white men invariably holding themselves above such a connection in any stage of degradation."

"The system [of amalgamation dens]," he concluded, "is the natural result of the negro emigration to this portion of the county, but, if present indications may be relied upon, it will not be allowed to grow on our hands."[26]

When another group of revelers went to police court in early March, the *Free Press* writer again blended fact with editorial in a scathing rebuke of "a peculiar and nameless offence against decency to which they are addicted." According to the short piece, the six defendants were arrested in a house with a lone bed, "which we are led to suppose they all occupied." This suggestion of a lone bed as the scene of a Bacchanalian orgy would reappear in a later article.

1. The Past as Prologue (1833–1863)

"The girls were white, as usual," the writer noted, "and the men black as tar. One of the former, a young girl named Mary Ann Vitiger, was discharged, on account of her youth and promises of reformation, and the rest were sent to jail for ninety days. It seems probable that after forty or fifty more of these reprobates are sent up they will learn to forsake their disgusting practices."[27]

Vitiger's "promises of reformation" did not materialize, and she ended up back in police court the following week alongside another teenager named Josephine Fox on vagrancy charges. The *Free Press* reporter described Vitiger as "about seventeen years old, and good-looking, but a common associate of negroes."

He was even harsher in his description of Fox, "a girl of sixteen or seventeen."

"About two weeks since she was arrested with some negroes and was found to be proscribed even among them," he wrote, "her person being affected with a loathsome disease which rendered her an object of disgust."[28]

The ire directed toward "amalgamation" extended beyond The Bush and the commercial sex trade. Mixed-race couples also came under attack. The reporting of one incident in particular provides a good example of how a certain segment of the general public came to view and treat mixed-raced couples.

The incident occurred in March 1860 in a railway depot just west of Pontiac when "a veritable nigger in company with a buxom white girl" boarded the train. All eyes turned as the couple entered the car.

"They took a seat together and settled down apparently for the mutual enjoyment of their journey and each other's company," wrote a *Free Press* reporter who must have heard the story from someone present at the time. "But as the train moved on their bliss was somewhat alloyed by the laughter and fun of the train boys and the indignant looks of the passengers. At last the sable husband complained to the conductor of the train, who administered a rebuke to the employees, which had the anticipated effect of heightening their merriment, which was not at all retarded by the grotesque merriment of the official to keep his face straight while administering the reprimand."[29]

It is notable that the most vocal reaction came from the "train boys" and that rather than scold the children the adult passengers allowed the verbal abuse to continue. Their inaction amounted to a form of approval, as if the boys gave voice to the emotions hidden behind their "indignant looks." Even the train conductor—the authority on the train—did not take the complaint seriously.

In late December 1862, another notable incident ended up on the front pages of the *Free Press*. Cordelia Bradley, the twenty-year-old daughter of Oakland County farmer James Bradley, ran away with one of Bradley's farm hands, a Black man named Louis Hill. Caught as they boarded the ferry in Detroit, the paramours were arrested and brought into police court.

A writer described the scene of the arrest as he imagined it happening. "Their dreams of unalloyed wedded bliss were nipped in the bud as the officer tapped the sable lover on the shoulder and informed him that he was a prisoner. As the truth dawned upon his mind through his black, wood covered skull, the effect was truly heart-rending (in an amalgamation point of view); the whites of his eyes rolled in their sockets like two balls of fire, the deep recesses of his soul were stirred within, and, in a tone of deep indignation, he demanded, as an 'American citizen of African descent,' to be 'let alone,' giving starting emphasis to his words by the gnashing of his teeth and the threatening, battering-ram motion of his genuine Ethiopian head."[30]

Once again, the *Free Press* writers used the incident of the "black viper that has stung the hand that fed him" to make a grand statement about racial equality. "These are the legitimate fruits of the mistaken philanthropy that would place the treacherous, and unprincipled … darkey upon an equality with the white man. Yet if he must be permitted to eat at the same table, move in the same circle, and attend the same church and school," the writer asked, "why not allow him to sleep in the same bed?"

The article ended with a statement that, according to rival editors at the *Advertiser and Tribune*, proved that the *Free Press* attempted to incite violent reprisal against Detroit's Black community.

"The young girl is a good looking Miss of about twenty years of age, and apparently possessing a good share of intelligence. There is, however, an evident determination on her part to share the fortunes of her ebony companion, and unless he is disposed of in such a manner as to exclude the possibility of such a denouement, they will doubtless follow in the footsteps of their illustrious predecessors of Pontiac notoriety."[31] Exactly what "disposed of in such a manner" entailed was left to the reader's imagination, but the comment's ominous undertones were evident.

The "predecessors of Pontiac notoriety" was a reference to the 1859 "elopement" of "Nigger Joe" and Sarah Judson, which triggered a series of headline articles in its own right. Unlike the Bradley-Hill case, "Nigger Joe" and his fiancé managed to reach Windsor, where they married, raised a family, and lived happily ever after to the ire of *Free Press* reporters who never missed the opportunity to use the case as a cautionary tale about "amalgamation."

The case became a minor sensation and was even adapted into the stage production, *Beauties of Amalgamation*, which played to a standing-room-only crowd in May 1859. The actor chosen to portray "Nigger Joe" even crossed the river into Windsor to study his subject at arm's length.[32]

Any sentence handed down by the police court magistrate paled in comparison to the condemnation the *Free Press* heaped on the star-crossed Cordelia Bradley in the December 24, 1862, edition. "The girl is forever lost to decency and respect. Even should her separation from her negro paramour be eternal, the finger of scorn will be pointed at her, to her dying day, as the white woman who disgraced her sex and common decency by consenting to become the wife of a black, ugly looking, disgusting negro."[33]

2

Behind Closed Doors: Law and Order in Detroit, c. 1863

The metropolitan Detroit police did not exist in February 1863. The task of maintaining law and order was shared by several distinct entities that included approximately two dozen Wayne County sheriff's deputies under the command of Sheriff Peter Fralick; ten constables, one elected by popular vote from each of Detroit's ten wards; and a city marshal with his lone deputy.[1] In addition, a U.S. marshal and his five deputies, headquartered in the federal building, investigated federal crimes and handled prisoner transfers from the western territories to the Detroit House of Correction.

Adding to the confusion, several men did double duty. David M. Freeman and Dennis K. Sullivan served as sheriff's deputies as well as elected constables. Deputies James Gunning and Julius Blodget moonlighted as the "Gunning and Blodget Detroit General Detective Police & Collections Agency." Fellow deputy John Van Stan, who would later become "Lieutenant Van Stan" and a key figure in the 1863 riot, hung his shingle as proprietor of "John Van Stan & Co.," a competing private detective agency.

As the elected constable of Detroit's Third Ward, forty-four-year-old David M. Freeman had the difficult task of keeping law and order among a mixed population of former slaves and Irish and German immigrants. He spent much of his time chasing down street toughs, some of whom lived in the byways and back alleys and eked out a hand-to-mouth existence through scavenging and petty theft. Many of them spent more than a few nights in the county "hotel" for "vagrancy." Freeman's beat also included several bordellos, such as Joshua Coon's "Milwaukee Exchange" at the corner of Beaubien and Atwater.

2. Behind Closed Doors: Law and Order in Detroit, c. 1863

Thirty-two-year-old Dennis K. Sullivan's beat consisted of the Seventh Ward, a trapezoid-shaped jurisdiction enclosed within Rivard and Dequindre streets to the east and west, Gratiot Avenue to the north, and the Detroit River to the south. But as a sheriff's deputy, he also came to know many of the characters in the Third Ward's vice world.

Much of Sullivan's work involved busting drunk and disorderlies. The humorous anecdote of Bridget Naggs provides a typical night's work on the beat in the wards of East Detroit. With a playful tone, an *Advertiser and Tribune* journalist described Nagg's ordeal in a piece titled "A GOOD DUCKING."

"An Irish woman named Bridget Naggs, who is well known to the Police Court, tumbled into the river last evening while intoxicated, near the foot of Woodward avenue," the article went. "Her cries which were indeed lustily made, attracted the attention of parties in the vicinity, who succeeded in dragging her out a little wetter and soberer than when she disappeared from the dock."[2]

Because their work often took place inside bordellos, the law enforcement officers of Detroit acquired a seedy reputation. A few days before the riot, an unnamed Detroiter writing under the pseudonym CITIZEN sent a scathing critique of police to the *Advertiser and Tribune*. "I believe few cities in the Union have more scoundrels and a poorer police than our city of Detroit," he said before describing the city's police as "a lot of pimps and bloats, who spend the first half [of] the night in houses of ill fame as guests, and the last half in assisting the inmates of other houses of ill-fame."[3]

Early law enforcement officers of Detroit could not wash away this stain, so when the first metropolitan police force was organized after the riot, the rulebook forbade officers from even entering houses of ill repute unless duty required it.

The city's fire marshal William Champ investigated cases of suspected arson. The position was one for which he was ideally suited. Champ had several years of experience in criminal investigation stemming from work as a Detroit city marshal, Wayne County deputy sheriff, constable of the Fifth Ward, and deputy U.S. marshal. In 1853, he opened the first private detective agency in Detroit, which he continued to operate until his appointment as fire marshal in 1856.

The fire marshal was a formidable character. Standing more than

J. A. GUNNING. **DETROIT** **J. S. BLODGET.**

GENERAL DETECTIVE POLICE & COLLECTING AGENCY.

GUNNING & BLODGET,
DEPUTY SHERIFFS, NOTARIES PUBLIC, &C.,

Will devote their attention to the transacting of the General Detective Police Business, Collecting, &c.

Office No. 2 Desnoyers Block, Jefferson Avenue, Detroit.

Detroit, Aug 24 1860

Mr J B Miller

We received your letter with papers to serve on Palmer in due time they were served by me but I owe you an apology for not serving them before as I have been so very busy I could not hardly attend to my private business Politics have been very high in our city for several weeks & yesterday they closed so far as our county is concerned & now we have only to look for Douglas interest & consequently have more leisure

The money you sent was quite sufficient indeed & you may consider no more obligation to you & should be happy to wait upon you at any time hoping that next time we will not be so much engaged in the (meanest of all meanness) Politics but when one gets excited how can they help it

---

Above and opposite: Before the formation of the Detroit Metropolitan Police, many law officers augmented their income with side jobs. Wayne County sheriff's deputies J.A. Gunning and J.S. Blodget operated the Detroit General Detective Police & Collecting Agency out of a private office on Jefferson Avenue. Because elected city constables were forbidden from serving papers and collecting debts, this work kept Gunning and Blodget busy. In this letter, Blodget ("B") writes to a client, J.B. Miller, who hired the duo to serve papers on one Palmer. He explains how political events in the summer of 1860 have kept them busy maintaining law and order between Lincoln supporters and "Douglas Democrats," but with things quieting down, they would find Palmer and deliver the papers (author's collection).

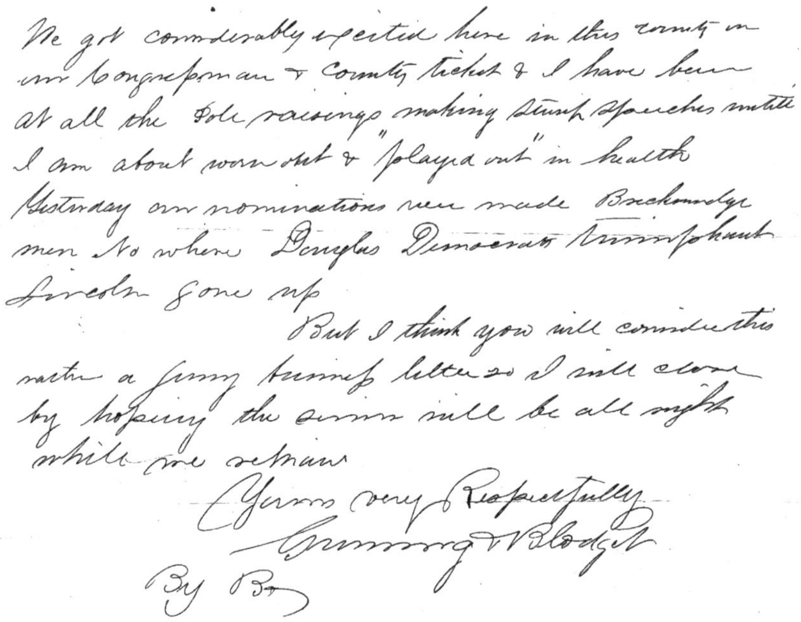

2. Behind Closed Doors: Law and Order in Detroit, c. 1863

[handwritten letter]

six feet tall, he was later described as "portly in figure, square shouldered and walked with his feet wide apart ... in complexion he was dark with gray eyes, brown hair, and a large nose."[4] Like his fellow lawmen, Champ was an avowed Democrat.

Champ's acumen as a detective became his identifying characteristic. Several times during the news coverage of the Detroit riot, both the *Free Press* and the *Advertiser and Tribune* applauded Champ as a brilliant investigator with a razor-sharp mind.

In February 1863, Wayne County Sheriff Peter Fralick was in the first year of his second two-year-term. His first term ended with a loss to Mark Flanigan in the 1860 election, but Fralick emerged victorious in the 1862 election and began his second stint as a county lawman the following January.

Following long-established custom, Fralick, his wife Mary, and their five children lived in the sheriff's residence adjacent to the jail. The complex, which included a yard and the city's police court, occupied a city block bordered by Gratiot, St. Antoine, Clinton, and Beaubien. Before the advent of the metropolitan police force, the jail had to house both city and county prisoners.

One of the major problems dogging Fralick in his first term was the antiquated, dilapidated, and overcrowded county jail. The overcrowding, in particular, confounded the sheriff and his "turnkey" Charles Bird. This problem has survived in a handwritten notation on the 1860 census: "The fact that we have no city prison or work house has filled our county jail with a great number of vagrants which compose a very great proportion of the present number [of inmates]." When the census takers visited in the Wayne County jail on July 25, 1860, the jail housed ninety-three inmates ranging in age from ten-year-old Mary Clapp to an eighty-nine-year-old known only as "Sixteen String Jack." Thirty-six of the "residents" were under eighteen years of age.

An amateur penologist of sorts, longtime jailer Charles C. Bird kept a monthly and yearly tally of prisoners entering and exiting the Wayne County jail. At the end of each month and each calendar year, the meticulous jailer submitted his lists to the *Free Press*.[5] Bird's list for the year 1861 provides a snapshot of crime in Civil War–era Detroit and underscores Fralick's complaints about overcrowding. Bird tallied crimes by the courts in which the perpetrators were tried; the following is a composite of those lists.[6]

Crimes in 1861	*Tally*
Disorderly and drunk	568
Assault and battery	437
Simple larceny	338
Disorderly persons within the meaning of Chapter 4, Compiled Laws	333
Vagrancy	133
Malicious trespass	79
Keeping house of ill fame	49
Burglary	45
Attempt to kill	27
Grand larceny	25
Adultery	24
Committed as witness	24
Passing counterfeit coin	17
Common drunkard	15
Passing counterfeit money	13
Resisting officers	13

2. Behind Closed Doors: Law and Order in Detroit, c. 1863

Crimes in 1861	*Tally*
Amalgamation	12
Making counterfeit coin	12
False pretenses	11
Fraud	11
Larceny from person	11
Compound larceny	10
Common prostitute	8
Forgery	8
Rape	8
Robbery	7
Robbing post office	7
Selling liquors to minors	7
Aiding in the escape of prisoners	6
Arson	6
Contempt of court	6
Deserting	5
Embezzlement	5
Violation of liquor law	5
Pick pocketing	4
Receiving stolen property	4
Seduction	4
Watch stuffing	4
Abusing dumb brutes	3
Breaking jail	3
Gaming	3
Manslaughter	3
Murder	3
Obscene language	3
Opening letters	3
Passing liquor to prisoners	3
Threatening language	3
Abusing parents	2
Attempt to break jail	2
Bastardy	2

Crimes in 1861	Tally
Breaking jail at Adrian	2
Escape from reform school	2
Highway robbery	2
Indecent exposure of person	2
Maiming	2
Mutiny	2
Treason	2
Contempt of court	1
False imprisonment	1
Incendiary	1
Killing dogs	1
Passing counterfeit bank bills	1
Passing worthless money	1
Perjury	1
Poisoning chickens	1
Poisoning his father, State prison for life	1
Receiving stolen property	1
Robbing mail	1
Violation of the game law	1

Some of Bird's classifications appear to be repetitious (fraud and false pretenses; robbing mail and "opening letters"; arson and "incendiary"), perhaps because different courts used different legal terms (prisoners incarcerated in the county jail went to trial in both state and federal courts). In some instances, Bird used descriptive terms to delineate specific crimes. For example, the lone case heard by the justice of the peace in Redford involved a man convicted of "poisoning his father" and sent to the "State prison for life." For some reason, perhaps because it was a patricide, Bird decided not to include this crime in the classification for "murder."

Some of the crimes reflect the social norms of the era: bastardy (child born out of wedlock); "abusing parents"; "obscene language." The two dozen cases of "adultery," which was considered a criminal offense, hints at the vigor with which such cases were pursued and prosecuted.

A cursory examination of Bird's list suggests that sheriff's deputies and ward constables spent a majority of their time busting up bar fights. They also spent a significant amount of time collaring the city's purveyors of sin, although it appears they went after bordello proprietors and turned a blind eye to street walkers ("common prostitutes").

The sheer number of inmates in the county lock-up suggests that the small contingent of sheriff's deputies and ward constables did a fairly effective job of keeping law and order and catching violators even without the presence of a metropolitan police force.

One particular entry illustrates the racial bias embedded in the criminal justice system at the time; in 1861 alone, the jail housed a dozen prisoners arrested for "amalgamation," or the coupling of Blacks and whites—more than those arrested for "common" prostitution. This indicates that officers considered the intermingling of Blacks and whites a greater offense than the sale of sex on the streets.

"Mr. Bird," a *Free Press* reporter commented, "has devoted much time to the preparation of the list, and it may be relied on as correct." If the reporter's faith in Bird was not misplaced, if his statistics were accurate, then a total of 2,360 prisoners spent time in the Wayne County jail in 1861, just under two hundred each month.[7]

Fralick lobbied for a newer, better facility, and the county commissioners listened; in January 1863, a new county jail opened on the same site as the old facility.

The new jail sported a three-story cell block containing a total of eighty-four cells, each five feet wide by seven feet long. Constructed almost entirely of stone and wrought iron, except for the window frames, the jail was considered fire- and escape-proof. A curtain wall two feet thick surrounded the yard, making the citadel-like structure virtually impenetrable.

Although the old sheriff's residence remained, it received a makeover that consisted of new hardwood floors and fresh wallpaper. Now, Fralick's thirty-five-year-old wife Mary could entertain her guests in style.

The new jail witnessed heavy foot traffic in its first month of existence. Prisoners accused of minor crimes such as stealing mail from the post office, adultery, and uttering "insulting language" rubbed elbows with alleged murderers, rapists, and thieves in the new and expanded cell blocks. The most common offenses included desertion, drunk and disorderly conduct, and larceny. Ironically, the jail housed just two "vagrants"—the population that caused Fralick to complain about

Exterior of the House of Correction as it appeared around 1880 on a stereo view card published by L. Black & Co. (New York Public Library).

overcrowding a few years earlier—in January 1863. They were joined by two witnesses spending a few nights in the county "hotel" to ensure they made it to the witness stand. In all, ninety-eight people spent time in the county jail during its inaugural month.[8]

The jail served as a temporary holding facility. Prisoners convicted of serious crimes were transported by train to the state prison at Jackson. Those convicted of lesser offenses were walked to the Detroit House of Correction, a new facility located at the eastern extremity of the Sixth Ward. The prison opened in 1861 and housed federal prisoners from the western territories as well as locals doing time for petty crimes. The person in charge of watching this motley group was thirty-five-year-old Connecticut native Zebulon Reed Brockway, the first superintendent of the House of Correction. A former warden in New York, Brockway was patriarch of the house from its inception in 1861 until 1876, when he returned to New York as superintendent of the New York State Reformatory.[9]

In February 1863, Fralick ended up in bed with a fever, so his duties fell to his second-in-command. Francis X. Cicotte came from

2. Behind Closed Doors: Law and Order in Detroit, c. 1863

Another stereo card published by L. Black & Co. captures a quiet moment inside one of the cell blocks. The photograph was probably taken when the inmates were either in the yard or in the shops working off the "at hard labor" portion of their sentences (New York Public Library).

an old and distinguished family. The fifty-one-year-old lived in the Third Ward at the corner of Gratiot and Beaubien with his wife Elizabeth, their six children, and one servant—a German immigrant named Sabrina Neil.[10] A lifelong Democrat, Cicotte was active in party politics and previously served as the city treasurer. He was also a successful entrepreneur. The 1860 census lists his occupation as "speculator" with real estate holdings worth $38,000.[11]

A majority of the cases on Bird's tallies ended in the police court of Justice Minot T. Lane.

Located in a small building called Mechanic's Hall at the edge of the county jail complex in Detroit's Third Ward, the police court handled lesser offenses such as drunk and disorderly conduct or violations of city ordinances.[12] The police magistrate heard arguments and handed down punishments, which usually entailed a fine or a short stay in either county jail or the new Detroit House of Correction. Typically, the defendant had a choice to either pay the fine or do the time. When the police magistrate was unavailable or when the docket exceeded the court's capacity, any of the city's justices of the peace tried minor criminal matters.

While the police magistrate and his six jurors disposed of most minor crimes in police court, Lane would refer serious crimes to recorder's court. As a result, transcripts of testimony in the era's recorder's court records often emanates from preliminary examinations in police court. In many cases, the police court reporter's handwritten transcripts are the only surviving records of testimony.[13]

In February 1863, Justice Lane was just about to turn fifty-six and had called Michigan home for more than three decades.

Born in New Hampshire on March 12, 1807, Lane ventured west in 1832, eventually settling in Michigan. He operated a successful farm in Macomb County until he won a seat in the state legislature in 1838. Six years later, Lane won a second term and joined the first Michigan congress to meet in Lansing.

When his second term ended in 1848, Lane moved to Detroit. He served as justice of the peace for eight years before taking a seat on the bench as Detroit's police justice in 1862.[14]

Police Justice Lane, like Sheriff Fralick, toiled in a cramped space until January 1863. Situated at the corner of the county jail complex, the old police court contained hardly enough room to conduct the day-to-day business of the court. The new building—erected at the same time as the new jail—contained a spacious courtroom thirty feet wide and seventy feet long, a chamber for Justice Lane, a general business office, and a separate room for jury deliberations.

A communicating passage led from the jail yard into the court building, so deputies could escort prisoners shielded from the public by the castle-like curtain wall. They did not enjoy such protection when escorting prisoners to and from recorder's court, which was located in city hall several blocks away.

Defendants who stood accused of serious crimes such as rape and murder usually found themselves standing in front of Judge Benjamin Franklin Hawkins Witherell. In 1863, Witherell presided over both the recorder's court and the Wayne County circuit court (serious criminal cases that occurred within city limits went to recorder's court; those that occurred outside of city limits but within Wayne County went to circuit court).

In February 1863, Witherell was in his forty-fourth year on the bench. Even at the advanced age of sixty-six, Judge Witherell was an imposing figure. He stood six feet tall and tipped the scales at two hundred and fifty pounds. Although his barrel-chest had sunk toward his waist and his jet-black hair had turned to a steel gray, his penetrating gaze and stentorian tone left little doubt who was the master of Detroit's criminal courts.

A local history buff, Witherell became known for his encyclopedic knowledge of the city's history. He even penned several articles published in the *Free Press* under the pseudonym "Hamtramck."

As a lifelong Democrat, Witherell was politically aligned with the *Free Press*. Considered an affable man and a fair judge, he was very popular among Detroit's law-abiding citizens but not as loved by its law-breakers, who nicknamed him "Big Fat Hog Witherell."[15]

Judge Witherell always wore black suits, possibly because he was in a constant state of mourning. By February 1863, he had been widowed twice, and his third wife Cassandra was under the weather.

Two figures in particular were mainstays in Judge Witherell's courtroom: Wayne County prosecuting attorney James Knox Gavin and defense attorney J. Logan Chipman. The two first met as students at the Lodi Academy, a sort of prep school operated by Professor Rufus Nutting in Washtenaw County six miles from the nearest town of Ann Arbor. Most of Nutting's pupils boarded with local farmers.

The twenty-nine-year-old prosecutor had a slim, wiry build. A later biographer described him as having a "high forehead, dark brown curly hair, worn long, with a large mustache and burnside whiskers of the same color, blue eyes, well-chiseled nose and a strong, resolute jaw."

After finishing at the Lodi Academy, Gavin returned to Detroit where he studied law and became an active participant in local politics. In 1857, Gavin's fellow Democrats nominated him for prosecuting attorney. After serving his first term, he lost the next two elections but won again in 1862.

A gifted orator and storyteller, Gavin was a popular and well respected among his fellow lawyers. His reputation as an incorruptible officer of the court stemmed from an incident in which he turned down a bribe of $50,000 offered by an influential citizen charged with the crime of seduction. Gavin refused the king's ransom and successfully prosecuted the case.

Gavin wouldn't take a bribe, but he was generous to a fault, which left him with empty pockets most of the time. "In manner and disposition," wrote historian Robert Budd Ross, "he was pleasant and generous, and he took little care of his money, which generally vanished shortly after it came into his hands."[16]

The steely-eyed prosecutor's most frequent, and most notable, adversary grew up with the law. Thirty-three-year-old John Logan Chipman's father Henry settled in Detroit in 1824, where he established a law firm and later presided over the recorder's court. Following in his father's footsteps, John studied law in Detroit but took periodic breaks from legal tomes to comb through the wilds of Michigan's Upper Peninsula in search of mineral deposits for the Montreal Mining Company.

Politically neutral in 1863, John Logan Chipman was no stranger to public service. He served as city attorney from 1856 to 1860, but by February 1863, he had stepped across the aisle to become one of the most celebrated and accomplished defense lawyers in Detroit. He spent much of his time in recorder's court, where he battled with his former school chum.[17]

Curiously, Chipman also had a role with the production of the Democrat-leaning *Detroit Free Press*. Charles Clark's Detroit City Directory of 1862–1863 describes him as "editor Free Press, lawyer."[18]

The three legal characters—Witherell, Gavin, and Chipman—were about to become key players in one of the most notorious cases in Detroit history, a case dubbed "the Faulkner Outrage." In the months leading up to the headline case, their focus became the city's purveyors of sin.

The forty-nine suspected brothel operators on Bird's 1861 tally represent the fact that city officials spent a good portion of their time fighting vice, which led to a few spectacular trials replete with some very scandalous testimony. A seat in the recorder's court gallery would become the hottest ticket in town. Nowhere else could Detroiters hear

2. Behind Closed Doors: Law and Order in Detroit, c. 1863

lurid stories told by prostitutes forced to kiss and tell. It was the nineteenth-century version of reality television, and it was wildly popular among habitual courtgoers who poured into Judge Witherell's courtroom.

Three cases in particular illustrate law and order in Detroit in February 1863; they underscore the racial tension in the air at the advent of "the Faulkner Outrage"; and they indicate the role the *Free Press* may have played in exacerbating those tensions.

At the beginning of 1863, J. Knox Gavin would prosecute Joshua Coon for running a brothel in the Third Ward.

J. Logan Chipman in a portrait photograph taken by C.M. Bell, 1873–1890 (Library of Congress).

Perched at the corner of Beaubien and Atwater, Coon's "Milwaukee Exchange" was adjacent to a barroom in which his prostitutes mingled with customers, a sitting room where they flirted, and three upstairs bedrooms where they consummated their short-term relationships. (The brothel was possibly named after the Detroit & Milwaukee Railway, the tracks of which formed the border between Detroit's Seventh and Tenth wards.) Called to the stand, one of Coon's regulars described watching women smoking, drinking, "sitting on men's laps and kissing them."

According to Flora Bell, a renter who testified at Coon's trial, four married women "boarded" in rooms above the bar at the high cost of $7 per week: Kate Hoffman, Kate "Pussy" Woods, Catherine Miller, and a woman whom she did not know by name. The exorbitant cost for rent, it appeared, represented the house take, as Bell quickly realized.

"One day I opened the door of one room and saw a man and woman in bed together that were not married and another day saw another man and woman in bed together who were not married. Mr. Coon new [sic] how the women got the money to pay $7 a week, they got it by receiving company." Bell went on to explain that Coon had to have known what took place behind closed doors because she saw him delivering drinks to the rooms.

Bell presented herself as an innocent resident who knew about the reputation of the building as "a house of ill repute" but she did not, curiously, explain how she managed to pay the rent. In fact, she pointed out that unlike the other women, she "furnished her own room."

Flora Bell may have been the fourth, unnamed renter. Six months after the "Milwaukee Exchange" case, Kate Hoffman, Kate "Pussy" Woods, and a Flora Brown were all arrested as "common prostitutes" working for brothel operators Frank and Flora Brundage.[19] In February 1863, Flora Brown may have called herself Flora Bell.

Bell testified that the women entertained both male and female "company" once or twice a day. Although she specified that she had no inside knowledge of "any person unmarried cohabitating together," she also said that she accidentally walked in on "Pussy" Woods and a man in *flagrante delicto* and once saw Woods go into her room "with several different men."[20]

She also saw men going into twenty-three-year-old Kate Hoffman's room. Bell did not know whether or not Hoffman had a sketchy reputation, but Hoffman's long-standing association with notorious madam Christine Thede suggested that she had worked in the business as early as 1860, when she lived above a saloon run by Thede and her husband.[21] Thede would be dragged into court several times in May 1863 on charges of running a brothel.

Any doubt about Hoffman's profession evaporated when Officer Dennis K. Sullivan testified. Sullivan said he had known two of the three Kates—Kate "Pussy" Woods and Kate Hoffman—for several years. He knew (only by reputation, he was quick to point out) both women to be prostitutes. Sullivan provided a flimsy excuse for going into a known brothel: "[I] was called to go there to see a sick person," he testified.

The extent of Sullivan's inside knowledge about Coon's "Milwaukee Exchange" was suspicious. The talkative detective, it appeared, said too much during his turn on the stand. At first he said he had "been in the barroom, been in the sitting room, also upstairs," but perhaps realizing his slip of the lip, he contradicted himself when he insisted he never left the barroom, never went upstairs, and never saw the women at work. Instead, he had concluded by the presence of known prostitutes that Coon's boarding house doubled as a whorehouse.[22]

Sullivan's fellow officer James Hepburn added the name "Kate Miller" the growing list of Coon's prostitutes. Like Sullivan, Hepburn was quick to point out that he only ventured into the house on one occasion.[23]

Gavin called two additional deputies to testify. John Starkweather and former officer William Ball both testified to having been inside the bordello; both testified to knowing the type of business transacted inside the "Milwaukee Exchange"; and both testified to knowing one or more of the residents as prostitutes. But like Sullivan and Hepburn, both said they knew these things from second-hand knowledge.

Ball testified to seeing the women perched "on gentlemens' laps" but "paid no attention 'to where they had there [sic] hands.'"

A former deputy sheriff, Ball said he entered the bordello "2 or 3 times per week sometimes every night" beginning in October 1862. Ball said he went there "for work" but only knew the establishment as "a house of ill fame" by its reputation and the reputation of its residents.[24]

The only witness who would admit to going upstairs was one of Coon's best customers, Valentine Lee, who testified to visiting the house no fewer than fifty times.

"[I] saw one girl in bed with a man her name is Kate Hoffman," Lee said. He explained that he had taken a friend named Alson Pennell to the house. Pennell and Flora Bell went upstairs, although "what he [Pennell] did [I] cannot say," Lee testified.[25]

The testimony cost Coon dearly. Found guilty, he did a lengthy stint in the state-run boarding house of Superintendent Zebulon Brockway.

The case also landed Coon on the front page of the *Free Press*. While the *Advertiser and Tribune* remained virtually mum about the case, the rival rag reported the arrest "OF A NOTORIOUS CHARACTER."

"A salutary example is needed for the preservation of common decency," the reporter suggested, "and as a warning to others who might get emboldened to follow in his [Coon's] footsteps unless proper and merited punishment is awarded for such flagrant outrages."[26]

• • • •

Neither of Detroit's major newspapers spilled much ink on the city's cat-and-mouse game with cathouse proprietors, so except for a few mainstays in the police court gallery, the city's war on vice remained behind courtroom doors. This changed whenever police broke up an "amalgamation" den, which became instant front-page fodder for the *Free Press*.

News of "AN AMALGAMATION NEST BROKEN UP" hit the front page of the *Free Press* on February 13, 1863. In six inches of text, the writer chronicled the raid on a notorious den of vice on the outskirts of the city, on Hastings Street about a mile and a half north of Gratiot.

The boarding house was owned and operated by twenty-three-year-old Martin Washington and his twenty-year-old wife Mary. According to the *Free Press* article about the raid, Washington's place was the headquarters for gangs of thieves who made a living snatching livestock from neighboring farms, while three women sold sex from the upstairs bedrooms.

The group went in front of Justice Lane the next morning. Despite the relatively minor and relatively common offense, the *Detroit Free Press* devoted a lengthy front-page piece to the case. The unnamed writer condemned the inhabitants as "filthy vagabonds" in the most racially-charged language, resorting to terms such as "cattle" and "gorilla" to describe the major figures in the case.

"The facts elicited on the trial disclosed a most disgusting state of things in practice at the den of the mulatto—who was the husband of one of the women, having been married in Windsor by the gorilla who figured so long in that place, in the pulpit, and at public meetings as 'Brudder Green,'" he wrote.

"Brudder Green" was a name that had appeared multiple times in the pages of the *Free Press*, which used him as a vehicle for condemning racial equality. In a short piece covering elections in Canada in 1861, the *Free Press* writer referred to Canada as "coffeedom" and put words

2. Behind Closed Doors: Law and Order in Detroit, c. 1863   53

in Green's mouth by describing him as someone who would "stand by the cullud pussun, and if he am elected, des all gwine to get officer, dar children will go to de same school, wid de white trash, and den dar will be no 'stinction ob color."[27]

The writer identified Martin Washington's three prostitutes as Mary (also known as Harriet) Washington, whom he called "the consort of Martin"; Margaret Champagne; and Sarah Campbell. Officers arrested all three for "vagrancy" and marched them to the county jail.

According to the *Free Press*' court reporter, appearance alone convicted the soiled doves. "Their personal appearance and the brazen indifference they manifested in court were enough to condemn them without further testimony. As such cattle never receive any mercy at the hands of this court, as they deserve none, they were all three sent to the workhouse for one year, in fault of the bail in the sum of $200."

Martin Washington evaded charges, to the chagrin of the reporter, who lamented, "A year's hard labor under Mr. Brockway would be a salutary warning to the black rascal that common decency must be respected."[28]

While Washington returned to his "den," the three women toiled in the "workhouse."

Brockway, the House of Correction warden, ran a tight ship. A penologist and noted prison reformer, Brockway emphasized the "correction" aspect of the institution. His staff provided both educational and spiritual guidance to inmates. "It is to be hoped," wrote the *Free Press* reporter, "that the fallen wretches who are now in custody will emerge from their confinement with a little more self-respect than has characterized their past behavior."[29]

The three "fallen wretches" emerged from the house a week later when Washington paid their bail and went right back to business as 'uncorrected' by their short stint behind bars.

• • • •

A week after the Washington affair, a raid on a Third Ward bordello or "dive" on St. Antoine between Clinton and Macomb streets—a block away from the county jail—gave rise to another page-one article under the "Local Intelligence" section of the *Free Press*.

The headline—"DESCENT ON A NIGGER DIVE: Disgusting

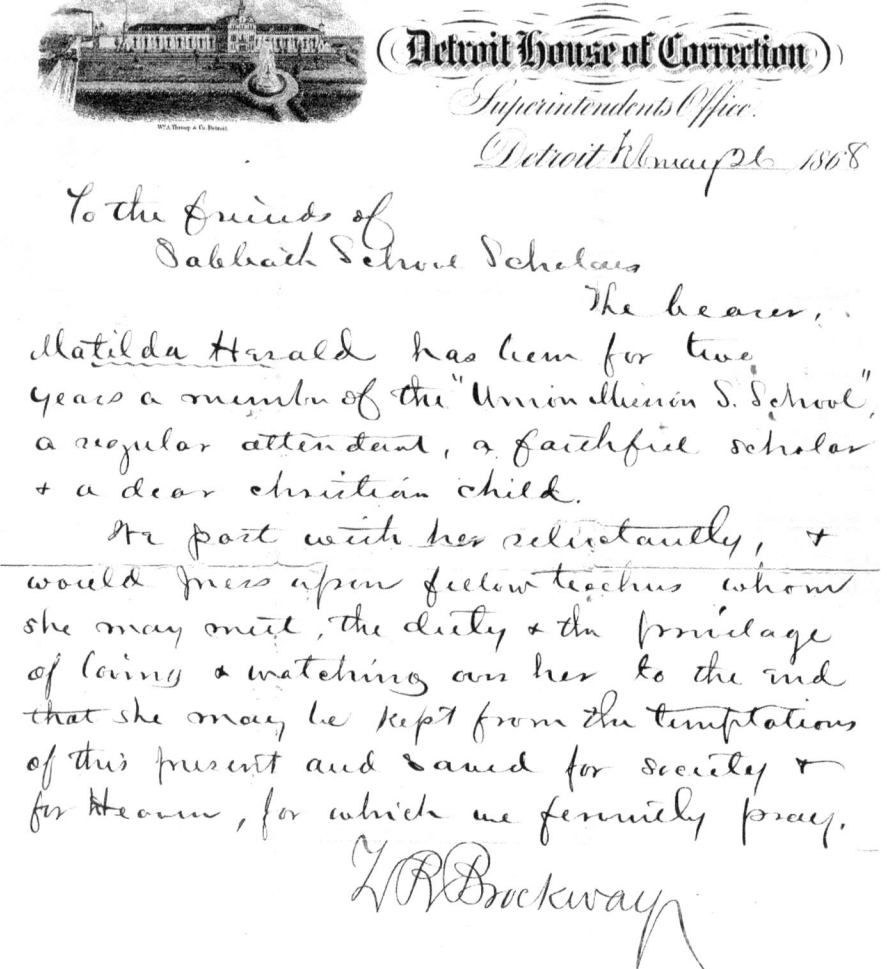

Zebulon Brockway, the first superintendent of the Detroit House of Correction, became a pioneer in the field of prison reform. He created a primary school that met three nights a week; he opened a prison library; he arranged for religious services on Sundays; and he ensured that the prison chaplain met one on one with each prisoner. Some of Brockway's initiatives were designed to keep wayward kids—whom Wayne County sheriff Peter Fralick called "vagrants"— out of the House of Correction. Brockway and a friend named James McMillan supposedly made weekly trips to the toughest neighborhoods in Detroit and surveyed the rudderless youth that they encountered. To prevent these street toughs from entering a life of crime and ending up behind bars, they established a Sabbath school. In 1868, Brockway penned this recommendation for one of the Sabbath school teachers, Matilda Herald (author's collection).

2. Behind Closed Doors: Law and Order in Detroit, c. 1863   55

Details of the Condition of the Inmates"—presaged the tone and content of the article.

"The number of low dens and dives where degraded creatures, white and black, of both sexes, congregate nightly for lewd, boisterous and drunken midnight revels, is behind belief," it read. "One of these places has recently been broken up by the police, their performances having been so noisy as to attract the attention of the respectable people living in the immediate vicinity."

The intent of the article became clear with the line that the reporter used to preface his description of the bordello. "The present case is but a sample of a host of others of like character."

Evidently not present during the bust, the reporter relied on a stock image to describe what he believed the officers found inside the "dive." His clever word choice obscured the fact that he was extrapolating the scene from others of "like character." Unless readers parsed the word choice—noticing the use of the conditional tense ("would")—they would have missed this vital point.

The reporter described the place as "a regular resort ... of the lowest and filthiest negro prostitutes and their male companions, for drinking, cavorting, dancing, fighting, and all the disgusting ceremonies for which such places are noted.... The house, which is all the ground floor, consists of but one room, the partitions having all been torn down for fire-wood, and in order to give full sway to the hordes of vagrants who made the neighborhood a perfect Babel by their drunken debauches." These would be the same "vagrants" that prompted Sheriff Fralick to complain about the overcrowded condition of the county jail.

The reporter then opened the bordello doors by describing what (he imagined) the sheriff deputies witnessed during the raid. A few intoxicated customers lay sprawled out on the floor, while others, half naked, wobbled past. "A negro fiddler and banjoist would occupy one corner of the hovel," the reporter noted, while the half-clothed, half-inebriated patrons were "dancing jigs, singing obscene songs, and going through all the various performances which the inventive brains of such abandoned outcasts can concoct."

The idea of possible "amalgamation" in the "dive" drew the strongest ire from the reporter: "here a white woman in disgusting proximity with a ragged, drunken negro, and in another place, perhaps, a white man in the same position with a filthy wench—the whole crowd being ragged, dirty, and generally alive with vermin, and in many cases, infested with contagious and loathsome disease."

Except that is not necessarily what the officers found between Clinton and Macomb, which the author acknowledged when he noted that "and this case is no exception. They are all alike—except, perhaps, that others might possibly excel in degradation, if that were possible." In other words, the description the writer just presented—a composite of scenes both real and imagined—"excelled in degration" to the actual scene.

In fact, the raid netted just two prostitutes, Lucretia Johnson and Mary J. Dorsey, whom the writer said "was infected with a disease known as the 'nigger itch'"—a reference to venereal disease. After a brief layover in Lane's police court, the two landed in the Detroit House of Correction for a year's stay.

The writer concluded his article with a sharp rebuke of the law. "Such a state of total depravity and obscenity as prevails in these dives is a disgrace to any community, and it should be visited with the utmost vigor of the law. A descent now and then on them by the police would be a salutary example, and, if it had no other good effect, it would at least caution them against such open and lawless infestations as now characterize them."[30]

The police may have reacted to this public shaming. The night following the "descent" on the Third Ward "dive"—the same day the "Descent" article appeared—sheriff deputies raided the Washington boarding house for a second time. Washington's three prostitutes had just returned from the House of Correction after Washington paid their bail.

This second raid on the Washington residence led to another page-one item in the *Free Press* under the headline "An Amalgamation Den Broken Up."

This time, the *Free Press* author did not rely on the conditional tense or composite sketches in describing the scene behind closed doors.

"The sight which met the officers, on entering, cannot be excelled in human depravity—three white women and three negroes being all in the same room, and all in the same bed," marveled the reporter. "The women were fair-looking, and, in another place and in different apparel, would have been considered as not inferior to the majority of their sex in personal attractions. They were taken entirely by surprise, the doors having been burst open, in order that no chance could be given for escape or concealment. Time was given them in which to put on their ragged and filthy clothing, and then the whole party, six in number, three men and three women, took up their march through the mud for their lodging-place, arriving there somewhere near midnight."

The sextet consisted of Washington and his wife and two prostitutes the writer now identified as Kitty Briggs and Sophia Graham. The writer described Graham as a sixteen-year-old "white girl … found beside the specimen of charcoal who reported himself as Austin Williams."

The writer, either out of error or design, misidentified one of Washington's retinue as Kitty Briggs, who was a well-known madam. At the time police raided the Washington house, Briggs ran a bordello in the Third Ward of Detroit. Her name came up in connection to the arrest of Dewitt C. Anderson for keeping a house of ill fame on Catherine Street, which was described as an establishment "of the lowest order of prostitution … to which negroes and depraved white persons of both sexes resorted for the purpose of lewdness and debauchery." Anderson was apparently collared while "at the house of the notorious Kitty Briggs" at the approximate time of the second Washington raid.[31] Briggs' name might have been added to the bust to further the Free Press "amalgamation" narrative.

"We believe," noted the writer, "they were arrested as disorderlies, but it is thought that a process will also be issued against them as amalgamationists. Some means will be found to make an example of them. They have flourished undisturbed long enough—now let them be punished as the stern necessities of justice and common decency demand. If a descent could be made upon some such infamous abode of crime every night, until they are all eradicated, it would be a greater blessing to the city than could be bestowed in any other way."

The writer lamented that the raid did not net any of the poultry pilferers but then explained that "it may be accounted for … in the fact that the night was intensely dark, and therefore a propitious one for their professional business."[32]

When Dewitt Anderson went to the county jail for operating a bordello, the *Advertiser and Tribune* ran a short piece under the headline "A DEN BROKEN UP." Unlike his colleagues at the *Free Press*, however, the writer did not feature the "amalgamation" angle. While he mentioned the proprietor's race in the first line, describing Anderson as "a colored gentleman in blue spectacles," he used neutral language in describing Anderson's customers and employees. "The house in question," he wrote, "is situated on Catherine Street, where for the past few months, have nightly congregated the lowest of both sexes who have kept up the most terrible howling until daylight."

"The 'gentleman' in blue spectacles," the writer said, employing quotation marks to suggest Anderson's less-than-upstanding character, was headed to recorder's court.[33]

Whereas the *Free Press* ran lengthy front-page articles about the Coon, Shepard, and Washington raids, the *Advertiser and Tribune* did not report on any of them. Whereas the *Free Press* editors devoted less than an inch of text to the Coon and Shepard brothel cases, they devoted more than six inches each to the three articles about raids on "amalgamation dens."

The difference can be summarized in one word: "amalgamation."

PART 2

Torch
(Monday, March 2–
Friday, March 6, 1863)

3

"The Faulkner Outrage" (Monday, March 2– Wednesday, March 4, 1863)

> The crowd ran collected and beat every one,
> Whose skin were not colored exact like their own,
> And swore they'd have "Falkner," [sic] and hang him that day,
> Or kill every "nigger" that came in their way.
> —From "The Riot" by Benjamin Cutler Clark, Sr.

The man whose alleged crime inspired the 1863 riot left a very faint trail in the historical record. Much of what has been written about him is contradictory and emanates from highly biased accounts, which makes unearthing the real man a very difficult task of historical detective work.

He had a dark complexion, although several sources indicate that he was light enough to pass for a white man, and, according to some sources, he considered himself a white man. The author of *A Thrilling Narrative* said that Faulkner actively discriminated against Black Detroiters by refusing to serve them drinks in his bar.[1]

Faulkner was not a native Michigander; he was from North Carolina, although it is unclear when or why he went north. He is not mentioned in the 1861 Detroit city directory, but by 1863, he owned and operated a tavern on Michigan Avenue, where the "horrible outrage" allegedly occurred.

In a *Detroit Daily Post* recap of the Faulkner case published in 1870, one journalist described Detroit as "like a powder magazine only needing a spark to produce an explosion," and William Faulkner supplied the "spark."[2]

• • • •

Case files 431 and 432 are the only two missing from the cardboard box containing recorder's court records from 1863. All of the other cases listed in the court docket are present.[3] It is possible that the files were taken to avoid some embarrassing information about the trial; it is equally possible that someone connected with the court took them home as curiosities; it is more likely that the two files were pulled for an official review of Faulkner's case later.

With the official paper trail missing, the local newspapers become the pre-eminent source about the alleged crime that led to the 1863 riot. Of the city's two main periodicals, the *Free Press* devoted considerable ink to the Faulkner case, so without the missing Faulkner files, it becomes the main source of information about the "outrage." A lengthy article in *The Detroit Daily Post*, published in 1870, presents a less biased albeit belated account of the case.[4]

According to the *Free Press*, the "Horrible Outrage" allegedly took place in the dark, back room of a saloon on the south side of Michigan Avenue near the market that straddled the border of the First and Third wards. The proprietor, forty-two-year-old William Faulkner, stood accused of raping a ten-year-girl named Mary Brown.[5] Trauma and bewilderment caused the youngster to keep mum about the incident, which allegedly occurred on February 16, 1863—a typically frigid, mid-winter afternoon in Detroit—for several days.

Mary was probably born Mary Moore in 1853.[6] Orphaned as an infant, she went to live with her mother's sister Rosa, a thirty-eight-year-old widow who lived on Croghan Street. In time, Mary began to see Rosa as her mother and took her last name. An Irish immigrant, Rosa worked as a washerwoman to support Mary and her step-sister, five-year-old Ann. Census records indicate that their neighbors on Croghan consisted of Irish immigrants and former slaves. She lived a stone's throw from Dr. John C. Gorten, the Black doctor who would treat many of the riot victims.[7]

On the morning of February 16, Rosa Brown sent Mary to deliver a letter to the post office. On the way, Mary bumped into Ellen Hoover, the twelve-year-old daughter of Dennis Hoover, a Black barber who lived on Beaubien Street. Since they were both headed in the same direction, the girls decided to walk together.

3. "The Faulkner Outrage" (March 2–March 4, 1863)

It was a frigid day, so as they passed Faulkner's saloon, Hoover suggested they go inside to warm their feet. What happened inside the saloon became a case of she-said, he-said, with the say-so of the ten-year-old forming the basis for all subsequent reporting on the case.

Brown's story changed a little with each telling. In the earliest reported rendition, she cast Ellen Hoover as Faulkner's accomplice. Once inside, Mary said, they were approached by Faulkner, who tried to persuade Ellen to go with him into the back room. Possibly using food as a carrot, Faulkner lured Ellen into the room while little Mary waited in the barroom.

Frightened by something she heard or saw, Mary retreated out the front door and waited on the curb for her companion. A few minutes later, Ellen emerged from the saloon and tried to coax her companion to go behind closed doors with William Faulkner. She promised that Mary would have "all the luxuries that she would wish" if she agreed.[8]

Brown refused, so Hoover grabbed her arm, pulled her through the front door, and pushed her toward Faulkner.

The silver-tongued barkeep tried to talk her into the back room, but when Mary again refused and went for the door, he stopped her and dragged her into the room. He locked the door and threatened to kill her on the spot if she cried out.

The *Free Press* account left very little to the imagination. "He then, after gagging [her], so as to prevent her giving any alarm, proceeded to commit one of the most diabolical outrages ever perpetrated." When finished, Faulkner ordered her to leave and again threatened to kill her if she squealed—a warning she evidently heeded since she did not come forward until ten days later, when her mother discovered physical signs of the alleged rape.

The specific injuries that led to Faulkner's arrest did not make it into newsprint, but the *Free Press* article from February 27 said that Mary Brown "hid the evidences of the horrible crime from her mother" out of fear and embarrassment.

Officer Dennis K. Sullivan arrested Faulkner for the alleged rape and lodged him in a cell at the county jail. While the turnkey turned the key on Faulkner's cell, Mary recounted the story to Justice Minot T. Lane and a *Free Press* reporter sent to cover the case. According to the reporter, who was allowed to eavesdrop on the interview, the girl's story deeply moved the jurist.

"The kind heart of Judge Lane was touched by her innocent simplicity," the reporter noted, "and the suffering little one was at once consigned to the care of a skillful physician for medical treatment."[9]

Faulkner was arraigned and offered bail of $3,500. Unable to procure the king's ransom, Faulkner returned to his jail cell where he would remain until the trial, set for the following week.

The saloon-keeper denied everything and said that on two separate occasions he had actually shooed Mary Brown out of his tavern and not into it. He claimed that he was victim of foul aspersions cast by a rival who wanted to acquire his tavern and used the two girls in a set-up. His explanation, however, did not echo from the walls of Lane's courtroom and into the next morning's papers.

Instead, the *Free Press* presented one-sided coverage of the case, in essence convicting Faulkner in print. The first barrage appeared in the morning edition of February 27, 1863. Devoting almost an entire column of the front page to the story, the *Free Press* editors selected a headline designed to invoke feelings of disgust among readers: "HORRIBLE OUTRAGE."

The subheading left little for the judge and jury to decide. "A NEGRO ENTRAPS A LITTLE GIRL INTO HIS ROOM AND COMMITS A FIENDISH CRIME UPON HER PERSON." Faulkner's swarthy complexion led the newspapermen to make assumptions about his race; beginning with the initial article of February 27, he became "the negro Faulkner" whenever his name appeared in the pages of the *Free Press*. Throughout the first four paragraphs, the author replaced Faulkner's name with "the negro" to emphasize the Black-on-white element of the alleged crime. Then, toward the bottom of the page, he added a clarification in the fifth paragraph: "William Faulkner … is a mulatto, not very dark-skinned, and would pass, if not scrutinized closely, as a white man."

In an interview fifty years later, veteran journalist Henry Utley recalled the angle the paper adopted for reporting on the "Horrible Outrage."

"We had a man on the *Free Press* whose name has escaped me," Utley recalled, "but who wrote the case up in a vigorous style, calculated to create sentiment for the girl. It had the desired effect."[10]

3. "The Faulkner Outrage" (March 2–March 4, 1863) 65

The unnamed reporter played up the little orphan Mary angle and emphasized the idea of the pure, wholesome white girl spoiled by a bestial brute in the form of "the negro" Faulkner.

"Mary Brown, the victim of the outrage," he wrote, "is a little girl between nine and ten years of age, an orphan, having lost her father and mother when an infant."

The writer described Rosa Brown as "evidently an honest, hard-working woman, though, from appearances, it would seem that she is poor, and depends upon her daily earnings for the support of her family."

He described Brown as "an interesting child. She will be ten years old in March next, not being very large of her age. She is extraordinarily intelligent, tells her sad story in a straight-forward manner, and there can be no doubt of its entire truth."

Mary's truth, as percolated through the *Free Press*, brewed a very strong, bitter cup for readers: a Black man had raped a pure, innocent babe in the woods.

And, according to the writer, Faulkner had done it before. "His former reputation has been exceedingly bad. For a long time, he has been in the habit of enticing young girls into his den for lustful purposes, and has, without doubt, been the cause of more than one girl's ruin and utter degradation.[11] He, of course, has his story in the matter, denying all the allegations of little Mary Brown. He says she had come to his saloon twice, and that he scolded her and told her not to come again. But the evidence of his guilt upon the lacerated person of his victim is stronger than the oaths of ten thousand negroes, even if he had the witnesses to testify to his innocence."

In other words, it didn't matter how many witnesses supported Faulkner's story; if they were Black, they were unreliable. Faulkner was guilty, tried and convicted in the pages of the *Free Press*.

This line about the "oaths of ten thousand negroes" suggests that even at this early stage in the case, Faulkner may have submitted a list of eyewitnesses who could attest to what occurred in his saloon that day, witnesses who might have testified that little orphan Mary did not kick and scream as Faulkner dragged her into the back room or that he did not go behind closed doors with her at all.

One witness in particular may have supported Faulkner's side of the story: a barfly who spent all of his waking hours in the saloon, even eating his meals there. Both girls agreed that this man, unnamed in any of the news reporters, was present in the saloon when the alleged "outrage" occurred, and Faulkner apparently believed that proof of his innocence relied on his constant patron. If contemporary reports about Faulkner refusing to serve a Black customer were accurate, then this man must have been white. On the other hand, the "ten thousand negroes" remark hints that this man may have been Black, which would explain the *Free Press* writer's condemnation; since his testimony would not fit into the *Free Press* narrative, it was subsequently dismissed as unreliable.

To the chagrin of the accused, authorities could not locate this man, perhaps because they considered him more of a suspect than a witness. A week after the trial, he was recognized and arrested as a possible accomplice, although no criminal charges followed.[12]

The writer nudged his readers toward a verdict by saying, "it may not be improper to state that those who have a heart that sympathizes with the friendless widow and outraged orphan would find no more deserving object on whom to bestow their attentions than Mrs. Brown and the innocent child which has been made the victim of this dastardly and inhuman outrage."

The author ended with a parting shot that may have contributed to the unrest that followed. "The whole affair, taken in all its aspects, is one for which every instinct of humanity cries out for vengeance. There is no punishment on the statute books of Michigan which would, in a hundredth part, atone for the heinous crime. Let a fair examination be had, and justice, though it be utterly inadequate, take its proper course."[13]

To a lesser degree than its rival in print, the *Advertiser and Tribune* also featured Faulkner's supposed race with the header of a February 27 front-page story: "A Serious Charge—a Negro Commits an Outrage upon a Little White Girl."

Curiously, the writer misidentified Faulkner as "William Fox" whom he described—three times—as a "negro."

The text of the piece suggested ambivalence toward "Fox's" culpability. In one sentence, the writer appeared convinced of the suspect's guilt. "The negro Fox and the woman [Hoover] went into a back room in the saloon," he wrote, "and after remaining there some ten or fifteen minutes, Fox came out, and seizing the little girl, literally carried her into the room from which he had just come, and there accomplished his fiendish purpose."

In the next sentence, however, the writer changed his tune. "The facts connected with this terrible outrage seem horrible, and, indeed, impossible. But if proven true, we hope the severest punishment the law can inflict will be laid without stint upon the head of the inhuman wretch who has thus blasted the life, as it were, of an innocent little girl."[14]

After no more than a single space between sentences, the crime of the previous sentence was now characterized as seemingly "impossible," and Faulkner's conviction not a question of "when" but of "if."

While the writer described Mary Brown as an "innocent little girl," this waffling suggests that the writer may have begun to question the logic of her story.

• • • •

Of the cases adjudicated in recorder's court throughout 1863, very few involved sex crimes such as rape or seduction. As fate would have it, J. Knox Gavin would prosecute three during the first week of March alone: the Schaaf seduction case, the Wineman rape case, and "the Faulkner Outrage." All three defendants were represented by J. Logan Chipman.

The Schaaf seduction was a sad story with a happy ending.

Nineteen-year-old Mary Smith worked as a "rag-picker" for Cornwell, Van Cleve & Barnes. Often poor immigrants, "rag-pickers" collected the detritus left by urban dwellers and resold it. Their "gold" consisted of rags, glass bottles, papers—anything and everything with nominal value.

At some point, Smith caught the eye of John Schaaf, a thirty-two-year-old foreman at the company.[15] Their conversation took on romantic undertones and, according to Mary, evolved into a "seduction." A felony in the mid-nineteenth century, "seduction" involved the use of coercion—often a promise of marriage—to obtain sex.

After several visits to Mary at the home of her married sister Elizabeth Tisler, John Schaaf proposed. Dispensing with formalities, the couple consummated the marriage before it had occurred. "I knew him about 4 or 5 weeks when it happened," Mary later explained. "He promised to marry me and then he had intercourse with me ... no other man ever had intercourse with me, [I] was a vergin [sic]."

According to Mary, they had intercourse "four times," and each time, Schaaf coaxed Mary by reiterating his intention to put a ring on her finger. "I would not have consented," Mary later said, "if he had not promised to marry me."

Schaaf subsequently reneged on his promise, and a few weeks later, Mary became convinced that she was pregnant. "I have had my courses for four years," Mary explained, and then "they have stopped 2 months, and mornings I feel sick at the stomach when I eat. My breasts have payned [sic] me ever since." Paternity was never a question to Mary, who insisted she "never had intercourse with any body [sic] but this man John Schaaf."[16]

Worse still, Mary believed that Schaaf had moved on to another lover and that she would be forced to raise the child by herself.

Mary Smith's "seduction" became news when the teenager swore out a warrant for Schaaf's arrest. The warrant landed Schaaf in a jail cell, which got his attention. Upon his release, he made a beeline to the residence of John and Elizabeth "Lizzy" Tisler in an attempt to talk Mary out of pressing charges and even offered her money to drop the case. She told him in no uncertain terms that the only payment she would accept were two short words uttered in front of a justice of the peace. Schaaf refused.

Schaaf returned to the Tisler residence the next day, hoping that Mary had changed her mind. While waiting for Mary, he told her brother-in-law John Tisler that he never intended to marry her and still didn't because he did not believe she was "in a family way." Tisler accused Schaaf of "ruining" his sister-in-law.[17]

Once again, Mary refused to drop the charges unless Schaaf made good on his promise. Once again, Schaaf refused, forcing Mary to talk about her "seduction" in court.

The trial commenced in February 1863. Mary, red-faced but undaunted, narrated the story of her "seduction," and her brother-in-law swore that Schaaf told him he never planned on a wedding, only a consummation.

3. "The Faulkner Outrage" (March 2–March 4, 1863)

The case merited only a few lines in the *Detroit Free Press*. Reporters shied away from the he-said, she-said details and resorted to euphemisms such as "enciende" and "in an interesting condition" to describe Mary's pregnancy.

Schaaf faced the music in court, which ended up with a solemn rendition of "Here comes the bride." Found guilty, he decided to make good on his promise after all.

"Finding himself thus driven to a close corner," noted a *Free Press* reporter, "the wanton swain determined to quash further proceedings by making her his wife. Accordingly the pair proceeded from the court-room to the office of Justice Kuhn, and were united in the holy bonds of matrimony. Thus was amicably settled a long course of legal proceedings, few of which it is believed are consummated so happily."[18]

The newlyweds moved to Ypsilanti. It remains unclear if Mary was "enciende" in 1863, but in the first few years of their marriage, the couple welcomed three children: Margaret in 1866; Catherine in 1867; and John in 1869.[19]

• • • •

Henry Wineman stood accused of raping twenty-seven-year-old German immigrant Mary Ann Gries. While Wineman did not receive so much as an anecdote in the dailies, his case nevertheless attracted the usual crowd that flocked to sensational trials, particularly those during which they might witness the airing of some pretty dirty laundry.

To the delight of the habitual court-goers in the gallery, Gries left very little to the imagination when she testified about the rape. Gries, who emigrated from Germany to New York two years earlier, eventually settled in Detroit and came to live with Wineman, a "confectioner" who rented rooms to several boarders including Mary Ann Gries.

According to Gries, Wineman made his first move by cajoling her into drinking with him.

He poured something he called "cherry whiskey" into a wine glass and told Gries to drink it. She may have later suspected that Wineman spiked the "whiskey" with morphine, because she testified that "the first liquor in the glass was a light yellow, the other he poured was a brownish color."

After Gries downed the liquor, Wineman handed her a lamp and asked her to take it to his bedroom. She obeyed, and a few minutes later, Wineman appeared in the doorway. "He ... took me by the shoulder and pushed me back onto his bed," Gries testified.

Despite obvious parallels between the two cases, the *Free Press* devoted a mere line or two to Wineman, whereas the Faulkner case consumed whole columns. Lines versus inches. The difference: Wineman was a white man who allegedly raped a white woman. Faulkner was assumed to be a Black man who raped a white girl.

• • • •

Faulkner's examination opened to a standing-room-only crowd, most of whom came to listen to the type of ribald testimony that characterized the Schaaf trial. The loud, boisterous group did not respond to Justice Lane's gavel, so he decided to hold the hearing in his office, at the same time insulating Mary Brown from reciting her traumatic experience in front an audience of morbid curiosity-seekers. Instead, she would rehash her story to Lane, Prosecutor J. Knox Gavin, Faulkner's defense attorney J. Logan Chipman, Faulkner, and a *Free Press* reporter.

Chipman had an ongoing relationship as an editor at the *Free Press*, which put him in a rather awkward position. While he did his damnedest to defend Faulkner, the *Free Press* editors would do theirs to condemn him in print. It remains unclear if this conflict of interest impacted Chipman's handing of the case, but it does present a possible conduit of inside information leaking to the press.

The *Advertiser and Tribune* did not have a man present, which led to a one-sided accounting presented by the rival paper.

The *Free Press* reporter would not repeat the details, instead teasing his readers with a placeholder: "The evidence was taken down by our reporter, but, from the nature of the offense was totally unfit for publication. It is sufficient to say that, if the story of this child is entitled to any credit, the crime was one of the most aggravated and fiendish ones ever recorded."

Although the reporter insisted that Brown's story jived with her earlier rendition, between the lines of his March 2, 1863, article is the unspoken suggestion that Mary's story had changed in Lane's office.

"Her statement was substantially the same as the account continued in The *Free Press* of Friday Morning," the reporter noted. "It could not, of course, be expected that a mere child, like her, would be as precise in all her statements as a person of maturity."

Evidently, one key detail did change, which caused the *Free Press* to retract a portion of the "Horrible Outrage" story. "The colored girl who went with little Mary to the saloon of Faulkner is not in any manner implicated in the foul transaction. It appears she was slightly acquainted with the prisoner, and went into his saloon merely for the purpose of warming her feet, without having any knowledge of his intention and subsequent acts."

In addition to the alleged victim, two additional witnesses testified: Brown's adopted mother Rosa and Dr. Charles H. Barrett, who examined Mary when the allegation surfaced, ten days after it supposedly occurred. Ellen Hoover did not testify at the preliminary hearing.

Rosa Brown's statement added nothing new to the record, but Barrett's testimony, according to the *Free Press* writer's account, "concurred in every respect with that of the girl, showing conclusively that her statement was not in the least exaggerated."

A trial appeared a foregone conclusion, so Chipman waived Faulkner's right to a defense at the hearing and did not cross-examine the witnesses. He indicated that the key witness in his client's defense would be Ellen Hoover, who Faulkner believed would verify that nothing happened to either girl that afternoon in his saloon.

The animosity toward Faulkner became evident from the demeanor of the small crowd that had gathered outside city hall. Incensed Detroiters shouted epithets at the accused and made ominous threats about a neck-tying party, a short rope, and a tall tree.

Deputies managed to escort Faulkner back to his cell at the county jail, where he would await his day in court, set for the following Wednesday.

He would have unexpected company in the person of Ellen Hoover.

Gavin requested that Lane issue bail of $300—a sum that he knew she could not pay and that would lodge her in the county jail until the trial. Reportedly, Gavin made this request because he wanted to ensure that Hoover showed up to testify in court, but he may have had one or more ulterior motives. Perhaps he feared that Faulkner or his attorney would attempt to exert undue influence or pressure, or perhaps he feared that Hoover's testimony might destroy his case against Faulkner.

Mary Brown walked out of Lane's office with her mother; Ellen Hoover with a deputy to escort her to jail. The Faulkner case took an unexpected and shocking turn as Ellen and her escort traversed the blocks between city hall and the county jail.

According to the *Free Press* reporter, "On the way to the jail the girl burst into tears, and, clinging to the officer for protection, asked, amid choking sobs, the following question: 'Will he kill me if I tell the truth?' Her fears being put to rest on that point, she voluntarily admitted her knowledge of all the material facts alleged by Mary Brown; stated that she was in the room at the time the outrage was committed; that Faulkner locked the door, and would not let either one of them out; and that she would testify to the whole proceeding, exactly as she saw it."

Lest anyone protest about coaching witnesses, the reporter added his bonafides: "These confessions of the only witness for the prisoner were made in the presence of officer Sullivan and our reporter, and there is no room for doubt that they are strictly true."[20]

If any "tampering" with the witness occurred, the journalist insisted, it was done by or on behalf of Faulkner. "That this girl had been tampered with, and either bribed or intimidated to swear falsely to screen the villain Faulkner, is beyond a doubt."

Hoover's story "exactly as she saw it," however, deviated from Brown's in one vital respect: Brown said that Hoover was not in the room when the "outrage" occurred, suggesting that the only person to witness Brown's rape may not have witnessed it at all. If the girls did not agree on what color shirt that Faulkner wore that day, then the deviation could be dismissed as trivial, but disagreement on such a significant detail threatened to undermine the veracity of both accounts—a possibility realized by the *Free Press* man.

The reporter tried to downplay this discrepancy by stating that it was "of no earthly consequence." He went further by explaining the trauma had left the girls confused. He noted that "both the girls were, as they had reason to be, in a terrible condition of fright, and the younger one did not probably notice at the time the presence of the other."

3. "The Faulkner Outrage" (March 2–March 4, 1863)

As a result of Hoover's revised statement, Faulkner's legal trouble compounded. He now faced two separate but related charges: "carnally knowing and abusing [a] female child under 10 years of age" for the alleged rape of Mary Brown and the rape of Ellen Hoover. Conviction on the first charge, which carried a life sentence, would make the second charge superfluous.

The *Free Press*' inside man penned a story that appeared on the front page of the Sunday, March 1, edition under the headline "THE FAULKNER OUTRAGE." He did not wait for the trial, the evidence, the case for the defense, or the inevitable guilty verdict. "The evidence of the negro's guilt is overwhelming, and cannot be controverted," he wrote.

He went on to lament the absence of a death penalty in Michigan and suggested that a guilty verdict would not bring justice in this case. "The only thing to be regretted is that there is no law sufficiently severe to punish him as the damnable crime which he has committed so richly merits. The gibbet or the guillotine alone would subserve the ends of justice in the case of the ten-fold worse than murderer, the black fiend, the monster Faulkner."

The *Free Press* emphasized the reporter's condemnation by republishing the article in the next morning's edition.[21] After the "Fox" story of February 27, news of the Faulkner case did not appear in the rival paper until March 6, and then only as a blurb. Either the editors of the *Advertiser and Tribune* chose to minimize the story, or they considered it less newsworthy than their counterparts at the *Free Press*. Regardless, there was a stark difference in how the dueling newspapers reported on Faulkner's case.

• • • •

Faulkner's arraignment on the Hoover rape charge took place in police court on Tuesday, March 3, but the *Free Press* presented case 432 as an anecdote to the alleged rape of Hoover's white companion. The *Free Press* kept the stove hot by placing news of the arraignment on page one, but the story occupied just about two inches of text. The article made no mention of a boisterous crowd or a lynch mob, so either the writer chose to ignore it or the alleged rape of a twelve-year-old Black girl did not create that same kind of stir.

Instead, they choose to report on items that furthered their assault on the city's Black community. The two inches below the Faulkner story was devoted to a story called "A COSTLY NOZZLE" about two Black Detroiters—James Jones and Philip Ward—tried in police court for stealing a copper nozzle and pipe from the steamship *Whitney*. The author concluded his piece with a pun: "The copper-colored thieves were convicted and sentenced to thirty days each in the Workhouse."[22]

4

The Case for the Prosecution (Thursday, March 5, 1863)

> The only pretext for this outbreak in fact,
> Was "Falkner" [sic] committed an [sic] now nameless act,
> Although given up to the law right away,
> The mob sought to lynch him in broad open day.
> —From "The Riot" by Benjamin Cutler Clark, Sr.

On the eve of Faulkner's trial, feelings ran high in the Third Ward. The *Advertiser and Tribune* blamed its rival paper for inflaming public opinion against Blacks by depicting them as the root of all war-related evils.

> The ignorant and unreasoning classes have been told by the paper referred to that this war is for the negro's welfare, and that all the national suffering is on his account; that white men are taxed to pay for negro freedom; that the white man's interests in Congress are neglected and only those of the negro attended to; that negroes emancipated at the South will come North and drive out white labor; that in giving an opinion that negroes were citizens, the Attorney General intended to compel white people to receive them upon terms of social and political equality. Soldiers have been represented as starving while thousands of slaves have been represented as supported in idleness by the Government, and we might add to these representations.[1]

• • • •

Without the missing Faulkner files, piecing together the goings-on at the trial becomes a Sherlockian feat of deductive reasoning. The *Advertiser and Tribune* did not cover the trial in any detail, leaving the *Free Press* as the sole source of reporting about the case. Their reporter sat among a throng who crammed the courtroom benches.

"The excitement which had been created by the nature of the charge against the prisoner," he wrote, "brought together an immense crowd at the court-room, every seat available in the room being filled to the utmost extent which it was possible for them to contain."

Deputy Sheriff Cicotte apparently anticipated trouble from the onset, so he detailed a group of deputies to maintain law and order in the court. Cicotte himself appears to have played a significant role in quelling any disturbances; the same *Free Press* reporter applauded him in follow-up article.

The two-day trial opened on the morning of Thursday, March 5, in recorder's court, Judge Benjamin Franklin Hawkins presiding. Prosecuting attorney J. Knox Gavin would make the case on behalf of the people; J. Logan Chipman and his second-chair Augustus W. Henssler would defend the most notorious man in the city.

Chipman was a familiar face in recorder's court and a well-known adversary to Gavin. In the months leading up to the Faulkner trial, Chipman defended bordello proprietors, thieves, murderers, and accused rapists John Schaaf and Henry Wineman.

An avowed Democrat, Chipman played an active role in city politics, chairing the Detroit Democratic Association. The lawyer's political affiliation made him a natural ally of the *Free Press*, but in the Faulkner case, they stood across the aisle from one another. While Chipman did his best to prove his client's innocence in recorder's court, the newspaper attempted to convict Faulkner in the court of public opinion.

Empaneling a jury consumed most of the morning session. Many of the potential jurors admitted to reading about the case and forming an opinion about Faulkner's guilt, which prompted Chipman to dismiss several with preemptory challenges. By the afternoon session, the lawyers managed to agree on twelve men, but critics would later argue that the impossibility of finding a dozen unbiased jurors meant that Faulkner could never have received a fair trial.

The case for the prosecution consumed the rest of the day in court. Gavin called four witnesses: Mary Brown, Ellen Hoover, Dr. Charles H. Barrett, and Rosa Brown.

Mary Brown recounted her story to a courtroom of spellbound observers. Although no trial transcript has survived to record what Mary said, the *Free Press* correspondent's description of Mary's testimony about the rape as "disgusting and sick-ning [sic]" suggests that Gavin wanted nothing left to the imagination. After hearing the

4. The Case for the Prosecution (Thursday, March 5, 1863)   77

Street scene in April 1865. The building at the left is the courthouse where the Faulkner trial took place (courtesy Burton Historical Collection, Detroit Public Library).

little girl's graphic description of the rape, the all-male jury of fathers, grandfathers, and uncles would want someone to swing for the crime. Gavin would give them Faulkner.

The *Free Press* correspondent was impressed by the ten-year-old's demeanor. "The little girl, Mary Brown, was first put upon the stand," he wrote. "As has been before stated, she is a child of extraordinary intelligence, of a good moral character, and trained from infancy, by a Christian adopted mother, to do that which is right, and abhor and refrain from anything wrong."

He went on to credit Rosa for raising Brown in an environment that treated lying as the eighth deadly sin. "All her [Brown's] actions thus far show that she has been nurtured and educated under an influence which would not, certainly, induce her to make other than an honest and truthful statement of the circumstances connected with this horrible outrage."

Mary Brown's testimony jived with the earlier rendition she gave at the preliminary hearing. Chipman's attempts to catch Brown in a contradiction also impressed the reporter, who described the defense attorney's cross-examination as "ingenious" but ultimately inadequate.

Brown parried each of Chipman's verbal lunges, which underscored "the palpable truthfulness of her testimony."

Dr. Charles Barrett followed Mary Brown to the stand. His testimony is lost except for a lone line from the only newspaperman who wrote about the trial: "[Dr. Barrett] testified [about] the results of his investigations, which fully confirmed all the statements of the girl and the mother as to the effects of the dreadful occurrence."

The "results of his investigations" likely referred to physical trauma he discovered during an examination of Mary. Without an official (trial transcript) or unofficial record (the after-action news report did not include specifics about Barrett's testimony), it is impossible to ascertain how he examined Mary and what he might have found, but physical markers of rape may include tearing of the vagina, bruising of the inner thighs, and a broken hymen. It bears noting that Barrett's "investigation" did not occur until ten days after the alleged rape.

Ellen Hoover's testimony hinged on a credible explanation for why she had changed her story, which had evolved from the first rendition in which she did not witness the rape to the second rendition in which she claimed to be in the room when it occurred. According to Hoover, Faulkner threatened to kill her, so she remained mum until she felt safe enough to tell the truth. Not that the "whys" and "wherefores" mattered, according to the *Free Press* reporter. "Her evidence, however, is not needed at all in the matter, but, as it is, goes to rivet the guilt more firmly upon the negro."[2]

Gavin ended his case with Rosa Brown, whose testimony was almost certainly designed as an emotional appeal. Since she did not witness the rape, her testimony may have consisted of nothing more than a human interest story about a niece orphaned as an infant and her guardian's troubles to make ends meet for her two dependents.

When Gavin rested the prosecution's case, Chipman asked Judge Witherell to let the jury see the scene of the supposed crime. He apparently wanted to show that Hoover could not have seen what she claimed to have seen. Although the *Free Press* downplayed Hoover's testimony as marginal and even superfluous, Chipman's request suggests he may have considered her testimony damaging enough to warrant an attempt to impeach it. The testimony of the older girl may have dispelled doubts about sending a man to life on the word of a ten-year-old.

4. The Case for the Prosecution (Thursday, March 5, 1863)

As jurors inspected the scene of the "outrage," deputies clamped a pair of "bracelets" around Faulkner's wrists and marched him off to the county jail. Faulkner and his escorts—officers John Esser, John Fenn, and James Hepburn—emerged from the courthouse into a mob of several hundred inflamed citizens who greeted the prisoner with hisses, jeers, and expletives. Moving Faulkner along as fast as possible, they made a beeline for the jail through a gauntlet of angry citizens throwing insults at Faulkner from the sidewalks and through second-story windows.

By the time the procession passed the German Congregational Church on Monroe Avenue, the crowd had swelled to about a thousand. Someone hurled a stone that struck Faulkner in the back of the head. He fell face-first into the paving stones.

The crowd engulfed the four figures. "The yells and shouts of the infuriated mob were at this time terrible," wrote the *Free Press* reporter who followed the angry crowd from the courthouse, "and it seemed as though it would be utterly impossible to proceed, the crowd hemming in around the officers and prisoner, determined that his blood should atone for the fiendish outrage he had committed. Every one appeared to be animated with the same feeling, even women, along the streets and from the windows of dwellings, cheered on the mob, waving their handkerchiefs, and calling upon them, as men and fathers, to hang, shoot, butcher, or kill him by any means in their power."[3]

While one of the officers brandished a revolver and threatened to shoot anyone who tried to abduct the prisoner, the other two pulled Faulkner off the ground and managed to rouse him. Each taking an arm, they dragged the wobbling man to the jail.

The officers foiled the crowd of angry citizens who formed a human barricade in front of the jail by taking Faulkner through a back gate leading into the jail yard. A combination of quick thinking, determination, bravery, and luck saved Faulkner's life from the lynch mob.

News of Faulkner's near-lynching hit the streets on the morning of Friday, March 6. The coverage in the city's two major newspapers hints at what the rival editors felt was most newsworthy. The *Free Press* devoted an entire column—more than a foot in length—to the "TRIAL OF THE NEGRO FAULKNER." The article provided blow-by-blow coverage of both the trial and the aftermath.

Up until this point, the *Advertiser and Tribune* editors had largely avoided reporting about the Faulkner trial, but by Thursday evening, they could no longer ignore the storm raging around the courthouse. They devoted a short paragraph—about two inches in length—to the story "GREAT EXCITEMENT," which focused on the unrest that occurred after testimony had concluded on Thursday. The article refers to the defendant as "Faulkner, the negro."

"The evidence," noted the *Tribune*'s article, "disclosed a state of facts that greatly incensed the large crowd that had assembled in and around the City Hall. The trial not being concluded, the prisoner was remanded to the jail, and on his way thither, under charge of an officer, he was followed by a mob and threatened with summary vengeance, and barely escaped with his life. He was safely locked up, and will be again brought before the Court this [Friday] morning, when it is apprehended, efforts will be made to wrest him from the hands of the officer, for the purpose of administering summary punishment."[4]

This was more than a warning; it was a prophecy.

• • • •

By the end of 1862, the war that everyone believed would end in days had dragged on for more than a year. The Union army had sustained several key losses and needed grist for the war mill. Congress obliged and passed a draft law in March 1863.

News of the new law hit the streets of Detroit on Thursday, March 5. Because Wayne County's volunteers were sufficient to meet the federal quota, the draft would not impact residents of Detroit.[5] Nonetheless, in the minds of many working-class German and Irish immigrants, most of whom resided in the Third, Fourth, and Seventh wards, this edict appeared proof of the doomsday-like predictions of the *Free Press*: that they would be forced to fight, and possibly die, to free a population that would come north and take their jobs.

The *Free Press* printed all thirty-eight sections of the bill in the Thursday, March 5, 1863, edition. The thirteenth section, which provided for the hiring of substitutes, raised the most eyebrows. It allowed a draftee to hire a substitute, who would march off to war in his stead, at a price of no more than $300. Drafters of the law apparently intended the price ceiling to prevent substitutes from charging exorbitant prices and therefore eliminating substitutes for anyone other than the very rich.

The section had teeth. "And any person failing to report after due service of notice, as herein prescribed, without furnishing a substitute, or paying the required sum therefor [sic], shall be deemed a deserter, and shall be arrested by the Provost Marshal and sent to the nearest military post for trial by court-martial, unless, upon proper showing that he is not liable to military duty, the Board of Enrollment shall relieve him from the draft."[6]

The provost marshal and his men, who were barracked at Fort Wayne, would be responsible for rounding up draft dodgers and malingerers. Angst directed at these men would reach a new high. In the minds of some working-class Detroiters, they would come to represent an unpopular edict by an autocratic government. The specter of forced conscription would materialize in the uniform of the provost guard wherever and whenever they appeared, so their presence on the streets of Detroit would add to an already volatile situation.

In the next day's edition, the *Free Press* editors unleashed a furious attack on Section 13 in a scathing editorial. Ignoring the proviso that allowed the secretary of war to fix a substitute fee of less than $300, they recast Section 13 as an attack on the underprivileged. "There is no good reason why one man should be exempt and another compelled to perform military duty, simply because one happens to have temporarily more money than another. If there is to be a discrimination of this kind, the poor—those whose families will be likely to suffer by their absence from home—should be the favored class. Those who are able to pay the three hundred dollars are able to support their families during their absence, but the hardship and wrong of the law, as it now is, falls upon the poor—those who are not blessed with a surplus of this world's goods. The injury to the community is far less to compel the rich man to serve in the ranks if drafted than the poor."[7]

To drive the point home, they offered the example of a recently-drafted German farmer with eight children all under the age of thirteen. "This man is drafted, and, as a consequence, his wife and children are driven to subsist upon the cold charities of the world, or starve. This is a gross wrong to society." The article did not mention the farmer's name but curiously drew attention to his ethnic background by

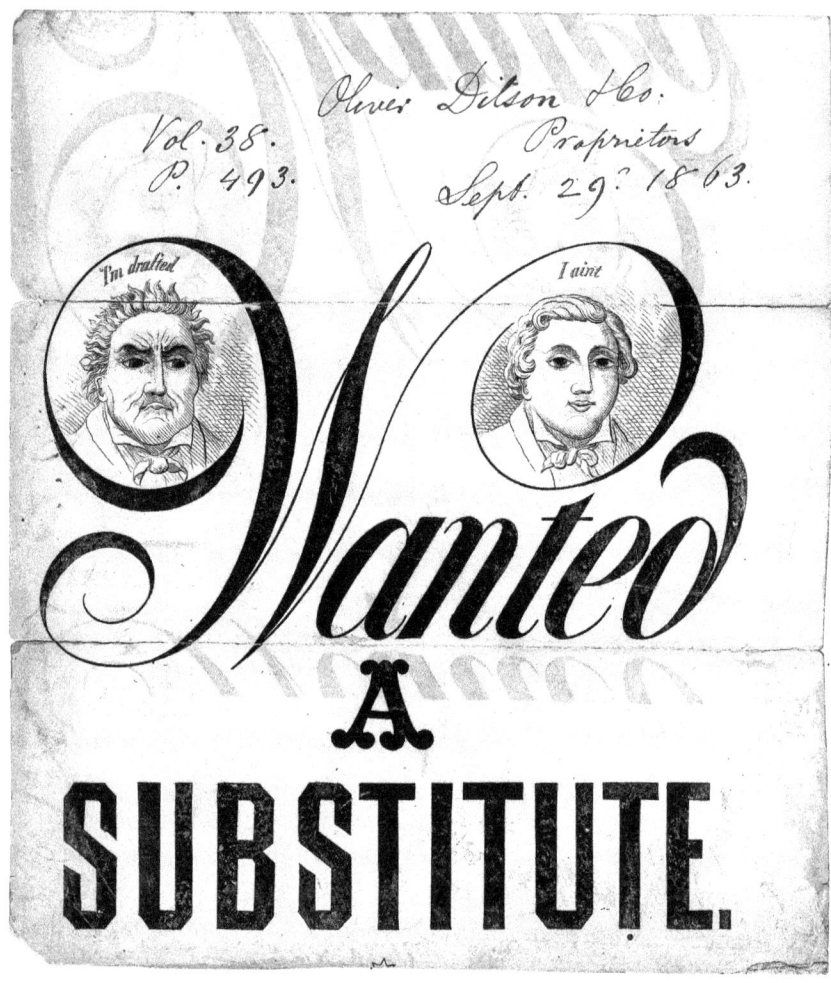

This cover for a piece of sheet music reflects the "rich man's war, poor man's fight" viewpoint regarding the substitute provision of the 1863 Enrollment Act. Note the artist's rendering of the working-class man looking for a substitute (left) and the possible substitute (Library of Congress).

describing him as "a hard-working, industrious German." If the *Free Press* encouraged the riot, as the rival paper alleged, then it appears that their target audience included German immigrants from the working class—the same population that targeted interracial bordellos in the Tenth Ward.

Advertiser and Tribune editors later condemned the *Free Press* interpretation of Section 13 as "the most shameless demagoguery" and

4. The Case for the Prosecution (Thursday, March 5, 1863)

PROVOST MARSHAL'S OFFICE
1st CONGRESSIONAL DISTRICT MICHIGAN.
Detroit, December 1st, 1863.

Notice

Is hereby given, that any person whose name is enrolled below, may appear before the Board of Enrollment any time previous to *December, 20th*, 1863, and claim to have it stricken from the list, if he can show to the satisfaction of the Board that he is not and will not be, at the time fixed for the next Draft, liable to Military Duty on account of *1st, Alienage, 2d, Non-Residence, 3d Unsuitableness of Age, 4th, Manifest permanent Physical Disability.*

☞ Persons who may know of any other persons liable to military duty, whose names do not appear on these Lists, or is incorrectly enrolled are requested to notify the Board or the Enrolling Officer of their District, giving the names and residences of such persons.

68d Sub. District,

First Class.

Allen, John B
Allen, Edward K
Abbott, Bara
Abbott, Oscar
Baylea, Andrew J
Beal, Elias
Bryant, William
Bryant, Wallace
Bryant, Samuel
Bovee, Henry
Bordine, Jacob
Bovee, David
Bailey, George W
Baker, Lucius P
Baker, Amos M
Baker, Levi W
Baker, John D
Bawl, Stephen J
Bovee, Arthur
Bovee, Hiram
Brown, Charles G
Chittenden, Seymor
Chaffee, Oscar
Convers, James O
Carpenter, Andrew J
Collins, James F

Carll, Patrick
Culver, George W
Cerow, Ransom
Collins, Peter
Combs, James V
Cleveland, Josiah
Curtis, Farons
Cross, Samuel
Carpenter, Frederick F
Ditton, Robert
Dedilice, Alonzo
Dye, John
Dye, Vincent
Downer, Jerome C
Deline, George
Deline, Edwin
Deline, Irа W
Finch, Isaac C
Fullerton, Henry H
Foster, Marion E
Foster, Daniel C
Fisk, Lyman C
Fisk, Amos
Ferman, William
Ferman, Dusenberry, J
Ferman, Asa T
Forbes, Timothy C
Fisk, Elisha
Gale, Isaac R

Griffin, Blake
Graves, Burritt W
Hulett, Frederick A
Herring, Daniel D
Hamlin, Heman
Hathaway, Jacob
Hathaway, Wilson J
How, Henry P
Howard, Daniel D
Howard, Almond
Heward, Darius M
Hunt, John L
Jordan, Judson L
Knapp, Henry F
Lingle, John
Langford, Edwin O
Lowth, John F
Lowth, Thomas E
Lowth, Nathan
Long, John
Lecock, Alexander
Latham, Edwin O
Lord, Jerome D
Leacox, John M
Lawrence, Chas R
Lord, Allen S
McMath, Francis
McLouth, Orville
Mickley, George P

Millins, Francis
Middleton, Philip
Middleton, Charles
Maynard, Haydon W
McLouth, Cyrus
Myers, Benjamin F
Moore, John M
Moore, Lewis P Jr
Moore, Charles F
Moore, Rily W
Nixson, John W
Nichols, Daniel D
Phillip, William H
Phillips, Saron P
Pontiva, David
Pawling, Hulbert
Pawling, Leonard
Porter, Charles C
Pratt, Hiram
Payne, John M
Porter, Charles W
Rickard, Samuel
Read, Enoch
Roberts, William
Roberts, Edward
Roberts, William H
Shay, Asahel B
Shepherd, James H
Salesbury, Levi O

Strong, Joseph T
Shaw, Charles J
Soper, George
Smith, John W
Small, Henry
Small, George
Spall, James
Smith, William Z
Thompson, Jeremiah
Telford, Joshua P
Thompson, Smith
Tyler, Almeron
Torbron, Gilbert
Vaughn, Samuel D
Van Ostrand, Theron
Van Sickle, Jacob M
Vedder, Aaron
Voorhes, William H
Warren, Austin A
Wert, William H
Warren, Johnathan W

Dover, Lenawee Co.

Second Class.

Allen, Thomas P
Ashly, William
Bayley, Hiram S
Bardine, David
Fennett, Louis B
Becannon, Joseph
Bailey, Benson E
Beals, Edward
Colgrove, Yeader
Cooley, Austin
Cammet, Elisha O
Colvin, Asa W
Collins, John J
Deline, Hiram
Fuller, Justus W
Foot, James M
Furgueson, Reuben
Foot, Ellery P
Grant, John C
Hitching, John O
Thompson, Walter
Hutchins, Norman M
Howard, George L
Ireland, David
Johnson, Jacob C
Johnson, Paris
Kerr, Mathew H

McLouth, Alva
Mulliken, Shurburn
McNight, John
McLouth, Wm W
McLouth, Peter
Phillips, Aaron M
Perkins, Newman
Palmer, Killwell N
Read, Jacob
Read, William F
Roberts, Phillips
Rowley, David T
Sweet, George
Seeley, James
Smalley, William C
Spooner, Amos B
Schooley, Hamilton
Soper, Carlisle B
Shanger' John M
Smith, John
Thompson ,George
Tabor, Daniel H
Telford, John W
Tobias, Charles M
Vreeland, Sylvester

By order of the Board of Enrollment,

MARK FLANIGAN, Provost Marshal.
HENRY F. KELLOGG, Commissioner.
GEORGE LANDON, Surgeon.

Draft notices like this one appeared all over Michigan in 1863 and inflamed preexisting tensions (University of Michigan Bentley Historical Library).

pointed out that the act also allowed generous exemptions for sole providers, such as the only children of widowed or infirm parents. As such, they argued, Section 13 actually favored the poor.[8]

They also offered a piece of advice for evading the draft: "Get married, all you youngsters. The unmarried men will be the preferred subjects for conscription." As for a suitable mate, the editors suggested "a lady, with at least $300, preferred."[9] The $300 would be necessary to hire a substitute should the nuptials fail to shield the groom.

Whys and wherefores aside, the timing of the Conscription Act could not have been worse for William Faulkner. While Detroiters, particularly working-class young men, contemplated the possibility of marching off to war to free the slaves, the "negro" Faulkner stood trial for his alleged rape of a white girl.

5

The Case for the Defense (Friday, March 6, 1863)

To avoid any attempts to intercept Faulkner en route, Cicotte had him escorted to the courthouse at 6 a.m.—three hours before the beginning of the morning session—where the most despised man in Detroit waited for Chipman to begin his case.

There was an eyewitness who could prove that Faulkner did not rape Mary Brown: a longtime customer who spent most of his waking hours in Faulkner's saloon. While it remained uncertain if the man had clear enough vision to see anything, Brown and Hoover admitted to seeing the man in the bar that morning. According to a *Free Press* correspondent, they testified to seeing "a white man ... lying on a lounge in a room adjacent to the one in which the outrage was committed."

"Faulkner appeared to be very anxious to secure the man as a witness," the reporter later said, "stating that he could swear to certain facts which would in a great degree qualify the testimony of the girls, if not entirely controvert it.... Both the girls agree in the statement that he was on the lounge at the time the crime of the negro was perpetrated." On the eve of his case, however, Chipman still had not located the witness whom the *Free Press* did not name.[1]

Chipman requested a continuance, which would allow him time to find the missing barfly and identify other witnesses who might help him convince the jury that Ellen Hoover's found memory was planted. Witherell, perhaps fearful that any delay might spurn the mob to storm the courthouse, denied Chipman's request.

Without the witness, Chipman faced a nearly impossible task: he had to convince twelve angry men that a ten-year-old fabricated the story of her rape. Her age complicated things. The twelve men in the jury box would see in Mary Brown the image of their daughters and nieces. This association would make it difficult for them to see her as a deceptive, conniving succubus. Chipman would need to accuse her of lying without calling her a liar. He would need to highlight the variances in the statements of the two girls.

Gavin, on the other hand, felt confident enough in his case that he did not plan on giving a closing statement. His case would rely entirely on the testimony of Brown and Hoover, who appeared credible.

Illness landed Wayne County sheriff Peter Fralick in bed with a fever, so Deputy Sheriff F.X. Cicotte took over as acting sheriff. While Chipman and Gavin prepared for court, Cicotte prepared to secure the courtroom. To maintain law and order, protect the courtroom figures, and prevent any would-be hangmen from nabbing Faulkner, he stationed a small detail of deputies inside the gallery.

Officers Dennis K. Sullivan and David M. Freeman were two of the deputies assigned to the courthouse that morning. As constable of the Third Ward, Sullivan would have heard rumblings emanating from barstools and would have recognized the potential for danger and the need for vigilance.

These harbingers of violence may have been communicated to residents of the Third Ward, which later gave rise to a conspiracy theory that the riot had been engineered by the city's Copperheads. According to one item published shortly after the riot, "city officials gave several negro friends timely warning 'to keep in, and not be about the negro districts of the city, for there would probably be trouble in that vicinity during the day.'"[2]

• • • •

Winter months were always busy times for Detroit's fire brigade and their leader, fire marshal William Champ. Frigid temperatures forced people to use their fireplaces more, and the buildup of soot made chimney fires the most common cause of fire, prompting Champ to take drastic measures. He issued a warning that violations of the fire ordinance would lead to strict punishments and worked with the city council to hire a chimney sweep who would be available "at all times." Nevertheless, of the twenty-one fires that Champ noted in his February report, seventeen were the result of dirty chimneys.[3]

High winds that blew through the area on Thursday, March 5, and Friday, March 6, created a very dangerous situation. Gusts could throw cinders from roof to roof; a simple chimney fire, otherwise easily contained, could become a blaze capable of destroying an entire city block.

On Thursday night, Champ's men worked in vain to extinguish a fire in a barn at the corner of Thompson and Grand River streets. The wind fanned the flames, which quickly ate the hay and turned the framing into charred toothpicks. The wind threatened neighboring structures, but firefighters managed to contain the fire even though the only source of water for engine No. 10 was a partially dried-up well.[4]

• • • •

A few blocks to the south of the courthouse, Joshua Boyd, Marcus Dale, Louis Houston, his brother Solomon, and Lewis Pierce prepared for work in Whitney Reynolds' cooper shop—one of the largest Black-owned businesses in Detroit. Reynolds' crew made barrels and casks used by local merchants to store beer, pickles, gunpowder, flour, and other commodities.[5] Reynolds had left before sunup for Oakland County to procure wood for the shop.

The son of former slaves David and Synthia Dale from North Carolina, Marcus Dale was born in Gallipolis, Ohio, in 1832. Ten years later, the Dale family moved to Detroit. When David Dale passed away, Marcus was forced to quit school and learn the cooper trade to help his mother and three siblings make ends meet.

Dale briefly attended Oberlin College, but when his money dried up, he returned to Detroit and went back to making barrels. In the ensuing years, he married Mary L. Williams, fathered three children by her, and became an ordained minister.[6]

As the sun rose over Detroit and Faulkner's trial opened for its final, climactic day, Dale and the other coopers gathered in the shop at the corner of Beaubien and Lafayette. They were unaware of the danger looming a few blocks north, outside city hall.

• • • •

The case for the defense hinged on a lone witness. Chipman questioned Ellen's mother Whiney in a desperate attempt to break down the revised version Ellen gave after Judge Witherell ordered her confined

5. The Case for the Defense (Friday, March 6, 1863)

to the Wayne County jail. By attempting to undermine Ellen Hoover's story, Chipman suggested that her new-found memory of the alleged rape was planted. According to the *Free Press*, however, the lawyer's efforts fell short. Testimony of Whiney Hoover "was not brought to bear on any important point."[7]

When Whiney Hoover stepped down from the witness box, testimony in *The People v. William Faulkner* came to a close. All that remained before the jury began deliberations were closing arguments.

Gavin, who planned to dispense with a closing argument and rest his case on the shocking testimony of Mary Brown and Ellen Hoover, gave a brief overview of the evidence they presented.

Chipman's second chair A.W. Henssler followed Gavin. Henssler focused his remarks on the testimony of Dr. Charles Barrett. He suggested that the medical evidence presented by Dr. Barrett was inconsistent with the brutal and violent rape as described by Mary Brown. Had Faulkner forced Brown face-forward against a chair or a table and forcibly penetrated her, the assault would have led to physical trauma not present during Barrett's examination.

Several times, audible outbursts from the gallery caused Henssler to pause while Witherell attempted to hush them with this gavel. The *Free Press* correspondent credited Cicotte's detail of officers for maintaining law and order in the courtroom.

"During the remarks of Henssler," he wrote, "the popular feeling of the dense crowd which thronged the court-room manifested itself in groans and hisses and uncouth remarks. It required the utmost effort of the police force in attendance to repress the demonstrations and keep order sufficient for the court to proceed with its business."

These "groans and hisses and uncouth remarks" must have vexed Henssler, who suffered from a long-term bronchial ailment that caused him to use opiates and made vocal projection a difficult and painful proposition.[8]

Chipman followed his co-counsel with an impassioned plea to the jury. According to the *Free Press* reporter, Chipman noted that "he had not gone into the case with any affection for the negro, as all knew his feelings upon that point, but simply that he might see justice done." By admitting that he overcame his own prejudice to "see justice done," Chipman used a powerful piece of rhetoric. If he could overcome his prejudice, he implied, they could overcome their prejudice. He implored them not to see Faulkner as "a negro" but as a fellow human being who deserved justice not at the hands of the mob outside the courtroom but by the twelve reasonable gentlemen inside it.

He asked them to ignore the popular sentiment against his client and instead examine the evidence, which he felt confident would lead them to conclude that Faulkner had not raped Mary Brown. Corroboration for Brown's story hinged on the statements of Ellen Hoover, but her version changed from one telling to another and contradicted Brown's story on one important point: she said that she was in the room when the rape occurred. This discrepancy alone created a reasonable doubt about the veracity of the victim's testimony.

The *Free Press* reporter described Chipman's closing argument as "ingenious, able, and eloquent."

Chipman's "ingenious" remarks apparently forced the prosecutor to make an impromptu summation. Gavin reiterated the importance of listening to the evidence and not the voices of the mob, which had grown larger by the minute. He condemned their efforts to nab Faulkner and characterized the attempt as subverting justice and usurping the court's authority.

Gavin finished his address around high noon, so Witherell recessed the court for a two-hour break. He asked Cicotte to clear the courtroom, and his deputies herded the court-goers onto the street, where they waited for the doors to open. The crowd swelled, and the *Free Press* reporter described them as "thirsting for the blood of the doomed criminal within."

When the courthouse doors opened at two p.m., a tidal wave of people rushed through them and packed the courtroom to watch the final scene in the drama. Judge Witherell addressed the jury and explained the law they would need to consider in deliberations, then sent them out of the courtroom to decide Faulkner's fate.

For Faulkner to be innocent, Mary Brown had to be lying, but why would the ten-year-old fabricate such as serious accusation? Without an alternative theory from the defense, jurors concluded that the girl was not fibbing. It took just five minutes for the twelve men to find Faulkner "guilty in manner and form as charged in the complaint."

Witherell asked the now-convicted rapist if he had anything to

5. The Case for the Defense (Friday, March 6, 1863)

say before he passed sentence. Visibly shaken by the verdict, Faulkner insisted he never laid a hand on Mary Brown, whom he believed lied about the rape for reasons he did not know or understand.

Faulkner went on to say that he believed the girls had played a role in an attempt to oust him from his property. Brown and Hoover, he said, had appeared in his saloon several times before the alleged molestation, and in each instance he had shoed them away. In what would later become a popular refrain for critics of the trial, the now-convicted rapist also protested that he did not have adequate time to round up defense witnesses. Chipman could not find their chief witness, a map peddler whom Faulkner believed lived somewhere in the vicinity of the Michigan Central Depot and who had apparently been in the saloon at the time of the supposed crime.[9]

Unmoved, Witherell characterized Faulkner's conviction as the only proper verdict based on the evidence presented and then noted that such a savage crime deserved the harshest sentence possible under Michigan law.

"I deem your crime the very worst of which a human being can be guilty, and one for which there can hardly be sufficient punishment," Witherell said, "and do, therefore, give you the full sentence of the law: to remain in the State Prison, at Jackson, during the remainder of your natural life."[10]

Faulkner's knees buckled. He dropped down into his chair, buried his head in his arms, and began to sob.

The audience in the courtroom applauded, prompting Witherell to quiet them with a few heavy raps of his gavel.

There was a question as to whether or not the crowd outside would consider the sentence "sufficient punishment." Fearing another attempt to grab Faulkner between city hall and the county jail, Cicotte sent an urgent request for the provost guard, billeted at Fort Wayne.

• • • •

In calling just one witness for the defense, Chipman apparently focused on undermining Mary Brown's credibility by highlighting inconsistencies in her testimony. He did not, however, present a theory for why Mary would lie in the first place.

In the days after the trial, Faulkner came to believe that his enemies paid Brown to fabricate the rape so they could drive him out of business. If Chipman presented any evidence of Faulkner's story, it disappeared with the trial transcript, but a minute advertisement in the March 6, 1863, edition of the *Advertiser and Tribune* provides a tantalizing albeit unprovable clue.

William Bromley, an auctioneer located at Michigan and Griswold, advertised "SALOON AND FIXTURES for sale cheap for cash." The timing and geography suggest these "fixtures" may have come from Faulkner's saloon; Bromley's auction house was near Faulkner's Michigan Avenue saloon, and the sale coincided with the date of Faulkner's trial. Of course, Bromley's sale does not prove conspiracy; Faulkner may have needed to liquidate his assets to pay his legal fees.

PART 3

Inferno
(Friday, March 6, 1863)
Timeline of the Riot

(Note: numbers correspond with numbers on the map. All times are approximate and based on fire marshal William Champ's report as well as eyewitness accounts from trial records and newspaper coverage).

1. **10 a.m.** Crowd gathers outside city hall (Woodward Avenue) during Faulkner's trial.

   12 p.m. Afternoon court session begins; crowd dissipates.

   2:30–3:00 p.m. Faulkner trial concludes with a guilty verdict. Fearing an attempt to lynch Faulkner, the Detroit City Provost Guard, under the command of 2nd Lieutenant John Van Stan, arrives from their barracks (at Clinton and Joseph Campau Avenue) to escort Faulkner from city hall to the county jail (Beaubien and Clinton). The crowd, now an angry mob, bombards the detachment with stones and paving bricks along the way.

2. **3:00–3:30 p.m.** The provost guards reach the corner of Gratiot and Clinton. Lieutenant Van Stan orders the crowd to disperse, which further inflames them. Van Stan then directs the guard to fire a volley of warning shots into the air. John W. Perkins later testifies that a crowd of about 300 gathered around the procession. He identifies Peter Doran as one of the rioters who hurled a rock at the soldiers when they reached the intersection of Monroe and Randolph sometime between 3:00 p.m. and 4:00 p.m.

   3:00–3:30 p.m. The assault on the provost guards worsens. Unidentified members of Van Stan's detail fire into the crowd, injuring several and killing local photographer Charles Langer. Some

Part 3—Inferno (Friday, March 6, 1863)

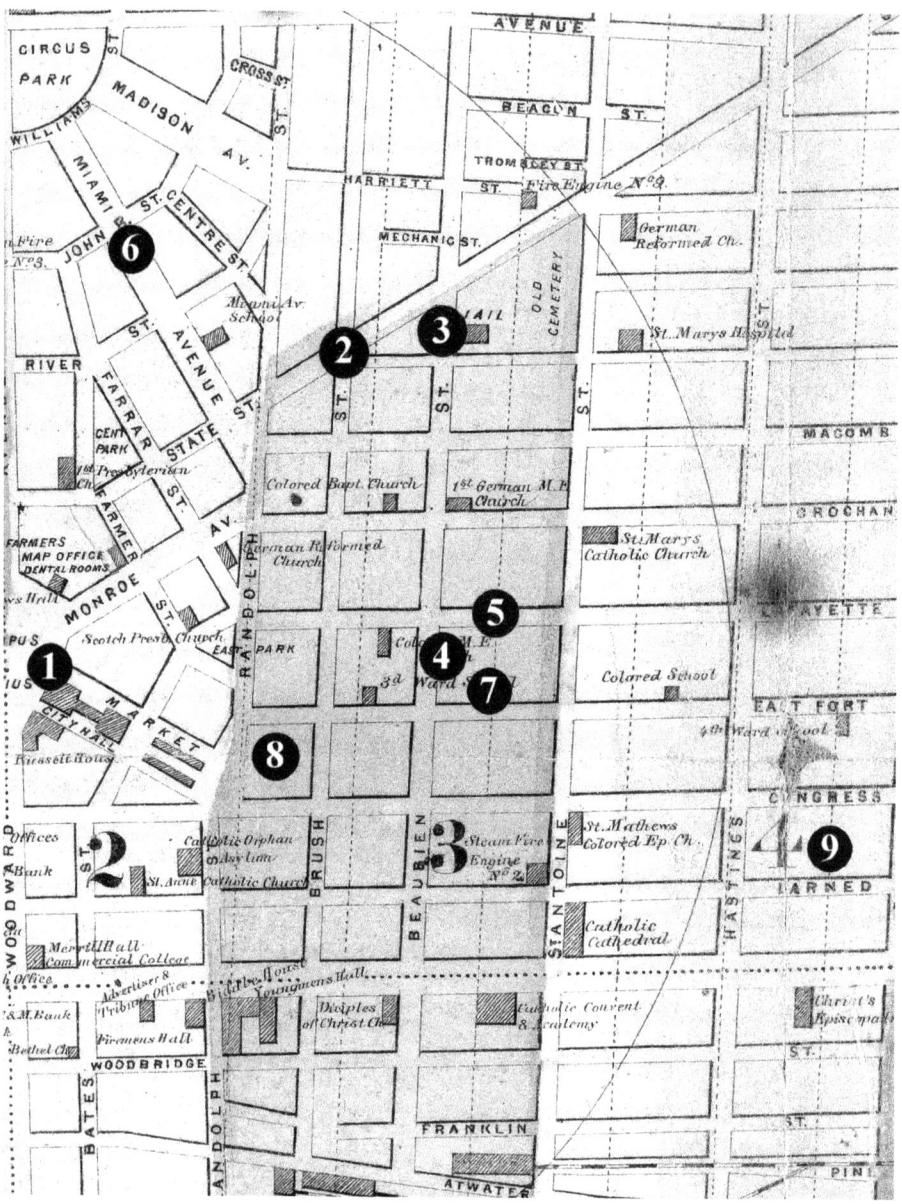

Detail from Silas Farmer's *Guide Map to the City of Detroit, 1863*, showing key events on March 6, 1863. Numbers correspond with events on the timeline (original from New York Public Library).

5. The Case for the Defense (Friday, March 6, 1863)   93

eyewitnesses recall seeing Van Stan brandishing a pistol and testify that Van Stan fired the shots that killed Langer.

3. **3:00–3:30 p.m.** Faulkner and his escorts arrive at the county jail; the provost guards return to their barracks. After ransacking and laying waste to Paton Alley, a cyclone of rioters moves down Beaubien toward Fort and Lafayette, the heart of the city's Black community.

3:30–4:00 p.m. Mob attacks house on Beaubien, smashes windows with rocks until Officer Dennis K. Sullivan intervenes; the mob subsequently attacks a residence on Lafayette Street before descending on Whitney Reynolds' cooperage.

4. **4:00–4:30 p.m.** The siege of Whitney Reynolds' cooperage begins.

6:00 p.m. Ebenezer Cutler, a sailor, testifies to seeing a mob of thirty individuals chasing and beating an "old man" (Joshua Boyd) at the corner of Beaubien and Croghan. Officer Sullivan wards off the rioters and takes the injured man into a nearby saloon. He tries to bar entry but a rioter named Krueger gets past him on the pretense of buying a glass of beer. While a crowd of about a hundred gathers at the front door, Sullivan manages to sneak the man out the back door.

5. **6:00–7:00 p.m.** Rioters attack the Lafayette District of the Third Ward, looting and setting fire to structures on Lafayette between and Beaubien and St. Antoine.

6. **7:00 p.m.** Rioters reach the intersection of Miami (Broadway) and John R.; authorities fear that the mob might attack respectable businesses and residences along Woodward.

7. **8:00 p.m.** Three dwellings and a barn on the north side of Fort Street are destroyed.

8:00 p.m. Fifty soldiers from the 19th Michigan Infantry arrive from Fort Wayne to quell the riot.

8. **8:15 p.m.** Rioters set fire to Gies alley, four tenement buildings on Congress between Brush and Randolph streets.

8:15 p.m. A train carrying five companies from the 27th Michigan arrives in Detroit; soldiers debark and with soldiers from the 19th Infantry begin sweeping the streets.

9:15 p.m. A house, barn, and shed located at Miami and John R. is looted and burned.

9. **10:00 p.m.** Rioters torch a barn on the south side of Larned Street between Hastings and Rivard. This is the last structure set alight during the riot.

11:00 p.m. The soldiers manage to clear the streets of rioters.

6

Blaze
(Friday Afternoon, March 6, 1863)

> To keep from a rescue, and take him to jail,
> The soldiers were ordered to come without fail,
> But they were insulted and stoned at—pell mell—
> Till some of them fired and down a man fell.
> —From "The Riot" by Benjamin Cutler Clark, Sr.

The "bloodiest day that ever dawned upon Detroit" began at about two o'clock on the afternoon of March 6. As the final courtroom episode of "the Faulkner Outrage" played to a full house—a standing-room-only crowd of the morbidly curious—a crowd gathered outside city hall. Its number swelled as the afternoon progressed.

The anticipated guilty verdict did nothing to assuage the mob, their ring leaders intent on grabbing Faulkner and taking him to the nearest tree or telegraph pole. To keep the now-convicted rapist safe from the frontier justice of a lynch mob, the small contingent of deputies would need to transport him several city blocks through a gauntlet of violent protestors. Fearing for the safety of Faulkner and his men, acting sheriff F.X. Cicotte consulted with acting mayor Francis S. Phelps, who requested help from the city's provost guard, billeted in barracks located at the intersection of Clinton and Joseph Campau Avenue.[1] Lieutenant Colonel Joseph Rowe (J.R.) Smith ordered Captain Erastus D. Robinson to comply with Phelps' urgent request.

The barracks housed three distinct groups: a detachment of 102 provost guards and officers under the command of Captain Robinson; a company of 114 soldiers from the 8th Michigan Cavalry under the command of Captain Elisha Mix; and a few men convalescing from battle wounds. When Robinson received Colonel Smith's order, several of his provost guards were away on duty, so he quickly patched together a unit that included provost guards, horse-soldiers, and the walking wounded and put Lieutenant John Van Stan, ex-lawman and private detective, in charge of the motley crew. Perhaps sensing what could happen and to prevent any itchy trigger-fingers from firing into the crowd, Robinson commanded Van Stan to supply some of his soldiers with blank cartridges.[2]

Lieutenant Van Stan divided the seventy men into two platoons and marched the patchwork group to the courthouse, having left the barracks an estimated ten minutes after Robinson received his marching orders.[3]

When the contingent of soldiers reached the courthouse just a few minutes later, the crowd had grown in size to include court-goers, the curious who had heard the din and came to investigate, and local street toughs—mostly German and Irish boys who ran wild in the Third and Fourth wards. The first two groups wanted to catch a glimpse of the notorious convict; the third group wanted to catch Faulkner as he came down the steps and lynch him.

Deputy Sheriff Cicotte met Van Stan at the base of the courthouse steps, and the two men came up with a plan: to form a hollow square around Faulkner and his escorts—Cicotte and deputies Charles Allen and William Close—and shield them as they made their way to the jail.[4]

Officer Dennis K. Sullivan recognized two of the faces in the mob: Bernard Groghan and William Krueger. Among the more vociferous of the group, they repeatedly jeered, "Kill the niggers, down them, kill them."

Shouting over a cacophony of jeers and insults, Van Stan formed his men into two parallel lines: the back line faced the courthouse and the front line faced the crowd. He then ordered the front line to move forward two paces, but the sheer size of the mob made it difficult for the soldiers to maneuver, so he ordered Lieutenant Babbitt to take a squad and clear the sidewalk.

The crowd reacted to the presence of the soldiers with more jeers, insults, and taunts. The blue tunics represented an unpopular war and an even more unpopular draft, which the provost guard would enforce by rounding up and prosecuting draft dodgers. Raising his voice above the din, Van Stan reminded his men to keep their cool.

When Faulkner emerged from the courthouse, the wave of humanity surged forward, prompting Van Stan to order his men to fix bayonets. The glittering quills of steel turned the hollow square into a porcupine, which kept the rioters at a short distance from the prisoner. With Faulkner and his deputy escorts in the middle, the hollow square inched forward with the crowd on its heels. The route snaked along Monroe to Randolph, right onto Gratiot, another right onto Clinton, a left on Beaubien, and right on a narrow alley leading to the jail.

According to a bystander named John W. Perkins, the crowd numbered about 300, including fourteen-year-old Peter Doran, whom Perkins spotted hurling a rock at the soldiers as they approached the corner of Monroe and Randolph.

Like Perkins, thirty-year-old photographer Charles Langer heard the shouting and went to investigate. Langer lived at the corner of Beaubien and Division and had walked several blocks south in order to see history in the making. The father of three did not realize at the time that he would become part of that history.

The crowd grew more violent as the procession neared the jail. The first brick was flung at the soldiers on Monroe Street, but by the time the hollow square reached the intersection of Gratiot and Clinton, the trickle of bricks, sticks, and stones had become a torrent. The rioters threw anything and everything they could find, including wads of crusted dirt and dead rats. One stone projectile hit Van Stan on the leg and threw him off balance. The former constable, however, managed to keep his footing and his poise.

Several rioters attempted to squeeze past the soldiers and grab Faulkner, but again Van Stan ordered his soldiers to fix bayonets. Dissuaded by eighteen inches of steel, they retreated, which gave Van Stan the few seconds he needed to redeploy his troops. He formed one platoon into a wedge and ordered the other platoon to proceed to the jail double quick, but the din of the elevated voices drowned out his orders and the first platoon misunderstood the command, prompting Van Stan to yell, "Why in the name of God don't you run with the prisoner?"[5] Eventually, the breakaway group heard the command and quickened their pace toward the jail, while Van Stan remained behind with the main body and attempted to block the mob from following.

The ejecta grew in intensity as the group reached the intersection of Beaubien and Gratiot, much of it hurled from a vacant lot next a blacksmith's shop located half a block to the south where Beaubien met Clinton. One rock struck a soldier in the temple. Dazed, he wobbled into the house of Jacob and Jane Hommel, located on the northwest corner of Beaubien and Clinton. "The blood ran from the wound very freely," an eyewitness named John L. King later said.[6]

King, a Californian visiting Detroit, wanted to catch a glimpse of Faulkner. He perched on the steps of a saloon across the street from the jail and waited for the soldiers to arrive. From this vantage point, King witnessed the entire episode develop. After the stone missile brought down the soldier, a few of his comrades fired their muskets in the direction of the blacksmith shop, although King believed they were firing blanks.

One of the soldiers later described his ordeal amid the mob on Clinton Street. "A huge pair of brogans" applied to "my suspender buttons behind my back" caused his "carcass" to rise "four feet from the ground…. Immediately afterward the half of a burned brick came in contact with my back, which landed me in the mud of Clinton street, where a full-sized portrait of the subscriber may be seen by those who are anxious to see the downfall of a man of parts but of small means."[7]

Thomas Buckner, who later told his story to the author of *A Thrilling Narrative*, described watching a mass of people coming down Croghan with several wagons laden with kegs of beer trailing behind them. "After this, while I was standing on the corner, with half a dozen other gentlemen," Buckner later recalled, "a rifle ball came whistling over our heads. After which we heard several shots, but only one ball passing us. In a short time after there came one fellow down, saying, 'I am shot in the thigh.' And another came with his finger partly shot off."[8]

Jane Hommel, who lived in a house on the corner of Clinton and Beaubien, had the best vantage point of all the eyewitnesses who later testified at the coroner's inquest. Through the window of the front parlor, she watched the scene unfold.

Deputy Sheriff William Close and 2nd Lieutenant John E. Babbitt pushed Faulkner through the thicket of rioters and through the jail doors. Babbitt later said that as they approached the door, three or four men attempted to grab Faulkner a second time. Close later described the plinking of objects against the iron door as it closed after Faulkner.

Meanwhile, Van Stan positioned himself on the corner of Beaubien and Clinton, literally in front of Jane Hommel, who had followed Van Stan by moving into the room fronting Beaubien, where she could observe all of the action. When a brick struck him in the hip with enough force to throw him off balance, he pulled his pistol and attempted to fire a round at the hoodlum. Hommel later described the Keystone Cops–type moment when Van Stan pulled the trigger but his gun did not discharge.[9]

Then, according to some witnesses, Van Stan ordered his men to fire in the direction of the blacksmith's shop; according to others, he ordered his men not to fire. Either way, it is likely that at least one soldier misheard the command and did the opposite.

His face bloodied from the glancing blow of a stone, Van Stan managed to hobble to the jail entrance on Beaubien, where he ordered his men to close ranks. At this point, Van Stan later said, he heard two or three shots and immediately saw a man, standing on the west side of Beaubien Street, fall to the ground. The man, photographer Charles Langer, died before he hit the ground.

Robert Warmsley stood shoulder to shoulder with Langer at the time the bullet struck him. According to Warmsley, Van Stan and one his soldiers had fired in rapid succession, but Warmsley insisted Langer did not fall until after the second shot, which he believed (based on the sound of the discharge) had emanated from a musket and not a pistol.

John L. King corroborated Warmsley's eyewitness testimony when he later recalled seeing a "stout, tall" soldier deliberately aiming his musket at the crowd and squeezing off a round. A few seconds later, Langer crumpled to the ground. Van Stan, King said, had his back to Langer at the time and physically could not have fired the shot.[10]

William Timm also saw Langer fall, but he believed Van Stan fired the round. A neighbor of the slain man, Timm knew the "daguerrean artist" by sight and stood about thirty-five feet away. Langer fell, Timm said, immediately after Van Stan fired his pistol in his direction. Only then did a few soldiers fire their muskets.

A farmer named Samuel Wilson saw Van Stan turn the corner of Clinton and Beaubien as he headed toward the jail. Wilson said Van Stan had his pistol in hand. When he reached the jail entrance, he fired into the crowd on the sidewalk across the street. Wilson said that the musket fire came immediately after the pistol shot, but he was certain that Langer fell before he heard the sound of muskets.[11]

Accounts vary as to the demeanor of the crowd after Faulkner had been delivered. Both William Timm and Samuel Wilson characterized the mob as deflated. Most of the trouble, Timm later said, had occurred before the procession reached the jail. With Faulkner safely behind bars, the animosity ebbed, so the soldiers had no need to shoot into the crowd. Wilson described the crowd as docile and did not believe the use of firearms was justified given the circumstances.[12]

Van Stan, on the other hand, said that the crowd was "very much excited and pelting the men with missiles," but Frank Auberry, a waiter at the Russell House, said that the crowd was calm until Langer fell, when they became enraged and rushed toward the soldiers.[13]

Van Stan gave the order to return to the barracks, and the soldiers left the scene double quick, leaving behind Charles Langer's body and a crowd of several hundred incensed Detroiters.

Deputy Sheriff William Close, one of the men responsible for leading Faulkner through the torrential rain of missiles, later criticized Van Stan for this abrupt about-face. Just a handful of sheriff's deputies were powerless to stop what came next.

In its day-after coverage, the *Free Press* also blamed the provost guard for leaving the city open to assault by German immigrants who wanted an eye for an eye after Langer's death, but this later assertion would prove inaccurate. Most of the rioters had English, Irish, and Scottish surnames.

Phelps, who was either on the ground in the Third Ward at the time or cowering at home, depending on who was telling the story, apparently realized the danger. He later explained, "I immediately repaired to the office of Lieut. Col. Smith and requested another force of 300 men to disperse the mob, who were continuing their riotous proceedings." With order number 2, Phelps granted the right "to fire on the rioters" if it became "absolutely necessary for the preservation of the public peace."

6. Blaze (Friday Afternoon, March 6, 1863)

But, as Phelps would go on to explain, there was a hitch. Smith "promptly gave the order, which was dispatched to the Barrack, and a communication from Capt. Robinson was received, saying that a rumor prevailed that an attempt was to be made to fire the Barracks by the conscripts in quarters there (which attempt was afterwards unsuccessfully made)."[14] Smith dispatched a group of soldiers from Fort Wayne instead, but the delay would prove deadly.

Edwin Jerome and his son, Edward Jr., watched in horror as Peter Smith egged on his fellow rioters. "Come, boys, down in there is a lot of niggers," Smith shouted, "come, let's give them hell."[15] It didn't take much needling to get Bernard Groghan and William Krueger to follow him.

Thomas Buckner overheard one of the rioters make an ominous comment. "If we are got to be killed up for niggers," he said, invoking the draft as an excuse, "then we will kill every nigger in this town."[16] They let out a collective war whoop and headed south on Beaubien.

7

Wildfire (Friday Afternoon, March 6, 1863)

> The mob, disappointed, now hied to a place
> Where some humble coopers, of the sable race,
> Were honestly working to earn their own bread,
> By rowdies were set on and left almost dead.
> They enter'd, and beat them with billets of wood,
> Then fired the cooper shop just as it stood,
> And as they attempted to rush from the flames,
> They met them with bludgeons to dash out their brains.
> —From "The Riot" by Benjamin Cutler Clark, Sr.

With Faulkner out of reach behind the stone walls and iron bars of the Wayne County jail, the rowdier elements of the mob turned their attention south. A tornado of rioters, most of them teenagers, according to Officer Dennis K. Sullivan, headed south on Beaubien, attacking any Black person they encountered.

Eyewitnesses, later testifying at the subsequent trial of the "rioters," identified specific faces among the amorphous, indistinctive mass of blurred humanity. During this phase of the riot, Cornelius ("Con") Dwyer, Robert Carey, and Timothy Drummond—described as a "deaf and dumb boy"—played a particularly active role in smashing windows.

Thomas Buckner raced from the jail to his residence on Beaubien, arriving just before the rioters passed by. "They approached my door in large numbers," he later recalled, "where I stood with my gun, and another friend with an axe, but on seeing us, they fell back. They approached four times determined to enter my door, but I raised my gun at each time and they fell back."[1]

7. Wildfire (Friday Afternoon, March 6, 1863)

Buckner and three of his assailants ended up in police court a few days later. Henry Freesee, William Gibson, and Gilbert Shiler faced assault and battery charges against Buckner, and in a bizarre turn of events, Buckner faced assault and battery charges against his three assailants. Justice Lane tossed the case.[2]

Frederick Wilson, who lived at the corner of Fort and Beaubien, recalled the moment he heard the banshee scream coming down the street. "I was aroused by the cry of 'A mob! A mob!' On hastening to the door, I saw thousands of men and boys coming down Beaubien street, yelling in a most hideous manner, as if all Pandemonium were turned loose. They let loose a perfect volley of all kinds of missiles at Mr. Buckner's dwelling."[3]

Frederick Wilson could see the berzerkers through his front window. "Doors, windows, and every part were under a shower of missiles. Axes, spades, clubs, and stones, and whatever they could lay hands on to do mischief with, were freely used."[4]

Dissuaded by the sight of Thomas Buckner's shotgun, the rioters gave up and moved further south on Beaubien, smashing windows as they went. At Beaubien and Layfayette, they laid siege to a house and cooper shop owned and operated by Whitney Reynolds, a former slave from North Carolina. Buckner raced up the stairs to a second story bedroom and watched as they descended on Reynolds' cooperage. The images he saw would haunt him for the rest of his life. "I could see from the windows men striking with axe, spade, clubs, &c, just as you could see men threshing wheat. A sight the most revolting, to see innocent women and children, all without respect to age or sex, being pounded in the most brutal manner. Sickened with the sight, I sat down in deep solicitude in relation to what the night would bring forth; for to human appearance it seemed as if Satan was loose, and his children were free to do whatever he might direct without fear of the city authority."[5]

A forty-nine-year-old former slave from North Carolina, Whitney Reynolds owned a cooperage and an adjacent house located at Beaubien and Lafayette. Two families lived in the house: Reynolds and his wife and Marcus Dale, his wife and their three children. Reynolds' twenty-year-old daughter Louisa, her husband Parker Bonn, and their infant daughter lived a few doors down.[6]

Earlier on the afternoon of March 6, Louisa and Parker Bonn

attended the funeral of an acquaintance. They returned home around 3:30. Louisa changed clothes and had begun preparations for supper when she heard what sounded like the howling of banshees. The loud, discordant noise grew louder as the rioters moved down Beaubien.

She glanced out the window to see the rioters pelting Thomas Buckner's house with rocks. Aware of the danger, Parker suggested that Louisa take their baby to her father's house. He would "shut up the house so that they would not think any one was home."[7] Louisa just beat the mob to her father's front door.

Contemporary newspapers and *A Thrilling Narrative* present the attack on Whitney Reynolds' cooper shop as a random act of violence, but the rioters may have had an ulterior motive for attacking this particular place in the Third Ward: the widespread belief that Reynolds kept a sizable sum of cash in the house.

According to the *Advertiser and Tribune*, a few days before the riot, Reynolds had received $700 from a recently completed job.[8]

The boys involved in the siege likely heard talk of Reynolds' stash because they had known, either personally or by association, several of Reynolds' workers. Marcus Dale testified to knowing Cyrus Sleker; Robert Bennette testified to knowing both Sleker and Alexandre Lefevre; and Lewis Pierce testified to knowing John H. Davis. These boys may have had more than mayhem on their minds; they may have been after Reynolds' cache of silver and gold coins.

Whitney Reynolds was away in Oakland on the afternoon of March 6, but six of his employees were busy at work in the shop: Robert Bennette, Joshua Boyd, Marcus Dale, Lewis Houston, his brother Solomon, and Lewis Pierce. Three women, four children, and two men were in the home next door: Mrs. Sara Reynolds, Louisa Bonn and her daughter, Mary Dale and her three children, Parker Bonn, and a visitor from Canada named William Jones.

As the rioters approached, the men could hear the eerie, blood-curdling chant, "Kill all the damned niggers. Kill all the damned niggers."

The six men clustered around the windows and watched as the mob materialized and ringed the building. Some of them carried makeshift clubs fashioned out of uprooted fence pickets. They began pelting the shop with the paving stones and bricks they gathered along Beaubien.

7. Wildfire (Friday Afternoon, March 6, 1863)

The shrill, discordant sound of shattering glass startled Robert Bennette, who looked up to see Cyrus Sleker and Alexandre LeFevre whipping bricks at the shop. Marcus Dale recognized John H. Davis. All three men had known their assailants for more than a year, although in what context remains unknown, perhaps as nothing more than neighborhood bully-boys. An eyewitness named Ada Smith added two names to the assailing mob: Edward Crosby and William Naylor.[9]

A few blasts from an old, rusty shotgun scattered the rioters like carpenter ants. They regrouped outside the house. Fearing for the safety of the women, the five men darted through a communicating passage into the house. With the shop's defenders gone, a rioter pushed through the door and started a fire, probably with a few red-hot coals. Wood shavings covering the floor worked as an accelerant, and the blaze turned into an inferno within minutes. The flames began to lick at the boards of the adjacent house, where the women and children tried to evade the stones and shards of glass flying through the windows.

"Let us surround the house," one of the rioters yelled, "and burn the niggers up."[10]

Edward Crosby, a young tough at home on the mean streets of Detroit's Third Ward, ran up to one of the windows with a fence picket. When he stuck his nose into the window, a cluster of shot peppered his face. He flopped to the ground and began moaning. He would survive but would be disfigured for life.[11]

Another load of buckshot ended up in the jaw of Morris Horan, although conflicting reports have blurred Horan's specific role, if any, in the attack. The *Detroit Advertiser and Tribune* at first described Horan as a bystander, then later as an active participant based on eye-witnesses who saw him brandishing a "bludgeon" and poised to strike when the cluster of shot peppered his leg. In a subsequent issue, the paper characterized this earlier depiction as a "misapprehension." The reason for the flip-flop was that the correspondent mistook Horan for Edward Crosby, who was the one waving the club.[12] Whether Horan was a savage rioter or an innocent bystander or something in between, reports about his injury indicate that someone inside the Reynolds' residence fired at least two volleys with a shotgun.

The maiming of Crosby further inflamed the mob.

Hearing the commotion, Father Ephraim Clark—the

eighty-year-old sexton of the African Methodist Episcopal (A.M.E.) Church a block away on Lafayette—went to the cooper shop. The aged sexton had a colorful past. Raised in slavery in South Carolina, he was sold to a Kentucky man who took Clark to war with him when he fought against the British during the War of 1812. Clark acquired his freedom when his master fell during Battle of Tippecanoe. He migrated north and settled in Detroit.

The mob immediately baptized Clark with a shower of stones, but his thick overcoat protected him until a brick struck him on the side of the head, knocking him to the ground. Rioters proceeded to kick him. Somehow, he managed to get into the house.

Clark later described the ordeal to the Rev. Sylvan S. Hunting, who presided over the Lafayette Street Unitarian Church. "After I got into the house, and sat down here," he said, "I thought, why does the Lord permit them to beat me, who have never hurt anybody the fifty years I have been in this city. The righteous must suffer with the wicked here, but up there, where I shall soon go, I shall be out of their harm. The good Lord will soon take me home. They can bruise and kill this body, but they can't hurt me."[13]

With the rioters forming a rough circle around the house, the inhabitants had nowhere to run. Mrs. Reynolds attempted to escape through the back door, but a barrage of stones forced her back inside the burning building.

Louisa Bonn described the torments of the trapped occupants to the author of *A Thrilling Narrative*. "Myself and child, mother [Mrs. Reynolds], and Mrs. Dale and her three children and brother, kept in the back part of the house while they were throwing stones, and then some one broke the front door open with an axe. Then the dining room caught fire."

The fire, Louisa explained, forced the residents to attempt an exit, but she would soon discover that the rioters had surrounded the house. "I started to go out the front door with my babe in my arms," she said, "thinking that, as I had not done anything at all to those fiends in human form, they would let me pass. On going to the door, a man met me with a large boulder in his hand, and would have knocked me in the head, had his hand not been caught by another man!" Two eyewitnesses would later identify Louisa's would-be attacker as Andrew Manning.[14]

7. Wildfire (Friday Afternoon, March 6, 1863)

In her statement, Louisa made a comment that indicted Detroiters for doing nothing to stop the rioters. "My husband, mother and other friends were all exposed to murderous assaults from those fiends; and to all human appearance there was not a friend in all the thousands that thronged and gazed upon our ruins."[15]

Louisa retreated into the house, but the "sheets of flames" forced her back to the front door. By this time, the roof had begun to collapse. Parker Bonn tried to calm his wife. The tolling of the fire bells, he suggested, would soon bring help.

The firemen never came, leaving the occupants dodging the licking flames, choking on smoke, and trembling in fear.

Sara Reynolds later recalled the moment she resigned to the hideous fate of dying in the inferno. "I found, on my daughter going to the front door, she had to hasten back to save her life from the mob, so I returned into the room and gave up to be burned up, for I saw from all appearances that if I went out in such a shower of stones, I should be certainly killed, and I just gave myself up to the mercy of God."[16]

Panic-stricken, Louisa screamed, the blood-curdling howl mobilizing Officer Dennis K. Sullivan and a bystander named J.B. Bloss who pushed their way through the crowd, darted into the house, and escorted Louisa and her child through the gauntlet. A forty-three-year-old seed merchant, Bloss would fight alongside Sullivan in saving Louisa and her child, and later others, from the angry hands clutching at them. They immediately walked her away from the scene and up the street. She was certain that both her husband and mother would die in the conflagration.

Still in her room, hugging to a trunk like a shipwreck survivor clinging to a piece of wreckage, Sara Reynolds heard Louisa's screams and assumed the worst. "I remained in this position and heard my daughter scream again," she later recalled, "and then soon it was over. I could not tell whether herself and babe had fallen speechless at the foot of the bloody assassin, or fell in the flames!"[17]

At that moment, Mrs. Reynolds heard someone in the crowd yell.

"The women will be protected," promised a disembodied voice, "[but] no protection for the men."

A few bystanders, whom Louisa later identified as Dr. Calhoun and "a Dutchman," raced into the house to lead the women and children to safety.

One by one the women slowly emerged from the house. Mrs. Reynolds went out first, still hugging the trunk. "I had taken care of the trunk," she later emphasized in her interview with the *Thrilling Narrative* author.

Mrs. Dale, squeezing her youngest to her chest, came next. The two older children clung to the hem of her skirt. "When the women approached the door," wrote the author of *A Thrilling Narrative*, "some fiend in human shape drew back a large club to strike them, but some spectators, having within them a spark of humanity, rushed to the women and rescued them—drawn probably by the screams of Mrs. Bonn."[18]

The men faced an agonizing choice. By this time, the flames had engulfed the house. They could die in the blaze or go outside to face a barrage of stones, brickbats, and probably a noose or two. Since a slim chance was better than no chance at all, the men decided to try their luck with the mob and rushed out of the house. Immediately, dozens of boys attacked them, stoning, beating, tearing, clawing. They fell like ten pins on the front lawn, beaten senseless. Even the aged priest did not escape the frenetic blur of fists.

William Jones, a visitor from Canada, first tried to go out the back door, but he ran into a group of "United States soldiers and others" armed with sticks and stones. Failing at the back door, Jones tried the front when rioters swarmed him "with all the fury of demons." Despite being knocked to his knees, beaten over the head, slugged in the stomach, and stabbed in the ribs, Jones made it through. Pursued by several rioters who ran after him yelling, "Kill the nigger, kill the nigger," he attempted to take refuge in the machine shop owned and operated by Isaac Ingersoll.[19]

Joshua Boyd made it as far as the fence at the back of the property. One of the rioters swung an axe at his head. The glancing blow gouged his scalp and left him slumped against the fence, insensate.

By the time Solomon Houston went out the front door, the fire had turned the frame into glowing embers. A familiar face in the crowd—a man Houston referred to as "a gentleman that I knew"—attempted to protect him from a savage beating. Houston later described this fateful moment. "Several laid hold of me," he recalled, "and said they were intent on taking my life; that they saw me shoot [the shotgun that peppered the face of Edward Crosby].[20] A German man rushed on me with a spade, and struck me twice with it over the head, inflicting a severe wound at each blow." The "German" was named Conrad Kalb, whom Houston later identified in court.

The "German" had raised the spade for a third time when one of the bystanders asked him what he intended to do.

"I intend to kill him!" the "German" responded.

"You ought to be ashamed to strike a man with such a weapon, whom you have never seen," the bystander scolded, "nor has done you any harm."

Something the man said resonated; the would-be spade killer threw the shovel down in disgust and let Solomon Houston pass. Houston was escorted to the residence of Lansing Thayer, a blacksmith who lived on Lafayette Street.[21]

Louis Houston followed his brother through the door. "The stones and bats were flying so that life was in danger at every step that I took," he later recalled. He crawled through a hole in the fence and came across the inert body of Joshua Boyd who had preceded him out of the burning building. Boyd had been gouged in the head by an axe, and his head and shirt were covered in blood. He was slumped against the fence, motionless.

For reasons never explained, Louis Houston went back to the house but soon realized the only way out was back through the fence. As soon as he squeezed through, a flying brick hit him in the head. He fell next to Boyd who by this time was lying on the ground.

A group of rioters surrounded them and took turns punching and kicking the stricken men. Leading the effort, according to eyewitnesses, were Antoine Downer and Timothy Drummond. Spotting the swarm, Dennis K. Sullivan and J.B. Bloss raced over to the spot. Pushing their way through the ring of boys, they found Boyd and Houston lying unconscious on the ground.

The chief instigator in this incident, according to Sullivan, was William Krueger. Sullivan later testified that Krueger brandished a bucket and egged on the others by yelling, "Kill him! Kill him!"

Sullivan and Bloss managed to rouse Boyd. Sullivan then helped him to a nearby saloon with Krueger and his minions following them, shouting insults along the way. "Kill him ... he is the man that fired out

The scene at Whitney Reynolds' cooper shop as envisioned by a *New York Illustrated News* artist. Note the man holding a stick at the left and leading the woman away from the mob. The woman was probably intended to be Louisa Bonn. The sketch inaccurately depicts the rioters as adults. A blurb in the March 28, 1863, afternoon edition of the *Advertiser and Tribune* used the sketch to criticize the *Free Press* accounts of the riot: "It is about as accurate an illustration of the affair as any novice with the pencil could have designed, who was a thousand miles away from the scene. The artist had probably read the *Free Press*'s imperfect and exaggerated account of the affair, and then drew upon his imagination to fill up the details. It would just as correctly illustrate a riot in Baltimore, Cincinnati, or St. Louis, as that which it purports to represent, and we therefore recommend the publishers to save the picture for future illustration of similar scenes that may occur in those cities or elsewhere." This sketch was reprinted in an 1883 edition of the *Pictorial War Record*, a New York–based periodical devoted to the Civil War.

of the cooper shop," Sullivan heard one of them shout. Houston, whom the rioters may have believed dead, remained lying inert in the ditch.[22] After a harrowing scene at the saloon, Sullivan left Boyd in the care of a friend and returned to the house.

Lewis Pierce had made it just out of the door when a stone struck him in the head, knocking him unconscious. When he regained consciousness, the fire had singed his arms and legs. He spotted a wheelbarrow nearby and pulled it over him. Like a turtle tucked into his shell, Pierce stayed under the wheelbarrow until officers Sullivan and

7. Wildfire (Friday Afternoon, March 6, 1863)

David Freeman rescued him.

A Thrilling Narrative is silent on how eighty-year-old Father Ephraim Clark—"the Prophet"—managed to escape the flames. The *Free Press* credited fire marshal William Champ with rescuing him. Unlike the younger occupants of the house, the Prophet had already sustained a brutal beating by the mob when he had entered the house. Champ found him crouched in a corner "trembling with fear, and praying for mercy."

Champ reassured Clark that he could and would move him safely through the rioters, but Clark would not move from his corner. According to a *Free Press* correspondent, fear had cemented him in place, although there may have been other reasons for his resistance to Champ. He may have been either unwilling to trust Champ's word or physically unable to move. According to *A Thrilling Narrative*, rioters had attempted to break Clark's legs when he arrived at Whitney Reynolds' residence.

HOW TO ESCAPE THE DRAFT.

In the wake of the New York riot, a *Harper's Weekly* artist drew this sardonic sketch titled "How to Escape the Draft." The Detroit riot of 1863 was often characterized as a result of angst over the new draft law, but the event was the result of a complex interaction of factors. Since Wayne County had already filled its quota, young Detroit men did not need to fear the new draft, and many of the malefactors were too young to enlist. Note the Leprechaun-like facial features of the rioters that the artist used to suggest their Irish heritage, leaving little doubt who he blamed for the melee. This scene, while depicting an event as it occurred (or as an artist envisioned it) during the New York draft riots, is reminiscent of the attack on Father Ephraim Clark, the aged sexton who was beaten outside the besieged cooperage in Detroit's Third Ward. Clark's attackers, however, used paving stones, pickaxe handles, boards, and rocks (Library of Congress).

The *Free Press* correspondent described the Prophet's so-called rescue. "Finding that entreaties were of no avail," he wrote, "the Marshal told several of the crowd to go in the back way and force him out. They did so, using no unnecessary violence, and even producing for him his clothes and other personal property, and then told him to go in peace, as they did not desire to harm an aged and infirm old man—that they were after the young darkeys, and not a feeble and utterly defenceless veteran of eighty years."[23]

The *Free Press* writer exaggerated and possibly even fabricated this rendition of Clark's escape, perhaps in an attempt to preserve Champ's reputation. Eyewitness Ebenezer Cutler would later testify to seeing an "old man" emerge from Reynolds' house and described the mob swarming him: "Antoine Downer with a crowd of others chasing a negrow [sic]—he was an old man grea [sic] headed—heard the crowd holler 'nigger, nigger,' saw him strike the nigger and kicking him when he was down." Clark was the only man in the house to fit Cutler's description.[24]

Marcus Dale was the last to escape the inferno. Half of his face was lacerated by a direct shot from a stone and the other half charred from the flames. "When he came out of the door," noted the *Thrilling Narrative* author, "some twenty dirty-looking Irishmen rushed at him with clubs, crying 'kill the nager.'"[25]

While the fire ate the rest of Whitney Reynolds' house, the survivors went in different directions, their tribulations just beginning.

8

Detroit Is Burning (Friday Night, March 6, 1863)

> Then they took the city without more delay,
> And fired each building that stood in their way,
> Until the red glare had ascended on high,
> And lit up the great azure vault of the sky.
> —From "The Riot" by Benjamin Cutler Clark, Sr.

A young *Free Press* reporter in March 1863, twenty-five-year-old Henry Utley followed his ears to Beaubien, where he witnessed some of the worst degradations in motion. In a profile written forty-five years later, Utley reminisced about reporting in an era before telephones, streetcars, or automobiles.

"It wasn't a case of sitting down in the office and calling your people up by telephone," Utley recalled. "Such an invention was unknown, and it was a case of tramp, no matter what hour of the day or night."

"At the first sign of trouble I was rushed to the scene," he continued. "Wherever a colored man was found he was dragged forth and beaten. Even women and children were not spared, many being subjected to the most brutal treatment. A popular plan was to set fire to houses in which people were known to be and then pelt them with cobblestones when they attempted to escape."[1]

• • • •

One of the truly heroic moments of the riot occurred outside Isaac Ingersoll's shop on Fort Street, where William Jones took refuge after surviving a savage beating outside Whitney Reynolds' house.[2]

Isaac Ingersoll, a builder whose brick-and-mortar was located at 66 and 68 East Fort Street, had stashed William Jones on the second story of his machine shop, where Jones had joined three other refugees. Jones' pursuers arrived seconds later.

Fed up, forty-four-year-old Lydia Ingersoll dashed out the door and attempted to shame the rioters. "You scoundrels," she yelled, "are you going to kill that man?"

Lydia Ingersoll's question, and perhaps the sharp tone in which it was shouted, hushed the crowd. "She ought to be shot for protecting the nigger," one of them whispered.

But no one harmed Mrs. Ingersoll or the wounded men convalescing upstairs.

Jones eventually recovered from his wounds. He credited Lydia Ingersoll's moment of bravery and her husband's kindness—which he attributed to divine intervention—for his survival. "It was to the humanity of Mr. and Mrs. Ingersoll," he said, "through the mercy of God, that my life was spared."[3]

Lydia Ingersoll wasn't the only Detroiter who refused to stand idle during the riot. Milton Frost, a furniture salesman and a city alderman, acquired a police night stick that he used to great effect. Lauding Frost's initiative and derring-do, the *Advertiser and Tribune* said that he "walked into the fracas with the coolness of an old hand, and by the use of arguments and club, materially assisted in quelling the disturbance and preserving property."[4]

Solomon Houston made it as far as the front door of Lansing Thayer on Lafayette when the mob overcame him. They knocked him to the ground and began mercilessly kicking when Thayer emerged from the house and demanded they stop immediately. He helped Houston into the house, where he remained until the next day.

While the flames licked at the framing of Whitney Reynolds' house, and Ephraim Clark and Lewis Pierce contemplated their options for escape, Officer Dennis K. Sullivan managed to move Joshua Boyd into a nearby saloon. Boyd was nearly unconscious and bleeding profusely from a gash in his scalp.

None of the contemporary accounts name the saloon or the saloonkeeper, but given Boyd's condition, logic suggests that Sullivan brought the critically-injured man to a spot a distance of a few steps. Three probable locations include the establishments of Henson Brown at 66 East Lafayette, Charles H. Roberts at 68 East Lafayette, John

Burns at 77 East Lafayette—all three located between Beaubien and St. Antoine—and Louis Sleaker at the corner of East Lafayette and Beaubien. Sleaker may have been the father of rioter Cyrus Sleker.[5]

About a hundred rioters formed an arc around the door of the saloon while Sullivan attempted to block entry. William Krueger, Sullivan later said, urged the crowd to rush the saloon, grab Joshua Boyd, and finish what someone had started with an axe outside of the cooper shop.

Krueger pushed past Sullivan and went inside on the pretense of buying a glass of beer. Later testifying against Krueger, Sullivan recounted the moment when Krueger emerged from the saloon. "When he went out, he said, 'the nigger is in there,' it cost him 10 cents to see him—to go into there and kill him." Sullivan did not know, however, if Krueger actually laid a hand on Boyd inside the saloon.

Apparently satisfied that Krueger had killed Boyd, the rioters left the saloon and moved south on Beaubien.

With the immediate threat gone, Sullivan left Boyd in the care of Peter Paul Lefevre—Detroit's Catholic Bishop and a trusted friend—and returned to what remained of Whitney Reynolds' residence to help the people—Lewis Pierce and Ephraim Clark—still trapped inside. Meanwhile, Lefevre loaded Boyd into a wagon and drove him to St. Mary's Hospital, but fearing further violence, Boyd's family ferried him across the river to Canada.

Felled by a flying brick and kicked mercilessly after escaping the fire, Louis Houston lay unconscious for several minutes. When he came to, he pulled himself to his feet and began to wobble down St. Antoine Street, where several of the rioters spotted him. They surrounded the terrified man and took turns punching and kicking him, but Houston lived to tell about the attack. "They commenced on me again," he said, "and with all kinds of weapons they beat me in the most cruel manner over the head till I heard some one say, 'he is dead!' then they left me alone."

For a second time, Louis Houston pulled himself from the ground. Noticing the bloodied figure hobbling along, a bystander suggested they go to the jail where Houston might be safe, but when they arrived, the "jailor" asked "what I came in there for."

The jailor's reaction incensed Houston. "Humanity sickens at such cruelty! Here I had lived and paid my taxes for the last ten or twelve years, and it was the first time I had ever been in prison; and then when a most brutal mob was raging through the city, the civil authorities doing not one thing to defend me; and when I went to the prison for protection of my life, was turned out to the exposure of the mob!"

Ejected from the jail, Houston ended up in the residence of Dr. Morse Stewart—a doctor who lived a block east of the jail and across from St. Mary's Hospital. Stewart treated Houston's extensive injuries. "My head was beaten almost to a pummel from the blows I received. I received three bad burns, which, with the wounds on my head, have caused me indescribable sufferings."[6] Like his brother, he would remain laid up for several weeks after the ordeal.

After being pulled out from under the wheelbarrow, Lewis Pierce stumbled to the house of William Jones, the city "scavenger" who lived on Lafayette (not the William Jones assaulted at the cooperage). Several rioters, including John Dollar, followed Pierce to the Jones residence. He tried to hide in an outhouse, but Dollar and a man Pierce later described as wearing "soldier's clothes" found him. They each grabbed a leg and dragged Pierce into St. Antoine Street.

With several rioters in tow, Dollar and the soldier dragged Pierce a block north to Croghan Street, where, he later said, "they fell on me, and with kicks and clubs, beat me till they thought life was extinct, and then went off and left me for dead!"[7]

Pierce spent several days on death's doorstep but ultimately survived. He later catalogued the numerous injuries he received at the hands and feet of the mob. "My head was bruised," he said, "so that for weeks my head and ears run with corruption. My knee cap was broke right in two by a stroke from some weapon. My body was so bruised that for two days I vomited nothing but pure blood."[8]

Louisa Bonn had survived a near-bludgeoning and escaped from a raging inferno, but her trial by fire had not yet come to an end. She ended up sheltering at the residence of Michael and Ann Clark on Lafayette Street. Certain that her mother had perished in the flames, she stood by the window to see if anyone else had survived. To her amazement, she spotted her mother, still hugging the trunk, wobbling toward her. Louisa raced out onto the street and helped her mother into the house.

Once inside, Louisa suggested they break open the trunk and retrieve the small sum that Whitney Reynolds had cached. Ann Clark handed Louisa a hammer, and with a few swings, she managed to break the lock.

They were going through the trunk's contents when several rioters, who trailed Mrs. Reynolds, formed a cordon outside the front door and began showering the structure with bricks and stones.

"Mrs. Clark and all of us were frightened to desperation," Louisa later described the assault. "She attempted to run up stairs, but Ma told her not to do that, but go out of the house. At this Ma opened the back door, and went down the yard, and jumped the fence, leaving the trunk and all its contents sitting behind the stove. My mother knew that the trunk had all my father's money in it that he was then just preparing to lay in a large stock of cooper stuff. She had dragged it several squares from our dwelling, that the mob had destroyed, to be compelled to leave it in the house of Mrs. Clark to be seized by those vile fiends."

Reynolds' trunk contained $1,200.

Louisa Bonn and Mrs. Reynolds, for the second time that day, escaped a house ringed by violent rioters. They wound up wandering the streets, cold, frightened, and without sanctuary. "My babe was entirely naked, with the exception of a little dress and skirt, having lost all his clothes, even to his bonnet, in the fire and trying to escape the mob," Louisa later explained.[9]

They wandered aimlessly for the next several hours, finally finding shelter at about 8 p.m. in the house of Edward Harberd, a Black "whitewasher" who lived on Mullet Street. Louisa still heard no word from or about her husband.

It would be a long night of worrying. Not until 3 a.m. on Saturday did Parker Bonn and Marcus Dale stumble into the Harberd residence after spending several hours dodging, evading, and hiding from rioters.

Whitney Reynolds returned to Detroit to find his house and business in ashes. He followed word on the street to the Harberd residence where he discovered, to his relief, his family safe. "This struck me with such force," he later said, "that when I came home and found my family all safe it filled me with such satisfaction that I did not feel the loss of the property scarcely at all."

Reynolds had lost all his material possessions, which, he later lamented, amounted to $1,200 in cash and $4,000 in property "all swept away in an hour for no cause, only the wickedness of a class of men who hate the colored man."[10]

• • • •

It took less than an hour for the rioters to reduce Whitney Reynolds' property into a pile of smoldering, charred timber. At about 5:30 p.m., they moved south on Beaubien, looting, pillaging, and burning as they went. Their vandalism followed a pattern. They would pocket anything of value—cash, jewelry, silverware—and then smash furniture on paving stones and tear open feather mattresses. They made funeral pyres of anything they couldn't or didn't want to carry away: piled-up pieces of broken furniture, shredded bedding, musical instruments. The Third Ward shimmered with bonfires.

Then, they burned the houses. As night fell, the glowing fires could be seen for blocks. The outline of buildings throbbed against the moonless night.

According to the after-action report of fire marshal William Champ, a majority of the structures that were destroyed—sixteen—were located on East Lafayette between Beaubien and St. Antoine. They laid waste to ten structures on the north side of the street, eight of which Champ noted belonged to Black residents, and another six on the south side. Champ described this area as "a most notorious resort for thieves, prostitutes and all the vilest portion of the colored portion of Detroit," raising the possibility that the rioters believed this area, like Paton Alley, housed "amalgamation dens."[11]

Although contemporary reports do not name all of the inhabitants burned out in the Lafayette district of the Third Ward, city directories suggest that Henson Brown's saloon and residence at 66 East Lafayette, the residence of a soldier named George Condon at 69 East Lafayette, the residence of cobbler Leopold Levy at 71 East Lafayette, the saloon of John Burns at 77 East Lafayette, and the home of a porter named Andrew McHugh at 78 East Lafayette all went up in smoke.[12]

Rioters torched the residence of a fruit and vegetable "huckster" named Romulus Morton and then set upon the house of Frederick Wilson.[13]

They stopped short of burning Wilson's house, but fearing for the lives of his family, Wilson gathered as much of his belongings as he could carry and joined the growing exodus across the river to Canada.

8. Detroit Is Burning (Friday Night, March 6, 1863)

Next came the residence of Thomas Holton on Fort Street between Beaubien and St. Antoine. Holton was at home with his wife and their child when he heard the chorus "Kill the niggers" accompanied by the percussion of shattered glass and the drumming sound of doors being kicked in. After a thunderous fusillade of bricks and stones, they set the house on fire, but Holton was able to lead his family safely out of the burning building.

The rioters chased them down Fort Street "with demoniac rage." Watching the scene develop, workers at a neighboring leather factory beckoned the Holtons, inviting them to pass through their building. Holton lived to tell his tale to the author of *A Thrilling Narrative*. "We took it as a great favor, for no one could tell in what direction to go—all the streets seemed to be filled with the mob."[14]

The Holtons made their way out of Detroit and spent the rest of the night shivering in the woods outside the city limits.

Holton's neighbor, Benjamin Singleton, was the next target. Blind, Singleton could hear but not see the havoc around him. They would have slaughtered the horse tethered to a hitching post in the front of Singleton's house because "it belonged to a 'nigger,'" but a white bystander stepped forward and said the horse belonged to him.

To the chorus of "Kill the niggers," the rioters set Singleton's house on fire. Unable to escape, he would have perished in the flames if not for "white ladies" who helped him to safety.[15]

Robert Burley, who lived across the street, recognized one of the boys as sixteen-year-old William Carlow. Other eyewitnesses identified Charles Hall, William Naylor, and John H. Davis. Realizing the danger, Burley fled before Carlow and company went to work looting his house. He would return later to find the residence intact but in disarray.[16]

Charles Fletcher had been chopping wood for a widow who lived on Miami Avenue, a few blocks to the northwest of his Lafayette Avenue address. Unaware that the mob had looted and burned his residence, Fletcher came home to find his home in ruins and his valuables gone.

The mob chased him into a back alley. Running for his life, Fletcher ducked into a tannery and hid in a vat, where the owner found him shivering in waist-deep water. He attempted to shelter Fletcher in a second-story room, but two of his pursuers found him hiding. They

Part 3—Inferno (Friday, March 6, 1863)

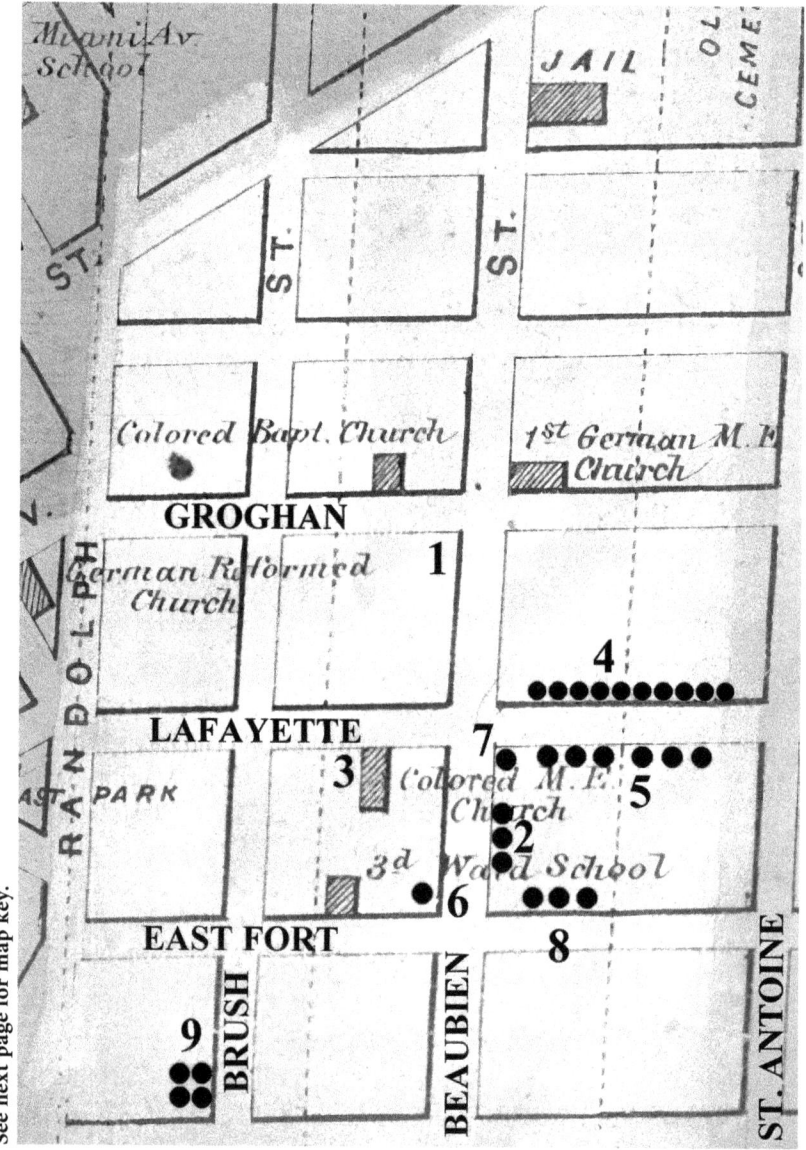

drove him down the stairs, out of the factory, and straight into a swarm of angry rioters, who beat him senseless.

Rioters lined up outside Ephraim Clark's A.M.E. Church, half a block down the street from the cooper shop. After showering the edifice with flying debris, they attempted to set it on fire, but Dennis K. Sullivan managed to thwart their attempt.

8. Detroit Is Burning (Friday Night, March 6, 1863)

Opposite: Riots seldom develop in a linear fashion. While it is possible that multiple locations were attacked at the same time, contemporary news reports indicate that the sacking of Third Ward residences occurred only after the destruction of Whitney Reynolds' home and business, which suggests that the more active rioters also played key roles in later episodes of violence and destruction. It also suggests that the violence radiated outward from the Reynolds property, perhaps in multiple directions at once. So D.K. Sullivan may have been warding off would-be arsonists on the steps of the A.M.E. Church at the same time that other rioters hit houses on Lafayette across Beaubien. Only one surviving contemporary account—William Champ's after-action report—provides a timeline for the attacks, so while the reason is evident, the rhyme is much less certain. Cross-referencing Champ's report with city directories, eyewitness accounts, court records, and newspaper accounts, it is possible to piece together a rough sequence of events. In his report, Champ identifies a few of the destroyed building as the work not of rioters but of opportunist thieves who used the confusion to steal. They are not included in the following sequence. The structures on the map are those that Champ identifies as the work of the rioters. (Note: all locations are approximate; Beaubien does not run strictly north and south but in a south, southwesterly direction.)

    1. (4 p.m.) Rioters attack residence of Thomas Buckner at the corner of Beaubien and Croghan.

    2. (4:30 p.m.) Mob besieges and burns Whitney Reynolds' residence and cooper shop on the east side of Beaubien (three structures in total located at 132 Beaubien).

    3. (5:30 p.m.) D.K. Sullivan thwarts threats to burn A.M.E. Church.

    4. (6 p.m.) Rioters sack and destroy ten structures on the north side of Lafayette.

    5. (6 p.m.) Rioters sack and destroy six structures on the south side of Lafayette, the residence of Charles and Mary Mathews (65 East Lafayette), and five other residences between Beaubien and St. Antoine.

    6. (7:30 p.m.) Rioters destroy Benjamin Singleton's house at the corner of Fort and Beaubien on the west side of Beaubien (119 Beaubien).

    7. (7:30 p.m.) Rioters destroy the residence of Romulus Morton at the corner of Beaubien and Lafayette.

    8. (7:30 p.m.–8:15 p.m.) Rioters sack and burn three dwellings on Fort Street between Beaubien and St. Antoine: the residence of Frederick Wilson at the corner of Fort and Beaubien (47 Fort); the residence of Thomas Holton; and the residence of Richard Evans, who is shot in the face (55 Fort).

    9. (8:15 p.m.) Rioters burn four buildings on Gies alley, between Brush and Randolph streets, by mistake. They intended to burn buildings on the east side of Brush Street between Brush and Beaubien (4).

Sullivan stood on the church steps, waved his revolver, and threatened to shoot the first person to throw a torch—an act of heroism that the *Advertiser and Tribune* credited for saving the structure.[17]

One of the most violent episodes occurred in the Fort Street residence of Richard Evans, a 79-year-old cook.[18] While Evans' wife watched in horror, a rioter pointed a pistol at Evans' head and shot him in the face. The ball ripped away part of his cheek. While Evans lay on the floor moaning, the rioters plundered his house and took anything of value. They left him for dead, set his house on fire, and raced off to the next house.[19]

Mary Jones stood on the street outside her Fort Street residence, forced to watch as the rioters set fire to everything she owned. Several times, she tried to dart into the burning building in a vain attempt to save some of her clothes, but she could not manage to fight her way through the thicket of malefactors blocking her entry.

Charles and Mary Mathews lived on E. Lafayette, although Mary would later state that Charles had been confined in "the Lunatic Asylum" at the time of the riot, leaving her home alone. Rioters burst through her front door and rifled through the house, pocketing anything of value and trashing the rest. They dragged the furniture to the street, where they smashed it into sticks and used it for a bonfire.[20]

An *Advertiser and Tribune* reporter witnessed an unverified attack on "a young colored woman" whom he did not name. According to the reporter, who claimed to witness the incident, the woman came to the door with a three-month-old in her arms and begged rioters to leave her house alone. "Her presence seemed to make them more savage, and with yells, screeches and horrid oaths, they rushed upon her," the reporter recalled in his day-after report. "The child was taken from her arms, thrown a distance of fifteen feet upon the ground, kicked and beaten, while the mother received similar treatment."[21]

The *Free Press* decried this as a fiction, "untrue in every particular." The germ for this particular story, according to a March 8, 1863, article, occurred when, "at the house on Beaubien street, which was set on fire, a woman was forced to the door from the intense heat with a babe in her arms. As she came out one or two boys threw stones and sticks of wood at her, which compelled her to recede a few feet from the door." The woman, who remained unnamed in the article, was evidently Louisa Bonn.[22]

The fire department did little to help. The *Free Press* offered the beleaguered firefighters an excuse for their inaction. "The steamers were upon the spot promptly, but would only be permitted to throw water on the homes of white men, to prevent the conflagration from becoming general. The mob threatened that the engines would be torn to pieces if they attempted to play upon any other buildings than those designated." To avoid losing valuable equipment, "it was deemed proper to cater to the wishes of the mob in that respect."

In at least one instance, a rioter made good on the threat when Bernard Groghan interfered with firefighters. Groghan "collared" chief engineer Thomas Oakley and, wrapping his hands around the frightened firefighter's neck, threatened to throttle him if he used the hoses to throw water onto the burning structures.[23]

In at least one instance, firefighters managed to push through the mob. When rioters threatened to destroy Steamer No. 2, George L. Whiting would have none of it. He jumped up on the engine. Shaking his fists and screaming threats, Whiting managed to keep angry hands off the firefighting equipment.[24]

With little to no interference from the fire brigade, the rioters ran rampant, setting dozens of structures on fire in the Third Ward between Beaubien and St. Antoine.

Sometime around 7 p.m., they moved farther south and set fire to several structures on Brush Street between Congress and Fort. They set fire to four brick tenement buildings owned by Frederick Gies, a grocer who had diversified his portfolio with real estate. His rentals catered to lower-income tenants, and the four buildings housed eight families who lost all their worldly possessions to the flames.[25]

The burning of a barn located in an alley between Lafayette and Fort triggered fears that the wind would blow red-hot cinders onto the roofs and destroy the neighboring market structures. With this threat to the assets of the white business community, the fire department went to work dousing the flames.

The firefighters then raced to the intersection of John R. and Miami but arrived after the flames had turned the building into a skeleton of charred framing. Nonetheless, the *Free Press* praised them for preventing further loss. "The entire corps behaved admirably, and worked their engines in a manner deserving of the warmest praise. Had it not been for their aid, thousands of dollars' worth of property, now in a good condition and perfectly safe, would have been in ruins."[26]

One of the last structures set on fire was a barn on Larned Street, between Rivard and Hastings. The flames consumed the entire structure and all of its contents.[27]

Citizens throughout the First, Second, and Sixth wards took matters into their own hands. Forming impromptu fire brigades, they climbed onto roofs and brushed away glowing cinders. They stood in doorways cradling shotguns.

Sometime between six and seven p.m., it became evident to acting mayor Francis Phelps that his tiny contingent of constables could not contain the mob, so he called for reinforcements. A telegraph went out to Ypsilanti with an urgent request for troops.

With the soldiers on the way, several local, independent units sprang into action. The Light Guard, numbering about fifty men, began patrolling the worst-hit areas of the Third Ward. The Lyon Guard formed a cordon around the jail to prevent any attempt to break in and snatch Faulkner. The Scott Guard patrolled the southern portion of the First Ward. At nine p.m., companies A, B, C, F, and G of the 27th Regiment—numbering around 400 men—arrived in Detroit. Colonel Dorus M. Fox and Colonel John H. Richardson wasted little time and marched their soldiers double-quick to the Third Ward. For all intents and purposes, Detroit was under martial law. Anyone caught on the streets was to be arrested.

Phelps' battle plan worked. Realizing they couldn't fight rifles and bayonets with sticks and stones, the mob rioters disbursed. By 11 p.m., the streets of Detroit were deserted.

Sheriff's deputies and constables under the city marshal spent the next few hours rounding up stragglers. Their sweep netted twenty-two, whom the *Advertiser and Tribune* labeled "rioters." After a brief examination, however, authorities concluded that the suspects did not take part in the riot and released them from jail the following morning.[28]

Over the next few days, Dennis K. Sullivan and David M. Freeman, whose years walking a beat led to an extensive knowledge about the denizens of the Third and Fourth wards, worked to identify and collar the real ringleaders.

• • • •

Berated, beaten, and burned out, many of the Third Ward's Black residents fled the city. Some of them took refuge in the forests outside city limits; some crossed the river into Canada. The exodus would intensify the next morning.

PART 4
Ashes
(Saturday, March 7–May 1863)

9

Cinders
(Saturday, March 7, 1863)

> The sight was most awful indeed to behold,
> See women and babes driven out in the cold,
> And old aged sires, that fought for the land,
> Beat almost to death by a desperate band.
> —From "The Riot" by Benjamin Cutler Clark, Sr.

While the orange glow of the Third Ward conflagration backlit the city's profile, sheriff's deputies spirited Faulkner out of Detroit. They put the prisoner in the back of a buggy, tossed a "buffalo robe" over his head, and took him to the train depot in Dearborn at 2 a.m. on Saturday, March 7, 1863.

At the depot, they removed the handcuffs and waited for the eastbound train headed for Jackson and the state penitentiary. Even at that early hour, a small crowd gathered on the platform. Conversation inevitably centered on Faulkner and the subsequent riot, which gave the anonymous prisoner a glimpse at the public furor over his crime.

Someone must have recognized Faulkner through his thin disguise. At each stop, a crowd of rubber-necking gawkers tried to catch a glimpse of one of the most villainous people by that point in Michigan history. Fear of a second lynch mob materialized in one fellow at the Ann Arbor depot. Shaking his fist at Faulkner, he yelled, "If I had you out of doors I would take your life blood in two minutes."

Despite several such encounters, the deputies managed to deliver their prisoner without a rope around his neck. A *Free Press* writer described the scene either as it occurred or as he imagined it occurred, even quoting (or adding) dialogue between the prisoner and his escorts.

"Faulkner, how do you feel on looking at your future home?" one of the deputies asked.

"I feel pretty happy," Faulkner supposedly responded, "now I shall have a house and steady employment, and I had rather be here than keeping a saloon in Detroit." The journalist's next comment was telling. "This community is perfectly willing he should be gratified in this last respect."[1]

It is hard to imagine Faulkner, who maintained his innocence all along, adopting such a cavalier attitude. Since the officers kept Faulkner's identity under wraps, literally, it is equally hard to imagine a reporter on the train let alone witnessing the scene. In all likelihood, the *Free Press* journalist put the words in the prisoner's mouth—one final way of vilifying Faulkner by depicting the convicted rapist as having a devil-may-care attitude toward his life sentence.

Faulkner was processed and officially entered the prison as a lifer. His commitment record contains a brief description: "very good English, features not dark for a mulatto."[2]

An *Advertiser and Tribune* writer, perhaps feeling scooped by the *Free Press*' account, commented with disdain on Faulkner's early morning transfer. "The mob should be taught that the authorities of the city are able to execute the laws without taking advantage of the night."[3]

• • • •

When the sun rose on Saturday, March 7, people returned to the streets, and looters returned to the Third Ward. Stand-in mayor Phelps had ordered soldiers to patrol every street, but according to the *Advertiser and Tribune*, they avoided the area framed by Beaubien, St. Antoine Croghan, and Congress, the epicenter of the riot.

During the first few hours of daylight, looters sifted through embers and ashes to find anything of value missed the previous night. "It is a little remarkable," lamented an *Advertiser and Tribune* reporter, "that no police force was placed around the ruins to prevent rowdy boys from carrying away the few articles of iron ware, old stoves, and other matters of some value, that were dug out of the ruins."[4]

• • • •

In the period from 4 p.m., when the rioters torched Whitney Reynolds' shop and adjacent residence, to 10 p.m., when the soldiers managed to herd the riotous cats, eight fire alarms sounded throughout the city.

In that six-hour span, the rioters managed to set fire to an estimated fifty-two structures, some reduced to smoldering piles of ashes and embers. Several families, such as that of Whitney Reynolds, lost everything. Nothing remained of Reynolds' shop and residence, which consisted of the three-structure complex on Beaubien between Lafayette and Fort.

On the south side of Lafayette between Beaubien and St. Antoine, six structures had been reduced to cinders. In reporting on the fire marshal's report, the *Detroit Free Press* characterized these as "shanties" and suggested that the city was better off without them. "They were of no considerable value, being one story shanties, and, aside from the disgraceful manner in which they were destroyed, the city is the gainer by being rid of a most notorious resort for thieves, prostitutes and all the vilest portion of the colored population of Detroit."

Across the street, the mob destroyed ten buildings, which the *Free Press* characterized as "of but little more value," and another two at the corner of Beaubien and Lafayette. Once again, the *Free Press* hinted that the mob had done the city a favor in removing "the resort of the vile and vicious of the colored people."

Two barns, situated in an alley north of Fort Street between Griswold and Shelby, were reduced to cinders, although the *Free Press* reporter suggested that this fire was not lit by the rioters but instead by opportunist thieves.

Between Brush and Randolph, four buildings in a multi-structure complex known as Gies alley went up in smoke. The brick, two-story tenements were "occupied by white people," so the *Free Press* correspondent indicated that the mob burned them by mistake since up to this time they had targeted houses occupied by Black residents.

The rioters went for "two negro tenements on this same alley," but to paraphrase Ben Franklin, the mob had thirty heads but no brains. In its furor, the ignorant hydra attacked Gies' tenement buildings instead.

Fire consumed most of a house, barn, and shed at the corner of Miami and John R. as well as another barn located on the south side of Larned between Hastings and Rivard.

The *Free Press* applauded the effort of the city's firefighters by proclaiming, "The Fire Department was very efficient at these several fires, and at 12 o'clock at night was again ready for operations against the devouring element."[5]

One citizen, Hiram McCain, praised the firefighters for preventing a much larger catastrophe. "The undersigned feeling very grateful to No. 9 Fire Engine Company, for the noble efforts made by them to prevent the spread to surrounding buildings of the fire originating in the buildings owned by Mr. Gies, on the alley between Fort and Congress streets, on the night of the 6th instant, and although it was beyond the power of any human agency to subdue the flames and prevent the total destruction of the buildings in which the fire first started, it was owing entirely to the splendid conduct and unassisted labors of that company, that the buildings on the opposite side of Brush street, were kept from being swept away by the devouring flames of the fearful conflagration; and I take this method of tendering my hearty thanks to the noble hearted firemen of that company, for their behavior and the good work they performed upon the occasion, and of intimating to them, one and all, that I have at least one unappropriated 'saw buck' that I am particularly desirous of converting into a circulating medium for their especial benefit."

The intended recipients of Mr. McCain's ten-dollar banknote or "saw buck" worked a hand-engine that was kept in a house on Gratiot between Beaubien and St. Antoine. That the company managed to keep the flames from spreading with a hand-pump instead of a more powerful steam-engine underscored their heroics and left McCain "feeling very grateful."[6]

Not everyone felt this way. Word on the streets of the Third Ward was that the firefighters dragged their feet until the mob began to encroach on the property of white people. One of numerous letters written by a concerned citizen calling himself "JUSTICE" and published in the *Advertiser and Tribune* (or written by an *Advertiser and Tribune* journalist and presented as a letter by a concerned citizen) accused the fire department of negligence in their failure to respond.

"During the whole time, from about 5 o'clock until 11," wrote J.B. Bloss, who helped Officer Sullivan rescue Joshua Boyd outside of the cooperage, "I was in various parts of the crowd, and I did not hear a remonstrance or a protest from any fireman or city official against the destruction of houses of negroes, or an effort to protect them from violence except officer [Dennis K.] Sullivan, who did his duty nobly."[7]

Some went even further. According to unnamed source who penned editorials under the name "An Observer," some of the firemen railed against protecting homes of Black Detroiters. The Observer named names, so fire marshal William Champ felt a need to defend his department.

Rather than counter the accusation of a less-than-color-blind fire department, however, Champ's statement appeared to support it.

"It is well known to many people and respectable citizens that violent threats were made," Champ said, "that is if the Fire Department threw water on the negro tenements, the hose belonging to the department would be cut and destroyed; and after consulting with several gentlemen who, I believe, were good, orderly citizens, and merely spectators at the scenes of violence being enacted, I thought that the true policy for the interest of the city, was to save the adjoining white men's property, which was most effectually and promptly done in every instance."

Champ went on to blame the lack of police for the discrimination. If he had had a sufficient number of officers to guard the hoses, "you can be assured that no distinction would have been made; but, under the then existing circumstances, of which I felt perfectly competent to judge, I believed it my duty, and the interest of the city, to shape the action of the Fire Department as to render the greatest good to the greatest number."

An *Advertiser and Tribune* editor did not buy a word of Champ's justification.

"Mr. Champ's note speaks for itself," he wrote. "It confesses that the house of every negro in the city could have been consumed without any interference from him. This may be the citizens' idea of an efficient Fire Department, but we doubt it. It simply means that the city was given up by the authorities to the mob."[8]

The *Free Press* supported Champ's position but went one step further by accusing the "respectable" citizens—those whom Champ said he consulted—for actually making the threats to the firehoses in the first place. "The steamers were upon the spot promptly at the time of the first outbreak of the conflagration, accompanied by the efficient and energetic Fire Marshal. While they were preparing to put a stream upon the burning building the Marshal was consulted by a large number of prominent men, who warned him not to endeavor to suppress the fire among the negro houses, but to save the property of the white people adjoining. They assured him that, while he would not be molested in the latter course, if he attempted the former the hose would be destroyed, and the engines thus rendered powerless. There being every prospect that these threats would be executed if the demands of the lawless mob were not plied with, the Marshal very property decided to save what property he could, and gratify, from necessity, the feelings and demands of the mob. When it is remembered that if the hose had been destroyed, the whole city would have been at the mercy of the devouring element, the decision of the Marshal cannot but be applauded."[9]

In this rendition, William Champ was the hero, not the goat.

The tug-of-war-of-words over Champ's culpability was tinted by politics. When evaluating Champ's role in the riot, as filtered through the two newspapers, it is important to note that Champ was an avowed Democrat, which meant that the Democratic *Free Press* was more likely to support him than the Republican *Advertiser and Tribune*.

• • • •

As the fires in Detroit's Third Ward died down, long-smoldering animosities ignited as Detroiters sought to affix blame for the shameful riot.

The city's leading citizens blamed law enforcement; Republicans blamed Democrats; the Republican-leaning *Advertiser and Tribune* blamed the Democratic-leaning *Free Press*; the *Free Press* blamed everyone and then pointed the finger at one particular individual.

The finger-pointing began the next day when Detroit's plutocrats crammed into the tiny county courtroom on Saturday, March 7, 1863, to pass a resolution that summarized their feelings about the riot, to bring the malefactors to justice, and to discuss measures that might be taken to safeguard the city and prevent any future riots. A committee was appointed and anchored by Wayne County prosecuting attorney J. Knox Gavin.

9. Cinders (Saturday, March 7, 1863)

"Lafayette," Detroit's first fire steam engine in a photograph taken in 1860. The spire of the old city hall can be seen at the left. On the Farmer map, Steam Fire Engine No. 1 is located at the corner of Wayne and Larned streets. Note the large water hoses. Rioters threatened to cut the hoses if firemen used their equipment to extinguish burning houses in the Third Ward (courtesy Burton Historical Collection, Detroit Public Library).

In his remarks, *Advertiser and Tribune* associate Edward C. (E.C.) Walker addressed the racial issue at the heart of the riot. "They [the rioters] were in no respect responsible for the outrage committed by the man Faulkner, who being seven-eighths white, the disgrace, if it had anything to do with the different races, rested more upon the whites than the blacks. The inoffensive blacks are made the object of this disgraceful mob."

Walker made an oblique reference to the assault on Whitney Reynolds' residence. "When they attempted to make their escape from the certain death which awaited them—the devouring element closing around them," he bellowed, "they were bruised and beaten in a most shocking manner, with the intent to murder. Innocent women, with babes in their arms, imploring the mercy of the mob, stricken down and rendered senseless, this, too, in broad daylight, and not an officer of the city government near to protect them."

The real troublemakers, Walker estimated, consisted of no more than twenty-five to fifty teenage hellions. While they ransacked residences, the crowd of thousands did no more than watch. When Walker noted that a platoon of twenty armed civilians could have squelched the riot, the audience responded with applause.

Then Walker blamed the authorities for failing to control the situation. "Where was the sheriff of Wayne County on this occasion? It is true, he was confined at home with sickness. But his deputies surely could not all have been sick."

The Rev. Dr. George Duffield focused his remarks on the hooligans who perpetrated the violence and indicted the greater community for neglecting those who he characterized as a "floating population." In support of his "takes a village" argument, the Rev. Duffield classified the rioters as "a class of boys and noisy young men trained up in the streets, many of them having no homes, and have been taught not trade or useful occupation; exposed to temptation and led on to crime—on the high road to ruin…. Society, in some respects, is responsible for this neglected class."[10]

The group adopted several resolutions, including a contingency to arm civilians. In the event of another riot, citizens were to gather at city hall with whatever weapons they could muster. This seemingly extreme proposition became necessary when the group formalized blame by stating "That this disgrace which has befallen our city might and should have been averted by a reasonable precaution on the part of the police authorities."

Another resolution called for reparations for those who lost property in the riot, paid for with a special taxation, but J. Knox Gavin suggested a more direct approach. He noted that people made homeless faced imminent need for shelter from inclement weather and therefore needed immediate aid. A hat was passed, and by the time it had circled the room, it contained $300.[11]

A later fundraising drive netted an additional $220 from fifty-nine individuals, including a $140 donation from a "A Friend" and $32 from a group calling themselves "Friends in Troy." Local attorney James F. Joy and Eliza Steward—the wife of a gas fitter—gave $25 each. The list of one-dollar donators contained the name "Mr. Barns." It is unclear which "Mr. Barns" donated the dollar, but it was probably *Advertiser and Tribune* editor Henry and not his more Democratic-leaning brother Jacob.[12]

The relief organizers opened up a donation "depot" inside a shop on Larned Street. In a letter published in the *Advertiser and Tribune*, they requested "donations of money, clothing for men, women and children, second-hand furniture, such as chairs, tables, &c.; bedsteads, beds and bedding, of all kinds, boots and shoes, stockings, all kinds of kitchen furniture, stoves, and stove furniture, hats and caps, provisions, &c." They needed just about anything and everything for the victims but cautioned donors to beware. Several gullible do-gooders had been buncoed by unscrupulous "imposters" who had falsely represented themselves as Good Samaritans.[13]

Acting Mayor Francis B. Phelps invited victims to his store, where he promised to give them food. In the ensuing days, Phelps claimed to have distributed a thousand pounds of bread and five barrels of bacon to dozens of people. Soon after, a rumor spread that Phelps had handed out moldy bread and rancid bacon.

Phelps attempted to dispel the rumor and defend himself by printing handbills and penning a letter to the *Free Press*, in which he invited skeptics to his shop, where they could sample his remaining stock.

The attempt backfired. The *Advertiser and Tribune* published Phelps' letter to the *Free Press* on the front page of the March 20, 1863, afternoon edition along with a lengthy commentary. In a pun-filled rebuke, the editor characterized Phelps' numbers as exaggerated and proclaimed the rumor to be true.

"The fact that he announces in the above card that he gave his mite 'without money and without pride,' has become a joke as *stale* as his bread, and as *rank* as his 'meat,'" noted the editor, who used italics to great effect. "We know not what kind of specimens this 'little stock remaining uncalled for' may prove to be, but we do know of several specimens that were given out under the direction of that official ... that upon examination, proved to be loathsome in the extreme, and unfit for food for man or beast. This is no 'malicious representation,' but a well established fact which can be attested by several good and responsible witnesses."

The editor concluded, "he will perhaps see that rather than to have compromised his character as a man of genuine benevolence, it would have been better to have 'saved his bacon.'"[14]

The city's Republicans, and their pet paper, the *Advertiser and Tribune*, blamed Democrats and their rag, the *Free Press*, for inciting the riot with inflammatory headline stories about the Faulkner trial—stories that had antecedents in the newspaper's racially-charged coverage of the war. Some angry Elephants even suggested burning down the *Free Press* office.

In its day-after coverage, the *Advertiser and Tribune* editors contemplated the cause of the riot in an editorial that pointed the finger at the city's rival paper. "Such being the ferocious and destructive character of the mob, where did it come from? We all know. The conversation of the vast crowd that lined the streets last evening, declared with unerring certainty, *this is a Free Press mob!*"

The editorial went on to catalogue the alleged assertions made by the *Free Press*. "The ignorant and unreasoning classes have been told by the paper referred to that this war is for the negro's welfare, and that all the national suffering is on his account; that white men are taxed to pay for negro freedom; that the white man's interests in Congress are neglected and only those of the negro attended to; that negroes emancipated at the South will come North and drive out white labor; that in giving an opinion that negroes were citizens, the Attorney General intended to compel white people to receive them upon term of social and political equality."

It continued, "These were known by the men who coined them to be utterly false, and were intended to excite the ignorant and prejudiced against the negro primarily, and secondarily against the Republicans who, it was alleged, were doing all this for the negro."

Free Press reporting, according to the editorial, amounted to nothing more than a political ploy to destroy the Republican Party. The paper used Blacks as a proxy in this attack by over-reporting, sensationalizing, and exaggerating stories about crimes allegedly perpetrated by Blacks. The editorial charged that "every time that some negro has committed an offense against the laws, the case has been grossly exaggerated in the journal referred to, and appeals made to popular violence."

As a parting shot, the editorial echoed Walker's condemnation of the police, who "did nothing." The understaffed and overwhelmed force had no help from deputized citizens because "a considerable number of the city authorities are the most violent negro-haters, and had little if any sympathy with the law and order party. This, or some other unaccountable circumstance, almost paralyzed the Fire Department, which never, since its organization, has been so inefficient."

9. Cinders (Saturday, March 7, 1863) 137

The *Advertiser and Tribune* also called out acting mayor Francis Phelps for not controlling the provost guard. "If the mayor called out these men, it was his duty to have controlled them. He would have been personally present at the jail, and ordered the mob to disperse by the reading of the riot act." A single squad, the editorialist noted, against a mob of thousands armed with sticks, stones, and bricks created a situation doomed to end in violence. "The incompetent authorities who put these men in such a position, without direction and without support, must share the responsibility of what followed."[15]

J.B. Bloss, who witnessed the riot and would later testify against the alleged rioters in recorder's court, presented an example of the *Free Press*' use of racially-charged language in a guest editorial that the *Advertiser and Tribune* ran the day after their scathing condemnation of the *Free Press* appeared in print.[16]

"Has not that paper," Bloss wrote, "held up to scorn and contempt and obloquy, from day to day—week to week, and month to month—the negro, or as they almost uniformly spell it, the 'nigger'?"

"As a sample I call attention to an editorial article in that paper of January the 17th, headed 'Is the Negro eligible to the Presidency?'… The argument is that under the decision of the U.S. Attorney General, affirming negro citizenship, that 'Niggers' have great advantages over foreign naturalized citizens. Seven times the word nigger and niggers occur in the article. It closes with a suggestion that the Republicans will hereafter place the 'American citizens of African descent' upon their tickets." Such articles, Bloss argued, were intended to undermine the Republican Party. Thus, Bloss concluded, the *Free Press* did not intend to incite the riot; instead the riot was a side effect of their political maneuvering.[17]

The ire of Republicans against the Democrat-leaning *Free Press* reached a fever pitch a few days after the riot when the Republican Association met and passed a resolution to boycott the newspaper.

"That we recognize in the recent disgraceful riot in this city, the legitimate results of the daily teachings and influence of the *Detroit Free Press*, and therefore we earnestly appeal to all loyal citizens, who may have heretofore patronized the paper, to withdraw from it their support." The Association insinuated that reading the *Free Press* amounted to nothing less than treason when it concluded, "It is a duty they owe to their Government, no less than to this community."[18]

The anti–*Free Press* rhetoric grew so strong that on Sunday, March 8, the paper ran a lengthy response to the haters, which it identified as "ultra-radical republicans."

"As we expected," the *Free Press* editorial began, "the ultra-radical republicans are endeavoring to create the impression and belief that the democratic party and *The Free Press* are in some way responsible for the scenes of violence which disgraced our city on Friday afternoon and evening."

The editorial went on to blame the war for deepening an already-existing racial rift. "The truth is, and these men know it, that politics have had nothing to do with the affair whatever. The deep feeling against the ideas of placing the negro race upon equality with the whites is confined to no party. It is the prevailing sentiment among the laboring classes of every shade of political opinion, and this feeling, always active, has undoubtedly been on the increase ever since the war began."

In linking the riot to the war, the *Free Press* editors belied their own contention that "politics have had nothing to do with the affair whatever." Just three months earlier, Lincoln—a Republican president—had repurposed the war from a conflict over states' rights to a conflict over slavery when he issued the Emancipation Proclamation on January 1, 1863.

"It is useless," the editorial continued, "to deny the fact that there is in the North an irrepressible conflict of races. With such a state of feeling, it only required a crime of the magnitude of the one of which Faulkner has been convicted to endanger the peace of the community. We could as justly charge our opponents with a sympathy for the crime committed as for them to charge us with countenancing or excusing the acts of the populace on this occasion. We have from the beginning deprecated and endeavored to repress this tendency to violence. We have counseled moderation and forbearance, and especially to avoid everything which tended to an outburst of this kind."

Then, in a pseudo-justification for the choice and tone of their news coverage, the editors added a caveat. "We have, however, as faithful sentinels, felt it our duty not to ignore the danger which we were sure existed, but on the contrary to warn the community, not only of its existence, but point out the only feasible plan of controlling and repressing it."

9. Cinders (Saturday, March 7, 1863)

In other words, the *Free Press* had really done a public service by identifying the "enemy within"—the city's inherent racial prejudices—with inflammatory articles that played up the racial angle, as it had done throughout the Faulkner trial.

In the ultimate attempt to deflect responsibility, the *Free Press* editors offered up a sacrificial lamb: Lt. John Van Stan. They accused the lieutenant of putting a match to a keg of gunpowder by ordering his soldiers to shoot in the direction of the crowd. "The outbreak would have been avoided, even with all of the excited feelings of the community, had it not been for the order of Lieutenant Van Stan to fire upon the people."

The writer then called on the authorities to bring the rioters to justice and added a scathing critique of the local constabulary. "If our city police authorities are unable to meet the emergency, it is the duty of the citizens to take this matter in hand, for the lives and property of every individual are in danger unless the guilty leaders in the riot of Friday are visited with the severest penalties of the law."

By suggesting that "it is the duty of the citizens to take this matter in hand," the *Free Press* writer appeared to promote the very vigilantism displayed by the mob that attempted to lynch Faulkner from the nearest telegraph pole.[19]

A follow-up item condemned the gathering of prominent citizens as a party of fat-cat plutocrats completely out of touch with reality. The editors took particular umbrage with the resolution pointing the finger of blame at "police authorities" and pointed out the hypocrisy in making such an assertion. "Nothing costs so little trouble, or requires so little brains, as fault-finding; especially by men who have *not* risked their lives in upholding the law of the land, against men who *have* so risked their lives."

The unnamed writer lambasted E.C. Walker, who stated that he could have stopped the small number of unarmed teenagers with a posse of twenty armed men. "We may be permitted to wonder that, if Mr. Walker felt so peculiar an ability to 'suppress these proceedings' with so small a force, he did not promptly offer his assistance to the guardians of the law. In fact, so far as we have been able to learn, the officers were left entirely unaided by these gentlemen who now so freely condemn them."

The *Free Press* lauded the acting sheriff Cicotte and his deputies for doing so much with so little. "It is equally so certain that the civil officers, under the charge of Mr. F.X. Cicotte, acting for Sheriff Fralick, who was on his back, sick," noted the writer, "displayed great heroism in protecting the negro Faulkner from the mob, and did all that a mere handful of men, in a sudden emergency, could do to suppress the riot."[20]

From the cacophony of raised voices, certain common denominators arose from the rhetoric: there was plenty of blame to go around, no one wanted to take accountability, the rioters needed apt punishment, and the city desperately needed a municipal police force.

The debate filtered down from city hall to the city's saloons, where patrons argued various points in between shots of whiskey. Nowhere was this debate more intense than in the watering holes of the Third and Fourth wards, where liquor loosened lips and led to the airing of long pent-up frustrations.

A good example of these mini-feuds occurred in a saloon run by rough-and-tumble Irishman John Bowers. A patron—an "Old German"—began to pontificate about the evils of the riot. Something he said (possibly blaming Irish immigrants for inciting the riot) rubbed Bowers the wrong way. Bowers, in the words of a reporter, performed "sundry riotous demonstrations on the head and back of the aged Dutchman." The incident landed Bowers in police court, where he was fined $25 "for not ordering the intruder out before giving the blows, instead of after."[21]

The heightened racial tensions led to at least one squabble on Saturday, which occurred somewhere in the vicinity of the A.M.E. Church on Lafayette.

According to one version, two soldiers and their sergeant from Company C of the 27th Regiment went to visit a friend who lived on Croghan. They bumped into a Black man, words were exchanged, and the man pulled a bowie knife. When one of the soldiers responded by pulling a pistol, the man quickly dropped the blade.

Another version has the three soldiers loitering on the street outside the church. The churchgoers, fearing a possible rekindling of violence, sent one of the parishioners to investigate. They exchanged words and nearly blows until deputy Chris Stadler, son of city marshal John

Stadler, stepped in. He arrested all four and lodged them in the county jail, but the soldiers were released almost immediately.

Later that day, two officers patrolling Grand River spotted a Black man loading a double-barrel pistol. Confronted by the officers, the man said that his boss told him to load the weapon and "shoot the first Irishman he saw." They took the weapon and escorted the man to jail.[22]

This was not an isolated incident. Acting mayor Phelps had organized a special detachment of police to patrol the streets and prevent outbreaks of violence. Their reports indicate that some of the city's Black population prepared for the worst by arming themselves.

One officer spotted a group of about a dozen men armed with guns on Kentucky Street and another reported seeing a larger group of thirty or forty men carrying guns, knives, pitchforks, and paving stones in the same vicinity. The officer asked the men to "keep indoors and not create any disturbance." The men told the officer that they had only come together for protection. That same officer later spotted a small group of white men, also armed with guns and knives, and ordered them to disburse. When they refused, he "put [them] in the hands of officer Sullivan."[23]

The officers averted a skirmish, but this non-incident almost certainly became the seed that grew into a giant melon in the hands of a news correspondent from Chicago.

"A negro rendezvous was discovered by the police in the upper part of the city to-day," he wrote in the first of two dispatches sent from Detroit on March 8. "There were thirty or forty in the building armed with shot-guns, pistols, and knives. As the police force in the neighborhood was insufficient to break it up, the negroes were ordered to disperse, which they refused to do, saying that they had organized only for self-protection. They were told that their course was unlawful; that the city was willing and able to protect them; that they must give up their arms and disperse. The negroes, however, still held out, determined to fight if interfered with by anybody."

In another item, the correspondent offered a ludicrous explanation for why so few Blacks died during and after the riot: "The reason so few negroes have died from their injuries is attributed to the fact that the blows they received were mostly on the head."

The *Advertiser and Tribune* editors condemned these reports as "a specimen of enormous lying," but nevertheless, Detroiters were sitting on a box of dynamite.[24]

The potential for further violence roused acting mayor Francis B. Phelps—maligned and pilloried by the press—to action. On Saturday night, he issued a proclamation, calling on all Detroiters to help in maintaining law and order. And he wanted them sober when they did it. Phelps had a reason for wanting the saloon-keepers to turn off the taps; the rioters may have fueled their orgy of destruction with spirits. When the crowd gathered outside city hall to see Faulkner, according to one eyewitness, a wagon train carrying kegs followed them.

"In view of the unlawful and riotous proceedings that have been enacted within the past twenty-four hours, I … do hereby request all good citizens to use their untiring endeavors to maintain the peace and quietude of the city, and also to discourage the unusual congregation of persons upon the streets, and, to further aid in preventing excitement, I require that, for two days, the keepers of saloons shall close the same at seven o'clock in the evening."[25] The saloon-keepers acquiesced; on Saturday night, Detroit became a dry city.

• • • •

The war of words between the *Free Press* and the *Advertiser and Tribune* intensified in the days following the riot. The feud took the form of punch-counter-punch with the *Free Press* typically throwing the first punch.

The day after the riot, the *Free Press* insinuated that a Black man may have taken part in attempting to burn a building at the corner of Miami and John R. and repeated the street gossip that people throughout the First Ward believed: that Blacks were the instigators of the arson. "He is accused of firing the place, but nothing is positively known at present," a *Free Press* reporter noted, "although many respectable people are convinced that the fires in the lower part of the city were caused by negroes."[26]

The *Advertiser and Tribune* editors counter-punched with an item titled "A Shameful Fabrication" in which they accused *Free Press* writers of creating fictitious news. "There is not a particle of testimony to show that any negro set fire to a building last evening, as charged by the *Free Press*, and the charge is preposterous."[27]

The *Free Press* editors also downplayed the violence of the riot and in doing so insinuated that the *Advertiser and Tribune* had sensationalized through exaggeration. "Not a single negro was killed, nor is there any probability but that all of the wounded will recover in the course of a few days. Only two were wounded so as to be confined on the following day. Those two were visited by our reporter on Saturday, and they were reported by the attending physician as being in a rapid state of convalescence."[28]

The two "wounded" visited by the *Free Press* man were unnamed in the article but most likely Charles Fletcher and Ephraim Clark, both of whom recovered. Since the article was published on Sunday, March 8, the reporter would not have had access to Joshua Boyd, who was across the river in Windsor at the time.

The *Free Press* writers depicted the rioters as buffoons and described a slapstick-like moment when the rioters ripped up a feather bed and gust of wind carried the feathers down the street. "An amusing incident is related as having occurred at one of the hovels which were being sacked. A large feather bed was brought into the street and torn to pieces. The feathers were scattered upon the street, and, the wind catching them up, they were taken into the air and floated in a dense mass around the immediate vicinity of the occurrence. The vast crowd, not exactly comprehending the nature of the substance, were panic stricken at the sight, and fled in confusion and dismay from the spot, not a solitary soul remaining in a space of half a block, some of them tumbling pell mell into the mud in their eagerness to escape. After they discovered that they had been frightened by such a simple process they returned, but not without feeling that their courage could not stand the test of even a white feather."[29]

The rioters were, at least in the *Free Press* reimagining of the riot, cowards terrified by "a white feather."

The *Free Press* also attempted a little spin control by declaring that the chief instigators of the riot weren't Germans, as they had originally reported, but a motley crew of "mostly rowdies, vagabonds and loafers … who incited the young desperadoes to the inhuman deeds perpetrated. These men, by their lawless example, instigated and led on the younger ones, and it is upon them that the fearful responsibility rests."[30]

They downplayed the destruction by characterizing some of the mob's targets as dens of criminal vice. Employing rhetoric from earlier, amalgamation-bashing articles, they hinted that some of the victims contributed to their own demise. "Some of them [the houses], we are informed, were inhabited by vile and filthy amalgamationists, whose habits were of the most disgusting, polygamous, and loathsome nature." As the vice capitals of Sodom and Gomorrah burned in a conflagration caused by a rain of sulphur and fire, so too did the Third Ward's bordellos.

The Democratic paper's editors may have had an ulterior motive for presenting the riot and its perpetrators in this manner. In 1870, a *Detroit Daily Post* writer claimed that *Free Press* editors downplayed the riot in an attempt to cover up their role in inciting it and to protect the reputation of the city's Democrats. "A stain had been inflicted upon the Democratic party of Wayne county; and the Republicans would not fail to reap an advantage in the State and Nation from this affair. Evidently the sensation had been overdone. So the *Free Press* now took a back track, and ridiculed the whole affair."[31]

10

Sermons (Sunday, March 8, 1863)

> I blush when I think that such deeds should take place,
> Not heathens or Turks, a civilized race,
> Not where savage nations alone have the rule,
> But here amidst churches, the Bible and school.
> —From "The Riot" by Benjamin Cutler Clark, Sr.

The area's preachers seized the opportunity to rework the tragedy into a morality play and rewrote their Sunday sermons.

The Rev. Sylvan S. Hunting, who helmed the Lafayette Street Unitarian Church, gave a moving address to a packed house. In a series of stirring anecdotes, Hunting catalogued the terror meted out to Third Ward citizens: Charles Fletcher, beaten senselessly by "a herd of tigers"; Louis Houston, set on by a wild pack of rabid dogs and "injured for life"; Boyd, who managed to escape slavery in Virginia but not the angst of his neighbors, struck in the head with an axe; "Father Clark" or "The Prophet," the elderly sexton of the A.M.E. Church who, like Boyd, had escaped slavery, beaten to a pulp.

One of the most graphic anecdotes involved the odyssey of Robert Bennette—a story filled with good and evil.

"Mr. Robert H. Bennett [sic] was at the cooper's shop, and barely escaped alive. He rushed through the crowd, was shot at, was stoned and clubbed, struck on the legs, fell down five times from the effect of the blows upon him, and at length reached the Biddle House, and was heartlessly ordered not to enter by the Clerk, which order he summarily disobeyed, and forced his way in, bleeding as if he had been butchered, and entered the dining room, where he met the proprietor of the house, who nobly protected him."

Hunting continued, shaming Detroiters for their cruelty. "A lady seeing the wounded man, hastened into the apothecary shop and said to one of the proprietors, 'A man is bleeding to death in the street!'—and he very coolly answered, 'How can I do anything for him?' To which the lady replied, 'I beg your pardon, sir, you cannot do anything for him, he is a negro.' Even after Mr. Bennett [sic] had reached Jefferson avenue, a well-dressed man called out to drayman, 'Why don't you hit that nigger with your whip?' whereupon the drayman raised the bottom of his whip and gave the man a blow."[1]

Hunting then indicted city officials in a series of scathing rebukes. The reverend did not name names, but he did not rely on irony or insinuation, either. In no uncertain terms, he characterized the local government as based on beer barrels and distilleries and criticized the law for pursuing just the suspects—minors—who could not vote in elections.

He ended with a dire warning: if the court system did not punish all of the perpetrators, including the adults, history would repeat itself in Detroit.[2]

A few weeks after scolding his parishioners, Hunting answered the clarion call, enlisted with the 27th Michigan as a chaplain, and marched off to war. He was there, providing spiritual guidance, when his regiment took part in the siege of Vicksburg, when they clashed with rebel forces at Spotsylvania and Cold Harbor, and when Lee surrendered to Grant at Appomattox.

Unlike Hunting's congregation, Black churchgoers ran a gauntlet to reach the church doors. On the Sunday after the riot, and on a number of succeeding Sundays, "vagabonds" (as the press dubbed them) congregated on street corners around Third Ward churches such as the A.M.E. These impromptu street preachers hurled insults and racial epithets at parishioners as they passed, prompting an outcry for protection that no one in officialdom apparently heard.

One of the complainants was Benjamin Franklin Hawkley, a former slave from Virginia. Described as an "old patriarch," the fifty-one-year-old told of curses thrown at him and the church leaders as they went into their place of worship.[3]

The *Free Press* editors commented directly on this state of affairs. "By all means they should be protected while going to and from their places of worship. The blacks, of course, must not demand that white men go off into the gutter to make a clear passage for them, but they have a right to at least a share of the respect accorded to other 'citizens.'"⁴ The word choice belied the writer's true beliefs: he belittled their citizenship by enclosing the word "citizens" inside quotation marks.

• • • •

J.B. Bloss, who witnessed some of the most savage incidents during the riot, gave a sermon of sorts when he penned a letter to the editor of the *Advertiser and Tribune*. Quoting scripture that he may have heard from a pulpit somewhere in the city, he described man's inhumanity to man during the Detroit riot. In his editorial, Bloss quoted many of the angry voices he heard. These statements present a good idea of the motives behind the violence.

> To a crowd who were trying to get into a house where a negro had fled for protection, I said: "Why do you want to hurt an innocent man? He has done you no harm." "Abolitionist! Abolitionist! That's a nigger man!" shouted the crowd. At another place I stepped up to a man who was smashing furniture, as it was thrown from a home. "Why do you do this?" I inquired. "These people never injured you." "D—m the negroes!—we are going to clean them out!—to exterminate them!" said the man. Another man, turning to me, said, looking at the burning houses: "They will draft again, will they? Draft, will they?" repeating it over and over. Near the City Hall, about past one o'clock, Mr. [J.G.] Swan was remonstrating against the proposition to take Faulkner from the officers and hang him. The crowd soon became greatly excited and cried "Abolitionist!—nigger man!—pitch into him!—put him through!" Swan fled into Beeson's store to save himself from attack.
>
> A negro was knocked down on Croghan street, severely bruised, and nearly insensible, and while lying on the ground a man came up and kicked him so violently in the face that the blood spirted [sic] on his own, exclaiming, as he did so, "you damned nigger," "you damned Lincoln voter," "pray, you damned nigger." A boy came up and gave him a kick in the face, exclaiming, "you American citizen of African descent." Mr. [David] Kendall, who, I believe, holds a city office, in speaking of the mob, said: "It is all right; exterminate them! Exterminate them!" Another man said: "When we have cleaned out the niggers, then we will clean out the Abolitionists." Some boys were pulling down a house, and I undertook to stop them. While doing so, Mr. Champ came up and said: "Don't say anything, don't say anything. You cannot do anything, and you may get yourself into trouble or get knocked down. All we can do is to save the property of white citizens. If we do not oppose their destroying the houses of the blacks they will not interfere with our saving other property." Perhaps this was very good advice, so far as I was personally concerned. I have no doubt it was kindly meant. But it suggested to my mind this inquiry:

Is the head of the Fire Department, and are the city officials, in sympathy with the mob? Another fact gave the inquiry greater significance. During the whole time, from about 5 o'clock until 11, I was in various parts of the crowd, and I did not hear a remonstrance or a protest from any fireman or city official against the destruction of houses of negroes, or an effort to protect them from violence except officer Sullivan, who did his duty nobly.

Bloss went on to indict the *Free Press* "teachings" for creating this furor. "What I believe and what I charge is," Bloss said, "that the recent mob is a legitimate result of such teachings. They cannot 'wipe their mouth and say, I have done no wickedness'—Prov. 30:20."

"But," Bloss added, "I do not say or believe they intended to raise a mob. They used the prejudices and passions of the lawless and violent for party purposes."

Nonetheless, Bloss concluded, again turning to scripture: "If a man should set a fire on his own premises, near my buildings, and the natural result is the burning of my house, he would be held accountable, though he did not intend to burn me out. The Prophet Hosea says, 'They have sown the wind and they shall reap the whirlwind.'"[5]

A congregation of a different type took place a few days later at the A.M.E. Church on Lafayette Street. Led by the Rev. John A. Warren, a group of leading Black citizens gathered to draft a resolution expressing their feelings about the riot.

Drafted by five men selected from the assembly, the resolution described the riot as "the decisive instrument of separating husband and wife, parent and child, with the loss of property of some of our most influential citizens, also many others, who were in destitute circumstances." Although the report did not name names, it was evident that one of the "most influential citizens" was Whitney Reynolds.

The report contained five resolutions condemning the riot as "inhuman and unlawful," praising those who stepped forward and tried to stop the violence, and denying responsibility for provoking the mob.

The committee singled out three individuals for jeopardizing their own safety to protect others: Officer Dennis K. Sullivan, who "stood in front of the reckless rioters, and prevented them from applying the torch to the A.M.E. Church, which they had indignantly sworn to fire, and in rescuing several colored men from the hands of the mob," and Job and Augustus B. Taber, "proprietors of the Biddle House, who kindly opened their hearts and their doors, to rescue one of the mangled flying victims from the frantic and blood-thirsty mob."

The final resolution spoke volumes about the absurd attempt of some Detroiters to fix blame on the Black community for their own demise. "That as citizens, we do not consider that we have laid ourselves liable to be censured as the instigators of these disturbances in this community, but on the contrary, have proved ourselves to be law-abiding and peaceable citizens."[6]

11

Inquest (Saturday, March 7– Tuesday, March 24, 1863)

> To keep from a rescue, and take him to jail,
> The soldiers were ordered to come without fail,
> But they were insulted and stoned at—pell mell—
> Till some of them fired and down a man fell.
>
> They enter'd, and beat them with billets of wood,
> Then fired the cooper shop just as it stood,
> And as they attempted to rush from the flames,
> They met them with bludgeons to dash out their brains.
> —From "The Riot" by Benjamin Cutler Clark, Sr.

Charles Langer died before he hit the ground, but the riot left six others—all from Whitney Reynolds' cooperage—teetering on the edge of life and death. Charles Fletcher, Lewis Pierce, and Joshua Boyd languished at St. Mary's, while Solomon Houston, Louis Houston, and Robert Bennette recovered in the home of Dr. Morse Stewart, who lived on Clinton Street across from the hospital. On Tuesday, March 10, Joshua Boyd became the second fatality of the riot.

The two deaths led to parallel inquests, Langer's conducted by Justice McCarthy and Boyd's by Coroner J.W. Daly.

Langer's inquest began on Saturday morning, less than twenty-four hours after his shooting. Acting for the coroner who was home ill, Justice Timothy McCarthy convened a jury in his office and called witnesses who stood near Langer when a bullet struck him in the chest.

Considering the truism that no two witnesses to the same incident will see the same thing, it is not difficult to imagine McCarthy's difficulty in finding who fired the bullet that felled Charles Langer.

11. Inquest (Saturday, March 7–Tuesday, March 24, 1863)   151

Less than four months after the Detroit inferno, an epic draft riot broke out in New York City. A wood engraving from a mid-July issue of *Leslie's Illustrated* preserves the moment in time when the provost guard fired on the mob. Although Detroit officers were accused of ordering their soldiers to fire, eyewitness testimony suggests a different scenario (Library of Congress).

The witnesses contradicted each other by offering widely divergent versions. Some of them swore that they saw Langer topple over immediately after Lt. Van Stan fired a revolver pointed in his direction. Others claimed that Langer crumpled to the ground after one of Van Stan's detail fired on his position.

William Timm, a neighbor who knew Charles Langer by sight, spotted him in the crowd about thirty-five feet away. He saw Van Stan and one of his soldiers discharge their weapons in close succession but insisted that Langer fell immediately after Van Stan fired his pistol and before the soldier fired his rifle.

Samuel Wilson stood closer to Langer and reported seeing Van Stan as "much excited," or in a highly-agitated state. "When opposite [the] jail, he turned towards the crowd on [the] sidewalk, and when directly opposite [the] deceased, fired, and deceased fell."

Local merchant Robert Warmsley followed the crowd to the jail, where he witnessed Langer's death. The sharp crack of a pistol report caused Warmsley to turn around. He saw Van Stan with a revolver in his hand, but he did not believe that the officer fired the fatal bullet. "[I] saw [a] soldier with musket raised and apparently taking aim, [he] fired, and deceased, who was passing so close that his shoulder touched mine, fell, shot in breast. [The] second shot was fired half a minute after first." Warmsley concluded, "Deceased did not fall until second shot was fired. In my opinion, musket was in [the] hands of [a] soldier, and [I] think I could identify him if I should see him again."

Joseph V. Scott also believed that the fatal bullet came from a musket in the hands of a private, not from a pistol in the hands of Lt. Van Stan. Scott said he saw one of the soldiers break ranks, move forward, aim his rifle, and fire.

Frank Auberry, a waiter at the Russell House, stood beside Langer when he heard Van Stan give the order to shoot in the direction of the crowd. He watched three soldiers lift their rifles to their shoulders and fire. "Langer immediately fell and exclaimed, 'Oh! I'm shot!'" Auberry said. He was positive of two things: Van Stan ordered his troops to fire and one of them, not Van Stan, shot Langer. Like Warmsley, Auberry claimed that he could identify the shooter.

John L. King had followed the procession from the courthouse to the jail and witnessed the entire sequence of events. King said that Van Stan had his back turned to Langer and therefore could not have fired the shot. He claimed that a tall, "stout" soldier shot Langer and thought he could identify the man if he saw him again.

King added a significant detail: Van Stan stood at the corner of Clinton and Beaubien, where he attempted to "keep them in order." This statement tends to support the idea that Van Stan did not give an order to fire into the crowd. Rather, the soldiers, perhaps frightened or angered by the barrage of bricks thrown at them, fired of their own volition.

Deputy sheriff William Close also saw Langer's shooting but insisted that Van Stan did not give an order to fire. According to Close, Langer stood about twenty feet from the soldier who shot him. After, Van Stan ran up to the soldiers and yelled, "Who shot that man?"

One of the more lucid and detailed statements came from Jane Hommel, who watched the entire episode unfold through the front windows of her residence at the corner of Clinton and Beaubien streets, directly opposite the jail. According to Hommel, Van Stan's men

11. Inquest (Saturday, March 7–Tuesday, March 24, 1863)

walked through a blizzard of sticks, stones, and other "missiles" fired from a vacant lot adjacent to a blacksmith's shop on Clinton Street. He ordered his men to fire and popped off one round from his pistol.

By moving from one window to another, Hommel followed Van Stan and his men as they turned onto Beaubien, where she saw Van Stan fire his pistol in the direction of the blacksmith's shop and a man in the crowd fall. It was the first shot fired, Hommel noted.

A bricklayer named Andrew Monroe verified Jane Hommel's statement. "The man was dead before the soldiers fired," Monroe testified. "He fell immediately after Van Stan fired." Monroe estimated that between four and eight soldiers fired, but only after Charles Langer fell.

John Rankin, a former soldier of the 2nd Michigan and one-time Van Stan subordinate, was even more direct: Van Stan "deliberately aimed his pistol at the crowd, and [I] saw deceased fall immediately after walking three or four paces." Rankin described the crowd as "perfectly quiet" before Langer fell and did not believe that any shots were necessary.

Van Stan's attorney George Hebden wanted to question Rankin. Perhaps realizing which way the winds were blowing, Van Stan came to the inquest armed with his lawyer, who believed that Rankin had an axe to grind with his former C.O. Hebden pointed out that Van Stan had busted Rankin numerous times and the inquest offered an ideal opportunity to square the books. Justice McCarthy would hear none of it. Since Van Stan wasn't on trial, McCarthy argued, there was no need for Hebden to impeach the witness.

John Alder, a soldier with the 4th Michigan Infantry, was in the detachment sent to escort Faulkner to jail. Alder thought he heard Van Stan order his men not to fire, but he estimated that the soldiers intermittently fired eight to twelve rounds anyway. He saw Langer fall but did not know who shot him.

During his testimony, Lt. John Van Stan emphasized the savagery of the protestors. He pointed to the contusion on his face where a brick struck him. As he continued to lead his men through the enfilading fire of bricks and stones coming from the direction of the blacksmith shop, he explained, he was hit by two more bricks: one struck a glancing blow on his cheek and the other slammed into his hip, throwing him off balance.

At the jail, Van Stan said, he ordered his men to close ranks. At this point, he heard two or three shots fired, one of which felled Charles Langer. As for his part, Van Stan admitted shooting his pistol as he stood in front of the jail, but he insisted he fired a warning shot into the ground and not into the crowd. He was the only witness to describe the crowd in front of the jail as in a highly agitated, excited state.[1]

Van Stan's second-in-command, John Babbitt, backed his superior officer. He insisted that the shots came from soldiers' muskets, not officers' pistols. No officer had fired, Babbitt said, because Van Stan ordered them not to. According to Babbitt, the hail of bricks and stones did not abate once Faulkner entered the jail; it intensified, which caused the soldiers to be on the defense.

John Palmer, one of the provost guards under Van Stan's command, said he was standing shoulder to shoulder with his superior officer when the shot (which Palmer believed came from a musket) was fired. If Van Stan fired his pistol at this moment, Palmer did not see it, which he characterized as an impossibility because Van Stan stood right next to him and had his back turned to Charles Langer.

Local physician Dr. John C. Smith took the stand to opine as to whether the fatal bullet came from a pistol or a musket. A postmortem examination determined that the projectile struck Langer in the midline by the second rib, tore through his right lung, and exited out of his armpit. Based on the wound track alone, Smith, who had seen many musket wounds, could not say with any certainty if the shot came from a pistol or a musket. A more oblong bullet would have created a larger wound track than he had seen in Langer's torso, he explained, but "a small pistol ball would pass through the body in the direction taken by the ball killing the deceased."

William Shaw, a soldier with the 8th Michigan Cavalry, dug a Minié ball out of a fence board directly behind where Langer stood when he was shot and believed it came from a soldier's musket, although there was no conclusive way to tie the bullet to either Langer or the smoking gun.

As divergent as their accounts were, the civilian witnesses all agreed on three points: the crowd outside the jail did not throw things at the soldiers or harass them as they had on Clinton Street, Lt. Van Stan did not have provocation to order his men to fire, and after Charles Langer fell, the crowd became enraged. These common denominators suggested that the itchy trigger fingers of Lt. Van Stan's soldiers may have inspired the human tornado that tore down Beaubien. In the minds of the rioters, the U.S. Army saved "the negro Faulkner" from a just punishment (a lynching) and murdered a white man in the process.

• • • •

On Friday, March 13, a parallel inquest began into the death of Joshua Boyd, who died as a result of the savage beating he suffered at the hands of unidentified assailants during the riot a week earlier.

Boyd came north to Detroit from Virginia a year earlier. Taking work as a cooper, he planned to save enough money to purchase the freedom of his wife and two children, who had remained behind in Virginia. By the time of the riot, he had managed to squirrel away almost enough money to free his family from slavery.

Boyd's tragic odyssey began when Dennis K. Sullivan pulled him from the ground and dragged him into a saloon. Successfully shooing away rioters that had gathered at the saloon entrance, Sullivan entrusted Boyd to Bishop LeFevre, who drove the stricken man in a wagon to St. Mary's Hospital. Fearing further violence, Boyd's friends took him across the river to Windsor, but when his condition did not improve, they returned him to St. Mary's, where he died a few days later.

Both the *Free Press* and the *Advertiser and Tribune* commented on Boyd's passing. In a succinct piece, the *Free Press* uncharacteristically softened their language by describing Boyd as "colored" and noted his reputation for hard work.

The *Advertiser and Tribune* offered a bit more of a biography but made no reference to Boyd's race. They, too, lauded Boyd for his integrity, hard work, and perseverance. The newspaper with the Republican bent suggested that Boyd's senseless death had victimized his family, who would remain enslaved. "This man, so industrious, so peaceable and honest," the writer noted, "has lost his property, lost the possibility of relieving his family from bondage, and lost his life, by the horrible persecution of a mob that would not be satisfied with anything but plunder and blood."[2]

Testifying at the inquest, Officer Sullivan described his rescue of Boyd. Alerted by the sound of loud groans emanating from a barn behind Reynolds' cooper shop, Sullivan found an "oldish man" curled into a fetal position, his head covered with blood oozing from a gash in his scalp. He helped Boyd to his feet, and together they hobbled into a tavern on East Fort Street. Like a following sea, several rioters trailed them, haranguing them with menacing taunts along the way. "Kill him! Hang him!" they shouted. A few voices emerging from the din led Sullivan to conclude that the rioters believed Boyd fired the shot that peppered the face of young Edward Crosby.

Sullivan described a harrowing scene outside the saloon. One rioter, with a clothesline with the end knotted into a noose, demanded Sullivan "give them the privilege of putting it around his [Boyd's] neck."[3]

Fellow officer David M. Freeman and bystander John J. Bagley, a tobacconist who lived a few blocks away from the cooperage, had witnessed the attack that left Boyd battered and bloodied. Neither man knew the names of the victims.

Freemen saw one man run from the burning building; rioters chased him down Beaubien Street. One brick to the back of the head sent the man hurtling to the ground. Freeman spotted an older man, Lewis Pierce, dart out of the building and attempt to take shelter from the flames under an overturned wheelbarrow. Freeman escorted the terrified man to a neighbor's house and then returned to the scene of the conflagration, where he spotted two men, Louis Houston and Joshua Boyd, prone with a ring of boys taking turns throwing rocks at them. Freeman collared one of the boys, which inflamed a bystander who demanded Freeman let the boy alone. During this exchange, a man whom Freeman described as having "long straight hair," Joshua Boyd, wobbled into the barn.

Louis Houston, who survived the attack and lived to tell about it, did not testify at the inquest. Later, he told his story to the author of *A Thrilling Narrative*. After fleeing the burning building, Houston spotted Boyd, "entirely lifeless, but ... being held up by the fence." According to Houston, Boyd had been "knocked on the head with an axe." After a while lying unconscious, he came to his senses and ran down the street, where the mob overcame him.[4]

Bagley spotted Houston at this point. At the inquest, he described seeing a "negro prostrate and apparently badly hurt" on Croghan Street. Bagley could not find an officer, so he rounded up a few bystanders and took the man to the home of Dr. Morse Stewart. Both Freeman and Bagley characterized the rioters as kids, Bagley stating that some of the boys were "apparently not over ten years of age."

Dr. John C. Gorten, who conducted the post mortem, provided a graphic description of Boyd's wounds. "The upper part of his face was beaten all to a jelly," Gorten said, "his nose was broken; he was burned from the right buttox [sic] above the hip to the knee; burnt about half an inch into the muscles." Gorten believed that "either of the injuries [the first degree burns or the blunt trauma to the head] would have proved fatal."[5]

• • • •

While witnesses testified in the Boyd inquest, jurors in the Langer inquest traveled to the barracks. Several of the witnesses said they could identify the soldier who fired the Minié ball that felled Charles Langer, so the commanding officer, Captain Robinson, staged a line-up that came under scrutiny because several soldiers were absent, including ten on leave and an unreported number of convalescents sent back to the front lines.

Robinson sealed the barracks to prevent anyone from leaving and positioned his soldiers in two parallel lines. Each of the witnesses paraded past the men and tried to recognize some facial feature they saw in the blink of an eye in a blur of movement a week earlier. The task was made more difficult by the fact that every one of the suspects wore the same uniform, so the witnesses could not use attire in an attempt to make a positive identification.

Once again, contradictions ruled the day. A few of the witnesses thought they recognized the guilty party, but each fingered a different man as the shooter. The identification became a farce when Robinson pointed out that one of the "guilty" parties had been a hundred and fifty miles away at the time of the Langer shooting and another was a straw man—a bystander inserted into the line-up.

On Monday, March 16, the last few witnesses testified in the Langer inquest. After a brief deliberation, the jury concluded that a member of the provost guard and not Lt. Van Stan fired the round that killed Charles Langer, but they could not place the musket in the hands of any particular individual.

A week later, the coroner's jury in the Boyd case came to an identical conclusion: "the deceased came to his death from wounds received during the riot, at the hands of unknown persons."[6]

Compared to the Langer inquest, the Boyd inquest was a relatively muted affair. Justice McCarthy called dozens of witnesses and brought the jury to the army barracks in a desperate attempt to identify Langer's shooter. Coroner Daly, by contrast, only questioned a handful of witnesses. The small number was in part due to the failure of bystanders to come forward and testify, but it also hints at the greater gravity given to the accidental shooting of Charles Langer than to the willful homicide of Joshua Boyd.[7]

To readers who could read between the lines of the newsprint, the difference between the two inquests was black and white.

• • • •

The fact that just a handful of Detroiters did anything to quell the riot only underscored the efforts of those who did. Dennis K. Sullivan's heroics did not go unnoticed. Both the *Free Press* and the *Advertiser and Tribune* lauded him as one of the good guys, and this positive ink led to his promotion to chief of the city's fledgling police force—a group of fifty officers and a sort of ancestor to the metropolitan police. A brief item in the *Advertiser and Tribune* noted that "the appointment of officer Sullivan to the responsible post as Chief of the Police will give great satisfaction to our citizens."[8]

The "Committee on Police" said of the newly-christened captain of police, "Mr. Sullivan has shown by his energy and efficiency, that he is eminently worthy of the appointment he has received."

The committee's edict also contained a stern warning should any of Sullivan's force devote too much of their time testing the quality of beer in the city's saloons or visually inspecting the city's prostitutes for venereal disease. "Any of the special police will be immediately dropped from the list for disobedience of orders, or neglecting to patrol their beats as required, and also for making unnecessary stops in saloons or improper places."[9]

Sullivan and company went to work busting the city's malefactors. One interesting case involved a thief who shimmied into the half-open window of a hotel room. He picked the lock of a trunk, which contained an assortment of fine clothes. He swapped his worn togs for those in

11. Inquest (Saturday, March 7–Tuesday, March 24, 1863)

the trunk and crawled back through the window. No doubt reveling in the thought of the hotel guest opening the trunk to find his threadbare clothes, the quick change artist ran into Sullivan, who clamped a pair of "bracelets" around his wrists and dragged him off to jail.

"A detective [Sullivan] extended to the burglar a pressing invitation to visit the jail," ran the playful prose of an *Advertiser and Tribune* journalist. "The rascal was forced to accept, and will shortly receive some hints concerning honesty."[10]

12

Witnesses (Monday, March 9– Tuesday, March 24, 1863)

> Whilst females were heard crying, "kill them"—Oh; shame,
> They urged on the mob, yet there's no one to blame,
> 'Twas got up to please our friends of the South,
> Now don't say a word—nay, don't open your mouth.
> We go in for the Union just as it was.
> And slavery also, and all the slave laws;
> Now do not think hard if we do behave rash,
> By burning those houses we pocket some cash.
> —From "The Riot" by Benjamin Cutler Clark, Sr.

William Champ's ebbing reputation further receded when he had failed to identify the firebrands in the mob. Detroiters knew Champ as a talented investigator with years of experience, so his inability to make an arrest led some to wonder how hard he had tried. The *Advertiser and Tribune* editors vocalized this concern when they wrote, "The Fire Marshal is known to be too good a detective and police officer—when he chooses to be—to plead that he 'didn't see it.' Why does he not do his duty to the city in this respect?" They followed this burning criticism with an even more caustic remark. "It would relieve his reputation of much of the odium acquired from the (to us) surprising stigma of being once cowed and prevented by fear from doing his public duty."[1] This was a comment on Champ's admission that he had backed down from rioters who threatened to trash fire equipment if it was used to save residences of Black Detroiters.

Sheriff's deputies and ward constables were more effective than the fire marshal in identifying the perpetrators. In the days after the

12. Witnesses (Monday, March 9–Tuesday, March 24, 1863)   161

riot, they pounded the paving stones of the Third and Fourth wards and interviewed hundreds of people. Gradually, faces of those responsible for the most flagrant acts began to materialize from the crowd. Aided by a rather large carrot in the form of a "liberal reward," the officers managed to round up the ringleaders. Within two weeks, they collared twenty alleged "rioters": Robert Carey, William Carlow, Edward Crosby, John H. Davis, Peter Doran, Antoine Downer, Timothy Drummond, Cornelius "Con" Dwyer, Bernard Groghan, Charles Hall, Jerry Hanifan, William Krueger, Alexander Lefevre, Andrew Manning, John Miller, William Naylor, James Robinson, Edward Skean, Cyrus Sleker, and Peter Smith.

Three additional malfeasants appeared in police court in separate arraignments. Francis Carr and Michael Hider stood accused of looting, while John "Conrad" Kalb faced the most serious charge of all: "assault with intent to kill and murder."

The collective arraignment and examination of the "rioters" occurred in a circus-like atmosphere. All twenty defendants and their counsel crowded into police court—a tiny brick structure adjacent to the yard of the county jail. Old adversaries James Knox Gavin, representing the people, and J. Logan Chipman, representing the defendants, once again faced each other from opposite sides of the aisle and made their arguments to Justice Minot T. Lane. Gavin wanted to prove that enough evidence existed to warrant trials in recorder's court, while his archenemy Chipman wanted to keep as many of his clients from a jury as possible.

It was an uphill battle for Gavin. While officers managed to collar twenty suspects, they could only muster half a dozen credible witnesses among the thousands present during the riot. Over the eight-day examination, they offered a quagmire of conflicting testimony.

A *Free Press* reporter lamented the lack of solid testimony when he complained that "one of the witnesses for the people, in the examination on Thursday, identified some three or four of the rioters, but could not possibly recognize more than that number. Yesterday the same witness took the stand and swore positively that he saw another party, who was in the prisoners' box both days, throwing bricks and paving-stones at a negro who was fleeing from the mob. There is not, of course, any doubt but that he saw the proceeding, but the mystery of the thing lies in the fact of his not recognizing him at all on Thursday, and positively swearing to the occurrence on Saturday." The reporter then added, "Even officers who were all the time endeavoring to pacify the mob with all the energy they possessed, are not, in several instances, able to identify a single man."[2] This was a jab evidently intended for Dennis K. Sullivan.

Sullivan's memory appeared sharper than the anonymous reporter suggested. He identified William Krueger as the one who pushed his way into the saloon on the pretense of buying a beer. He ran out of the saloon bragging that it had cost him ten cents to see the bloodied visage of Joshua Boyd. J.B. Bloss corroborated Sullivan's story but could not identify any of the others in the dock.

Dr. John C. Gorten identified Timothy Drummond as one of the more active rioters. Described as "the deaf and dumb boy," Drummond ran with Con Dwyer and Robert Carey, the trio smashing windows as they tore down Beaubien Street. Other witnesses testified to seeing Drummond kicking a Black man who was face down on the street and John Miller for chasing down and beating a young Black boy.

Testimony likewise fixed blame on Con Dwyer for hurling a stone at Faulkner as soldiers escorted him to jail following the trial and then for hitting and kicking an unidentified Black man and on Andrew Manning for whipping stones at a Black woman with a baby in her arms.

Bystander William Sullivan, the principal witness against Manning, said he dodged a barrage of flying debris to rescue the terrified woman. John Venn, who watched the assault on Whitney Reynolds' cooper shop, corroborated Sullivan's testimony. Manning, according to Venn, pelted the woman with rocks after she escaped the burning building. Venn also said he saw Manning throwing rocks through the shop windows.[3]

Both Edwin Jerome and his son, Edwin Jerome, Jr., identified Peter Smith as the young tough who, running toward the jail, tried to incite his fellow rioters by yelling, "Come, boys, down in there is a lot of niggers, come, let's give them hell."[4] According to a local carriage maker named William M. Lyon, Smith approached him during the riot and asked him how he liked it. "I didn't like it all," Lyon responded.[5]

Other eyewitnesses fixed blame on one or more of the defendants

12. Witnesses (Monday, March 9–Tuesday, March 24, 1863) 163

for various acts of malfeasance. Edward Crosby and Bernard Groghan chased down a Black man and repeatedly hit him. Alexandre LeFevre disrupted a fire engine as the flames consumed Frederick Gies' grocery store. Antoine Downer brandished a club and yelled, "Come on, we will kill the damned niggers."[6] Peter Doran pulled a picket from the fence surrounding the cooper shop and a swung it at the windows. James Robinson attempted to torch a building. Eyewitness Lorena Lang—a twenty-nine-year-old denizen of the Third Ward—said she saw Jerry Hanifan in the crowd and knew it was him because of the type of clothes he wore, but then she admitted to a "defect in one eye so that I can not see out of it."[7]

Like Downer, Robinson had a big mouth. An eyewitness said he heard Robinson yell, "Hurry, and bring in the coals." He then attempted to fan the fire with his hat. Another eyewitness said that Robinson wanted "the niggers cleaned out."

Carlow, Davis, Doran, Hall, Skean, and Sleker had all been seen throwing bricks, rocks, and whatever else they could find at houses in the Third Ward. Marcus Dale knew Sleker and identified him as one of those who laid siege to Whitney Reynolds' cooperage.

In addition to Marcus Dale, two other inhabitants of the cooperage at the time of the attack testified: Lewis Pierce and Robert Bennette.

Bennette was at work when the human tornado descended on the shop. A brick through the window startled him, and he gazed out the window to see two familiar faces: Cyrus Sleker and Alexander Lefevre. "I looked and saw him pick up a brick and throw it—he then went back into the house—there were a great many around, many engaged in throwing." Bennette also saw Lefevre "throw at the 3 men who were running out of the house."[8]

Lewis Pierce, who had known John H. Davis for more than a year, testified to seeing him hurling stones at Whitney Reynolds' cooperage. "I was in the rear part of the house when I saw him throwing when we got the women out of the house through the front door." He also said that Davis pelted him with stones when he attempted to flee the structure through a back door.[9] After the siege of the cooper shop, Davis went to the home of a friend sometime between six and seven o'clock. August Sprege said that Davis had blood on his hands.[10] Likewise, Thomas Skillman saw Skean "with his shirt sleeves bloody."[11]

When the examinations ended a week later, hard evidence—hard to find among the mass of conflicting testimony—winnowed down the number of "rioters." Only the thinnest threads connected John Miller, Edward Skean, and Cyrus Sleker to the riot, and these threads broke under scrutiny. Gavin had no conclusive evidence against Robert Carey, Jerry Hanifan, or Peter Smith, either. All six were discharged.[12] Despite some damning hearsay, Alexandre Lefevre and James Robinson were likewise dismissed, and Bernard Groghan was nowhere to be found.

During the examination on Tuesday, March 24, Bernard Groghan, who stood accused of one of the more violent acts, slipped out of court and immediately fled the city.[13] Not until a letter arrived at the *Free Press* offices a few weeks later did his whereabouts—too far out of reach for the long arm of Justice Lane and Officer Sullivan—become known.

A *Free Press* reporter depicted the discharged suspects as victims of greedy reward-seekers who supplied inadequate or even false information in exchange for payment. "Why these young men, most of whom were respectable, and never before saw the inside of the jail as prisoner, were arrested," he wrote, "it is difficult to conceive." With his tongue firmly planted in his cheek, the reporter supplied a reason. "It is hardly possible that there are those base enough to endeavor to convict innocent men in the hope of obtaining the reward for the apprehension and conviction of parities engaged in the riot. Yet it is generally believed that, but for the reward, not more than one-half the number of arrests would have been made."[14] So it wasn't the reward until it was.

Eleven of the original twenty defendants were held for trial in recorder's court.[15] Lane set their bail at $1,000 each, but unable to pay this king's ransom, they would spend the days leading up to the trial in the county jail.

Carr and Hider faced charges of looting during the riot, Catherine Prusher for fencing the stolen items.

John "Conrad" Kalb, dubbed the "prince of rioters" by a creative reporter, would hear the most somber music in court. Faced with a charge of "assault and battery with intent to murder," he stood to spend a good portion of his twenties behind bars. The *Free Press* reported that "the evidence against him was clear," and he appeared primed for a role as the riot's scapegoat.[16]

In late March, officers collared William Crosby, believed to have

12. Witnesses (Monday, March 9–Tuesday, March 24, 1863)

been an active participant in the riot. Crosby had evaded capture by fleeing to Canada, but when he crossed back over the river, constables slapped a pair of "bracelets" over his wrists and dragged him to the county jail. Described by the *Advertiser and Tribune* as "a hard pet ... said to have been very conspicuous in leading on the mob of the late riot," William Crosby would go to trial alongside the other accused rioters in May.[17]

• • • •

On March 18, Dennis K. Sullivan received a watch—a "chronometer balance silver hunting watch"—in recognition of his bravery ten days earlier. Detroit's plutocrats had passed the hat to pay for the expensive token, which cost $75.

The inner case contained a laudatory inscription acknowledging Sullivan's heroics during the riot.

> Presented to DENNIS K. SULLIVAN,
> BY THE CITIZENS OF DETROIT,
> For his FIDELITY as an officer in protecting life
> And property in the late riot.
> March 18, 1863

J.B. Bloss presented the watch to Sullivan in the mayor's office.

"Your fellow-citizens," Bloss said, "desirous of expressing their gratitude, have contributed this testimonial of their regard for you as a worthy and efficient officer; but more particularly for your fearless conduct during the late riot, in protecting the lives of the unoffending, when chased and beaten by an infuriated mob; and guarding their property, which the rioters endeavored to destroy by fire. I take great pleasure in being the bearer of this token of their regard, and their approval of your conduct on that occasion. You did your duty nobly."

Bloss' remarks, preserved for posterity in parallel articles that appeared in the *Advertiser and Tribune* and the *Free Press*, contain a subtext embedded in the reference to guarding property "which the rioters endeavored to destroy by fire." Most of the Third Ward structures fired by the rioters burned to the ground, so the "duty" that Sullivan did "nobly" likely referred to his efforts in stopping the rioters from torching the business district.

"It is not simply that you did your duty that we thus commend you," Bloss continued. "But that you did it *heartily, earnestly*, with resolute determination; showing that your action was the spontaneous impulse of your humanity." Bloss waxed poetic about Sullivan's moral compass, which he compared to the steady rhythm of time and the rightward movement of the watch he presented.

> You did not stop to inquire whether there was danger to yourself. You saw danger to others, and threw yourself into the breach. It was manly, brave, heroic.
>
> Trusting that the high regard and confidence we repose in you may never be weakened by any act of yours, I now present you, from the citizens of Detroit, this watch. Take it, and wear it as a token of their regard and esteem; and may the pulsations of your heart ever beat as true to the right, as this does to the rising and setting sun.

Sullivan accepted the watch and gave a brief statement.

> Deeply imbued with the sentiment of gratitude for this beautiful and useful memento of kindly consideration and appreciation by my fellow-citizens, of my humble services as an officer of police, I tender you my sincerely thanks.
>
> Through you, also, I desire to convey to the liberal donors the profound sense of obligation with which I am inspired. To know one's duty, and to do it, with an abiding conviction of the responsibility imposed in times of stormy excitement and difficulty, may be said, in general terms, to constitute the highest attainment of the citizen and the patriot. To be made the recipient of such tokens of regard, accompanied with such graceful expressions as mark your address of confidence and approval, might fill the bosom of the refined and appreciative with happiness. To one, who, certainly, can make no just pretensions in either direction, it is overwhelming.
>
> It is mine, therefore, in the simple language of truth, to repeat, I am profoundly grateful.
>
> While I thus give utterance to my feelings of obligation, I should be wanting in honor were I to withhold my solemn pledge to you sir, and to my fellow-citizens at large, that I will ever, whether in official position or in that of the humblest denizen, in this, the city and country of my adoption, devote my best energies and efforts, faithfully and honestly, to the performance of every duty, private and public, which the times and the circumstances may require—that the sustaining of the constitution and the laws of my country and the preservation of peace and good order in the community among whom my lot may be cast, shall be paramount to all considerations and issues of a private or individual character.
>
> It only remains for me to express the hope, in which I know you will concur, that a merciful Creator may preserve us, in all future time, from a repetition of the sad and disgraceful scenes through which we have recently passed.[18]

13

Black, White, and Sepia (March 1863)

> Now be it remember'd that Falkner [sic] at right,
> Although call'd a "nigger," had always been white,
> Had voted, and always declared in his shop,
> He never would sell colored people a drop.
>
> He's what is call'd white, though I must confess,
> So mixed are the folks now, we oft have to guess,
> Their hair is curl'd and their skins are so brown,
> If they're white in the country, they're niggers in town.
> —From "The Riot" by Benjamin Cutler Clark, Sr.

Before, during, and after Detroit's "Great Riot," Faulkner personified the racial tensions festering among some of the city's residents. That a middle-aged barkeep may have raped a ten-year-old caused a stir; that a Black man may have raped a white girl caused a riot. Faulkner became the scapegoat for the city's racial angst.

But was Faulkner Black?

For the Democratic-leaning *Free Press* editors, there was never any doubt. In their reporting of "The Faulkner Outrage," *Free Press* writers invariably described Faulkner as "the negro Faulkner."

Yet in his remarks at the meeting of the city's scions on the evening of Saturday, March 7, Edward C. Walker described Faulkner as "seven-eighths white" and noted that "being seven-eighths white, the disgrace [the alleged rape] if it had anything to do with the different races, rested more upon the whites than the blacks."[1]

If, as Walker pointed out, Faulkner was not in fact a "negro," then the *Free Press* coverage of the trial either by accident or by design further exacerbated already-existing racial tensions.

It was a point that the rival paper was quick to identify.

The *Advertiser and Tribune* broached the subject of Faulkner's race in an article published on March 7 under the headline.

The writer began with an apologetic note. "The statement was made upon the first arrest of Faulkner, and has been acquiescent in by this journal for want of better information, that Faulkner is a negro. He is a dark skinned man with blue eyes and straight hair."[2]

Then came the zinger. "He is not, however, a negro. He claims to be Spanish and Indian." This was an important distinction. E.C. Walker described Faulkner as "seven-eighths white"; if the one-eighth derived from a Black great-grandparent, he would have been classified as a "mulatto" in the era's parlance. If, on the other hand, Faulkner owed his dusky complexion to a Spanish or Native American ancestor, then the 1863 riot was based on a false assumption about Faulkner's skin tone.

Not only was Faulkner not a "negro," according to the *Advertiser and Tribune*, but he discriminated when pulling a tap in his tavern. "He has never associated with the negroes, and had not been claimed by them. He would never allow any of them to enter his saloon, and has exhibited great hostility to them as a race."

As a further proof, the *Advertiser and Journal* pointed out that Faulkner "voted uniformly in the Democratic ticket," insinuating that no Black man would vote for the party that tended to support slavery as an institution.

The writer ended his piece by pointing out the horrible irony raised by E.C. Walker: "How doubly prominent this fact sets forth the atrocious outrages perpetrated upon the colored people in this city on his behalf."[3] Although the writer did not mention the *Free Press*, this was nevertheless a stinging rebuke of the rival newspaper's writers.

This idea that the race riot resulted from a mistaken assumption was reiterated in the pages of the *Advertiser and Tribune* throughout March. A pair of letters to the editor directly addressed this issue.

The author of the first letter, signed with the enigmatic pseudonym VINDEX, described Faulkner as "a white man (in law), and a ranting Democrat, a negro hater—for Faulkner was amongst the most malignant of his class of 'fanatics.'" VINDEX pointed out that even

Faulkner's lawyer, avowed Democrat J. Logan Chipman, believed in his client's innocence.

"This alleged crime," VINDEX continued, "is made the excuse for an indiscriminate, brutal and murderous attack upon the unoffending negroes of the city, by the part to which the alleged criminal and his attorney belonged, and his offence was made the excuse for murdering two or three negroes, for attempting to exterminate our whole negro population."

VINDEX concluded, "Such is the position in which the Copperhead Democracy of Detroit have placed themselves by their blind hatred of negroes and their contempt for law and order!"[4]

These assertions were reiterated eight days later by his fellow letter-writer, UNION, who even used some of the same descriptions. Both letter writers, for example, said that Faulkner "has not a drop of negro blood in his veins." UNION also said that Faulkner was "at the time of his arrest a registered voter in the Third Ward, and a virulent Copperhead Democrat, hating a 'nigger' and an 'abolitionist' as intensely as the most malignant rebel sympathizer in his party."[5]

The *Free Press* ran no such articles about Faulkner's background. Even after the trial, when Faulkner's race became a topic of heated debate, the *Free Press* failed to drop the epithet "negro." To do so may have been to admit the error, and the *Free Press* editors may have been eager to side-step their role in inflaming public opinion against Faulkner and Detroit's Black community. In a piece published the day after the *Advertiser and Tribune*'s "FAULKNER NOT A NEGRO" piece, the *Free Press* writer maintained his stock epithet when lauding acting sheriff F.X. Cicotte for "protecting the negro Faulkner from the mob."[6]

The *Advertiser and Tribune* further muddied the waters with a follow-up piece insinuating that Faulkner was the illegitimate love child of Charles James Faulkner, a Virginia planter who had been a U.S. congressman and ambassador to France. In March 1863, when his alleged offspring stood trial for rape, Faulkner served on the general staff of Confederate general Thomas J. "Stonewall" Jackson.

The short article came under the heading "AMALGAMATION" and took a shot at *Free Press* writers for suggesting that the coupling of Blacks and whites resulted from "Republican teachings" about racial equality. "The *Free Press*, a few weeks since, was filled with virtuous indignation at the influence of Republican teachings as developed in the elopement of a negro with a white woman. It now turns out that the mulatto [William Faulkner] was a natural son of Charles James Faulkner, of Virginia, ex–Minister to France, and so far from his actions being due to Republican doctrines, that he was only carrying out the principle to which he owes his existence."[7]

Translation: Faulkner's "actions" (his alleged rape of Mary Brown) did not result from "Republican doctrines" but from the repetition of his father's alleged indiscretion. In other words, like father, like son.

It's impossible to know if Faulkner's alleged blood ties to the gentleman from Virginia was based on evidence or speculation, but in identifying Faulkner as the illegitimate offspring of a Virginia planter and in describing him as "mulatto," the author contradicted the "FAULKNER NOT A NEGRO" piece by conceding that somewhere in Faulkner's family tree was an ancestor of African descent.

The anonymous author of *A Thrilling Narrative* made no specific claims about Faulkner's background, instead describing him as "to all intents a white man." The writer declares this assertion "behind doubt, for he was a regular voter, and the journals of the city that understood his politics state that he voted

Charles J. Faulkner in a portrait taken sometime between 1855 and 1865 (Library of Congress).

the Democratic ticket." As proof, the writer cites Faulkner's own attitude toward Blacks as seen through an unnamed source. "And an old veteran of over one hundred years of age declares that, in conversing with F. he said: 'If he thought he had one drop of colored blood in his veins, if he could, he would let it out.'"[8]

This description is eerily similar in content and wording to the *Advertiser and Tribune* article "FAULKNER NOT A NEGRO," suggesting that either this portion of *A Thrilling Narrative* is based on the earlier news item or that they shared a common source. The account contains verbatim portions of other *Advertiser and Tribune* pieces, suggesting that the author drew source material from Detroit's Republican-influenced newspaper. The author may have been affiliated in some way with the *Advertiser and Tribune*, perhaps as an editor or writer.

The writer of *A Thrilling Narrative*, written and published in 1863, enjoyed access to sources and scuttlebutt long lost to history. Yet the author's motives may have clouded this unique vantage point. The wording—"to all intents a white man"—appears to concede that Faulkner may have been part Black, but representing Faulkner as a "white man" served two purposes: it distanced Detroit's Black community from the alleged rape of Mary Brown and underscored the absurdity of leveling value judgements based on skin color. Rioters and writers alike tended to perceive things as black and white when the reality was not so simple.

Benjamin Cutler Clark, Sr., versified this argument in his poem "The Riot," presented as an epilogue to *A Thrilling Narrative*. "Now be it remember'd that Faulkner at right, / Although call'd a 'nigger,' had always been white, / Had voted, and always declared in his shop, / He never would sell colored people a drop."

Clark added a sardonic editorial: "He's what is call'd white, though I must confess, / So mixed are the folks now, we oft have to guess, / Their hair is so curl'd and their skins are so brown, / If they're white in the country, they're niggers in town."

Clark's poem indicts people for "guessing" Faulkner's race based on his dusky complexion. People, he insinuates, had judged the content of Faulkner's biography by the sepia tone of its cover.

Regardless, the *Advertiser and Tribune* article "FAULKNER NOT

A NEGRO" would have legs that carried it into subsequent accounts. In describing the riot in an 1863 item, a *Jackson Citizen Patriot* writer said of Faulkner's identity: "Instead however, of the prisoner being a negro, it appears that he is a half-breed Spaniard and Indian; a registered citizen of the city, and has always voted the democratic ticket." The author then added a jab to the Democratic-leaning *Free Press* by stating what the original piece left unsaid: "that must be sweet consolation for the *Free Press* and kindred publications."[9]

It is unclear if Faulkner ever claimed "to be Spanish and Indian," but the uncertainty of his ethnicity is evident in later records. His 1863 prisoner registration describes him as "not dark for a mulatto." The 1870 census records his race as "B." His marriage record of the same year indicates that he was white. An 1877 account of Faulkner's death published in the *Advertiser and Tribune* described him as "colored."[10]

Ten days after the *Advertiser and Tribune*'s article "FAULKNER NOT A NEGRO," the *Free Press* finally addressed the question of Faulkner's race, in part to refute a statement made by *New York Tribune* founder Horace Greeley. "The mob in Detroit," Greeley argued, "was virtually plotted at Richmond, fomented in New York, and led by democratic ruffians, the allies of Jefferson Davis…. It apparently began in an attempt to take from the custody of the lawful authorities—not a negro, but a Spanish Indian, who never even associated with the blacks, who had been guilty of a horrid outrage on a white girl."

"Faulkner was, in fact, a negro," the *Free Press* editors countered. "His boast was that he was from Virginia, and connected with the Faulkner family of that State. The mob were not democrats. Many of the Germans who took part in it never voted a democratic ticket in their lives."[11]

Despite an earlier retraction, the *Free Press* had reverted to German-bashing even though the majority of those arrested for riot had English and Irish surnames.

• • • •

Despite accusations of fomenting racial unrest, *Free Press* reporters did not soften their language. The paper's treatment of alleged victim Julia Ann French contained a litany of racial epithets.

Fifty-eight-year-old Julia Ann French attempted to press charges against a woman and her daughters for pelting her with stones during the riot. Neither the court nor the *Free Press* looked upon her complaint as legitimate. The *Free Press* depicted French as a litigious woman who was not beyond fabricating evidence to settle a score.

The *Free Press* article about the French case devotes a considerable amount of ink to describing Julia Ann French as an ogress. "Mrs. French is by no means a female whose charms are calculated to win for her admirers, either male or female. Her proportions, naturally elephantine, have been extended and distorted from the effects of frequent and long-continued indulgence in the favorite negro beverage known as 'tangle-leg.' Add to this the fact that the small-pox has left its deep-seated imprints in her naturally repulsive and furrowed cheeks."

French, her head covered in bandages, recounted the alleged assault to Justice Lane. After hearing the complaint, Lane demanded proof. He ordered her to remove the bandages and show him the bruises.

The *Free Press* correspondent playfully toyed with the notion of "black" in his description of the climactic moment when Mrs. French unraveled the bandages. "With great reluctance the persecuted female bared the bruised parts to inspection, but, contrary to expectation, there was no perceptible difference in the appearance of the bruised and unbruised parts—all were of one uniform color, and that color most essentially black."

A number of witnesses testified that no one had assaulted French; French responded by accusing them of perjury.

Adding insult to alleged injury, Lane fined Julia French $5.[12]

• • • •

In early May 1863, two meetings were held at the Baptist church on Croghan Street to determine the feasibility of Black Detroiters enlisting in a Massachusetts brigade. The *Free Press* article covering the second meeting made liberal use of racially-charged terms such as "nigger," "darkie," and "shade."

The rhetoric became particularly florid in the description of the participants. "Not a solitary nigger appeared upon the scene of action until nearly 9 o'clock, at which time the doors were opened, the gas lighted, and an occasional shadow in the doorway would demonstrate the fact that another had been added to the dark congregation."

The reporter singled out George De Baptiste for criticizing the *Free Press* in his remarks to the group. "The nigger actually waxed warm with eloquence, characterizing the paper as incendiary, treasonable, hellish, and such other choice epithets as happened to enter his copper-colored skull." Word choice proved De Baptiste's point.

The article ended with a direct reference to the riot and a sharp barb at Black Detroiters who fled to Canada. "It is pretty safe to say, however, that no matter what may be the result of these meetings Detroit does not stand in any great danger of losing any considerable numbers of her colored population. The fact may as well be told first as last, Detroit niggers don't care about risking their precious necks where even bricks, much less ballets, are used in a careless and dangerous manner."[13]

Racially-charged rhetoric remained particularly strong in stories concerning "amalgamation," such as a piece on an arrest that occurred in August 1863. "In one house men and women of all shades and complexions were found piled promiscuously in one bed. The parties were arrested and taken before the Police Court, on Monday, as vagrants."

The author characterized their "conduct" as "a disgrace to any community laying the slightest claim to civilization, as they were properly given the severest penalty which the law allows. The people are not yet quite prepared for practical amalgamation, although there are many who profess to believe in the theory."

The court apparently agreed; each of the "parties" received a year in the House of Correction—a harsher penalty than that meted out to most of the rioters.[14]

• • • •

In the civil war of Detroit newspapers, the *Free Press* prevailed in sending news coverage of the riot outside of Michigan—a fact lamented by *Advertiser and Tribune* editors, who decried the rival paper's account as exaggerated or downright fabricated. "Much of the sensational portion of the *Free Press* account, which has been extensively copied, did not take place at all, whilst many actual occurrences where wholly overlooked, and others greatly exaggerated, as it was compelled to admit in its subsequent issues."[15]

The bit about admitting exaggerated reporting was probably a reference to the *Free Press* claim that the riot was made up of German immigrants angered by Langer's death only to retract the statement in a subsequent issue. The *Advertiser and Tribune* would counter that their coverage of the riot was the only accurate account, even though it contained several factual errors: listing twenty-two men labeled "rioters" but who weren't rioters at all; describing Solomon Houston as the proprietor of cooper shop, when the cooperage belonged to Whitney Reynolds; and misplacing the cooperage at the corner of Beaubien and East Fort.[16]

Despite *Tribune* criticisms of inaccurate reporting, the *Free Press* account flowed outside of Detroit, and newspapers around the country began to comment on the riot. Like the two papers in Detroit, their politics inevitably flavored their reporting. Republican newspapers ragged on the *Free Press* and accused them of fomenting the riot.

The *Springfield Republican*, for example, accused the *Free Press* of widening preexisting animosities. "Bloody riots like this are the legitimate effect of the teachings of some of the Copperhead journals, who use every sophistry to create hostility between the negroes and the whites, especially the Irish and Germans. The *Detroit Free Press* has been one of the first and most persistent sheets at this kind of work."

Other papers were less direct. The *Buffalo Express* pinned the riot on "the journals and managers of a certain party in the country," and the *Chicago Tribune* characterized the riot as "the legitimate fruitage of the rebellious teachings of secession newspapers and traitorous stumpers."[17]

14

Whitewash: The Trials of the Rioters (April–May 1863)

> 'Tis said that those houses and inmates were bad,
> And hence the excuse that the outragers had,
> Yet was it the true love of virtue alone,
> That made the mob anxious to pull a church down?
>
> Strange as it may be, yet 'tis true without doubt,
> Mobs do not discriminate if once let out;
> So when they had fired the huts of the poor,
> They ran with the torch to their rich neighbor's door.
> —From "The Riot" by Benjamin Cutler Clark, Sr.

The trials began in mid–April, two weeks after the police court circus. More than a month had passed since the riot, and hammers could be heard throughout the Third Ward as traumatized residents began to rebuild their homes and victims of the riot looked to the recorder's court of Judge Witherell for justice.

The charges fell into three categories: "larceny at a fire," destruction of property, and "riot." Several defendants faced multiple charges, leading to a crowded court docket throughout April and May.

One common feature united all of the rioter trials: the difficulty in obtaining a jury. In the immediate aftermath of the riot, feelings ran high. Some of the residents wanted to turn a blind eye to the real mayhem caused by the youngsters, and it became almost impossible to find twelve men to take an objective look at the evidence.[1] This led to lengthy delays in the subsequent court action.

• • • •

Of the dozens who looted property, only three were ever held accountable in court: Francis Carr, Michael Hider, and Catherine Prusher.

14. Whitewash: The Trials of the Rioters (April–May 1863)

Prusher operated a saloon. During the riot, she lured Carr and Hider into her saloon and plied them with free drinks, then coaxed the semi-inebriated boys into rummaging through homes and bringing her anything of value.

The two boys had been caught with their hands in the cookie jar. Following descriptions provided by Benjamin Singleton and Richard Evans—Black residents of the Third Ward whose houses stood in the way of the tornado—Officer Sullivan identified Carr and Hider as the possible looters. Any doubt evaporated when Singleton and Evans identified goods in the possession of Carr and Hider as their personal property. In Singleton's official complaint, which he signed with his mark (an "X"), he accused Carr of stealing "one decanter of the value of one dollar." Evans' complaint against Hider, who signed with his mark (a "+"), specifies three items: "one shawl of the value of six dollars, one coat of the value of ten dollars and one shirt of the value of one dollar."[2] The trail of the purloined property also led to Catherine Prusher, who attempted to sell some of the hot goods.

The *Advertiser and Tribune* condemned Prusher's opportunism. "It is gratifying to know that severe punishment will be visited upon the heads of those who teach children to defy the law and to abhor peace."[3]

Since neither Carr nor Hider could conjure up a reasonable explanation as to how they had acquired the looted items, they threw themselves on the mercy of Judge Witherell and pled guilty. The court sentenced them to six months each in the Detroit House of Correction—a relatively heavy penalty for three pilfered garments and a glass bottle. It is possible that the complaints, which form the backbone of the recorder's court file, do not contain a comprehensive list of the stolen merchandise. Alternatively, Gavin may have agreed to keep some of the more valuable items out of the official paperwork as part of a plea agreement. This would have been easily accomplished since neither complainant could read the documents they had signed.

Catherine Prusher did not spare the court and pled not guilty to a charge of "recieving [sic] stolen property." The brief trial began and ended on April 9 with a verdict of "not guilty." Who said what during the proceedings has not survived into the historical record, perhaps because of the verdict.[4]

• • • •

The second group of trials related to the riot began a few days later. Hall, Naylor, Crosby, and Davis each faced charges of torching the "dwelling houses" of Benjamin Singleton and Whitney Reynolds. The trials of Crosby, Davis, and Naylor began on Monday, April 13, and consumed the rest of the week. The trial of Charles Hall would take place in October.[5]

Isaac W. Ingersoll, a builder whose brick-and-mortar was located on Fort Street, witnessed the rioters attacking Whitney Reynolds' cooper shop. "The first I saw of it," he testified, "was a lot of little boys throw[ing] stones into the cooper shop window." Someone—Ingersoll did not know who—threw a torch into the building and the crowd scattered. Of the eight to ten boys who did not "skedaddle," Ingersoll identified Edward Crosby, who threw stones into a side window and "then went up to the window and peeped into it." At this point someone inside the building fired a gun at Crosby, the cluster of balls tearing through his jaw and peppering his shirt with holes.[6]

During Chipman's cross, however, Ingersoll wasn't so sure of his identification. Standing about two hundred feet away, he could only say for sure that the kid wore a hat.

Ada R. Smith also picked Crosby and William Naylor out of the riotous crowd that descended on the cooperage. Smith was on Franklin Street when she heard chattering that "they were killing people uptown." Curiosity apparently trumping any thought of personal safety, Smith went to see for herself. The cooper shop was surrounded by forty to fifty rioters, whom Smith characterized as predominantly boys. She spotted Crosby charging the window with a club ("about 5 feet long, about as thick as a fish rod") apparently about to smash through it when she "heard the report of a gun … saw Crosby put his hand in his mouth." Smith approached the wounded boy. "As I looked into his face," she recalled, "[I] saw his coat on his shoulder was cut with shot."[7]

The jury only had to glance at the defendant to verify Smith's identification. Permanently disfigured, Crosby would carry the scar of that moment with him for the rest of his life.

About forty feet from where she stood on Beaubien Street, Smith saw several boys busting down the door of the cooperage, including

14. Whitewash: The Trials of the Rioters (April–May 1863) 179

Charles Hall and William Naylor. She saw Naylor "take matches from his pocket and light [the] shavings" or scraps of wood covering the floor.

Gavin's star witness was Dennis K. Sullivan, who watched the lynch mob materialize at the jail. The boys, which "were principally close to the age of 17 or 18," were "hallowing kill the nigger … pull down the nigger houses," Sullivan recalled on the stand.

This core group, which Sullivan numbered about twenty, "started down Beaubien toward the river." At the corner of Lafayette and Beaubien, they began pelting a house with anything they could find—stones, paving bricks, even wooden fence boards. Sullivan "saw a collored [sic] man drive a horse and a waggon [sic], saw him knocked off the waggon [sic] with a stone."

While the mob attacked the front of the house, Sullivan moved around to the back, where he found the terrified residents. He "knocked out some boards out of the fence and helped them get away." Although the handwritten notes of Sullivan's testimony do not elaborate as to how the constable used these fence slats, it appears likely that he cleared a path with a few baseball-like swings.

The mob then moved down Beaubien to the cooperage. Sullivan corroborated Smith's testimony when he described the shooting of Edward Crosby.[8]

Thomas Skillman and his wife Margaret were visiting at the home of a friend on Fort Street when they heard the commotion coming down the street. From across the street, the Skillmans watched in horror as the crowd began stoning houses. Skillman identified Charles Hall, whom he described as "a man I am well acquainted with," as one of the ring leaders. Hall ranted "kill every nigger" as he fired stone missiles at the house across the street. Skillman followed the mob to the cooper shop but apparently drifted too close to the action; "a brick bat hit me on the arm," he recalled.[9]

Margaret Skillman verified her husband's testimony about Charles Hall. She, too, heard the damning racial slur Hall shouted as he threw rocks. Mrs. Skillman also recognized Naylor and "Mr. Doran's two youngsters," one of whom—Peter—would go to trial with the second group of rioters.[10]

Testimony ended with J.D. Weaver and David M. Freeman, both

officers of the law present during the riot. Weaver, a deputy sheriff and constable, recounted seeing Crosby receive a face full of lead when, literally, he stuck his nose where it didn't belong. Weaver also corroborated Ada Smith's testimony about Naylor and Hall breaking through the cooperage door and torching the place. Freeman's brief turn on the stand served to verify Naylor's role.[11]

The evidence against Edward Crosby was overwhelming. The jury had little trouble in reaching a verdict of "guilty," but they could not decide about William Naylor. This hung jury led to a second trial two days later. Despite the testimony of several credible witnesses who identified Naylor as the one who lit the fire that destroyed Whitney Reynolds' business, the jury still could not agree. The third time would not be a charm for William Naylor. His third trial, which took place five weeks later, led to a guilty verdict.

Witherell sentenced Crosby and Naylor to a fine of $250 or one year in the Detroit House of Correction. In addition to this princely sum, Lane required both boys to submit "bonds to keep the peace for one year": $500 for Crosby and $200 for Naylor.

Since none of the witnesses could identify John H. Davis with any certainty, he beat the rap when the jury returned a verdict of "not guilty." He wasn't off the hook just yet. He and his co-defendants still faced charges of rioting.

The charge against Charles Hall lingered until October, when a jury could not decide on his guilt or innocence despite a number of eyewitnesses who had seen him at the cooper shop.

• • • •

The next rioter in the sequence of trials was John "Conrad" Kalb, who faced the comparatively more serious charge of "assault with the intent to kill and murder."[12] The evidence against Kalb hinged the testimony of Solomon Houston, who identified Kalb as his assailant during the mob's siege of Whitney Reynolds' cooper shop, and Earnest Friend, a bystander who witnessed the attack.

The trial began and ended on April 16. The trial record—a slim folder of just four pages—contains no transcript of testimony, but Solomon Houston's testimony from the trial of the rioters presents a good idea of what he may have said during the Kalb proceeding.

14. Whitewash: The Trials of the Rioters (April–May 1863)

The evidence against Kalb was overwhelming, and the only real question was the extent of his guilt. After the brief proceeding, the jury found him guilty of assault and battery but not attempted murder. The evidence clearly indicated that Kalb attacked Solomon Houston but Gavin failed to prove that he intended to kill his victim.

Lane sentenced him with a hand slap: a $50 fine or three months in a work house in addition to a bond of $500 "to keep the peace for one year." He made both payments and avoided spending so much as a day behind bars in the Detroit House of Correction.[13]

• • • •

In early May, a letter from Camp Hall, Virginia, arrived in Detroit. Addressed to the "Editor of the *Detroit Free Press*," the note solved the mystery of Bernard Groghan's whereabouts.

> Being in your city at the time the late riot occurred—knowing nothing and caring less about the cause of the disturbance—I was beset by the Right Hon. Minot T. Lane, your Police Justice, and his myrmidons, and only succeeded in eluding their ill-directed activity by leaving the city. It was not until then that I learned the cause of the riot, and was heartily sorry that I had not known it sooner, and taken an active part in dealing out summary justice to those miserable, degraded beings who dared to assail childish innocence and virtue in so brutal a manner.
>
> I would say to Minot T. Lane, that if his department is reduced to the necessity of defending and upholding such miserable creatures, in such devilish crimes, to exercise their sluggish minds, and employment for their sincere offices, I would feel honored by being notified when the next riot comes off, and will use every effort to give them a substantial cause for arresting me.
>
> Hoping Minot T. Lane and staff will fully appreciate the motives that actuate me in writing to you—as it is intended for this worthy self, and still more worthy aiders, abettors, and bottle-holders—and hoping they will comply with my request in giving me due notice of the "joust," wherein I offer what they so eagerly desire, viz.; exercise for their bullet-headed, lop eared co-workers, I bring my letter to a close. And, if you deem it worthy of insertion in your valuable sheet, I shall consider myself, sir,
>
> Yours, most obliged,
> H.B. Grogan [sic]
> Chief Wagonmaster, Ninth Army Corps[14]

Bernard Groghan had not, as many believed, fled to Canada. Rather, he enlisted with the Ninth Army Corps. Sometime during a break in the action, he penned the sharp rebuke of Minot T. Lane and his "myrmidons" for shielding Faulkner from the lynch mob. Groghan's willingness to participate in the next "joust" and give Sullivan, Freeman, and the other "bullet-headed, lop-eared" officers "exercise" undermined his claims of innocence and could even be construed as a partial confession.

The wording of Groghan's letter shows its writer to be far from an uneducated, unsophisticated ignoramus. His use of the term "myrmidon" to criticize sheriff deputies for their blind allegiance to the powers that be hinted at an education far superior to his fellow rioters. It also hints at the possibility that Groghan may have played a significant role in leading the rioters on their rampage.

The editor of the "valuable sheet" deemed the alleged rioter's missive "worthy" and inserted into the May 7, 1863, edition.

The article ended with a laudatory note. "It is a matter of congratulations ... that Mr. Grogan [sic] has improved in his behavior as to secure the position which he so conspicuously flourishes as an appendix to his somewhat notorious autograph."

• • • •

The small crowd of thirteen accused of "riot" went to trial during the week of May 26. The fourteenth defendant, Bernard Groghan, remained missing since he had absconded from the police court examinations in March, although his sarcastic letter indicated that he was driving one of Uncle Sam's wagons when his fellow rowdies went to court.

John "Conrad" Kalb, Cornelius "Con" Dwyer, and Andrew Manning all changed their pleas to guilty at the outset of their trials. Kalb received a hefty financial fine, which represented his cumulative legal punishment for the two offenses (assault and battery and "riot"); Manning received a month in the Wayne County jail. Dwyer's punishment somehow escaped notation on the court docket, but it probably amounted to a fine or brief prison stint.

At the police court examination, Ebenezer Cutler, a sailor in town at the time of the riot, picked Antoine Downer out of the crowd of defendants. "[I] saw Antoine Downer with a crowd of others chasing a negrow [sic]—he was an old man grea [sic] headed—heard the crowd holler 'nigger, nigger,' saw him strike the nigger and kicking him when

14. Whitewash: The Trials of the Rioters (April–May 1863)

he was down." Although Cutler could not identify Downer's victim, he did note that the unfortunate man had emerged from a burning building at the corner of Lafayette and Beaubien streets. The building was Whitney Reynolds' cooper shop, and the victim Ephraim Clark.[15]

Despite Cutler's evidence, the case against Antoine Downer amounted to one lone sentence in the court docket noting that he paid the court a $300 personal bond to appear. Apparently, he evaded a trial by forgoing the bond money and leaving town. John Dollar evaded the court record entirely. Although his name appears in the case file, the court docket contains no entry for a plea, a trial, or a punishment, which suggests that Gavin may have decided not to pursue the charges against him.

Without much evidence to prosecute, Gavin dropped the charges against John H. Davis as well, winnowing the court docket to seven: Carlow, Crosby, Doran, Downer, Drummond, Hall, and Naylor.

William Naylor sidestepped the "rioting" charge. His third trial for the comparatively more serious charge of burning houses coincided with the trials of the "rioters" in late May. Found guilty, Naylor received the stiff penalty of dual fines: $250 and an additional $200 bond for "keeping the peace." Hall's trial wouldn't commence until October, leaving Carlow, Crosby, Doran, Downer, Drummond, and the absent Groghan left to answer for their actions in court.

Dennis K. Sullivan recounted the events of the riot, naming Groghan, Krueger, and William Crosby as among a crowd yelling "kill the niggers, down them, kill them" outside the courthouse. After Faulkner's delivery to the county jail, Sullivan said, they joined the mob "smashing furniture" and setting fire to houses on Beaubien Street.

The case against William Crosby fell apart when Sullivan, on cross-examination, admitted, "To my knowledge I can not say, Mr. Crosby was in the crowd in front of the jail, do not know whether he [was] intoxicated." His cameo appearance in the history of Detroit ended when the jury found him innocent.

Sullivan also described finding a bloodied and battered Joshua Boyd lying in the alley behind the cooper shop amidst the angry crowd that had knocked him down. According to Sullivan, Krueger—who brandished a bucket in his left hand—was yelling, "Kill him! Kill him!" He did not, however, see Krueger assault Boyd.

The constable managed to push past the rioters to find a man lying in the fetal position and bleeding profusely from a gash on his head. Sullivan helped Boyd to his feet and rushed him to a nearby saloon with several rioters yelling, "kill him … he is the man that fired out of the cooper shop" following on their heels. The angry mob believed the stricken man responsible for peppering Edward Crosby's face with shot and they had blood in their eyes. Krueger, according to Sullivan, yelled to the crowd that they should pull Boyd from the saloon and kill him. Sullivan estimated about a hundred rioters formed an arc around the saloon door as he attempted to block entry.

"Mr. Krueger," Sullivan testified, "came to the saloon, said he was thirsty and wanted to drink some lager beer. He then crushed in under my arms. When he went out he said, 'the nigger is in there,' it cost him 10 cents to see him—to go into there and kill him."

Krueger apparently boasted about killing Boyd for the cost of a dime. On cross, however, Sullivan admitted that he did not know whether Krueger had assaulted Boyd inside the saloon. "[I] do not know," Sullivan said, "if he laid hands onto the nigger." The court record contains an alteration that underscores racial attitudes of the era: the word "nigger" is stricken and replaced by "negro." Throughout the court documents, Sullivan refers to Joshua Boyd as "the colored man," so the stricken racial epithet is probably the work of the person responsible for transcribing testimony for the official court records: recorder's court clerk Francis Hughes.[16]

Because the constable did not know if Krueger's statements amounted to anything more than bravado and idle boasts, Gavin decided not to pursue the charges and the *People v. Krueger* ended with an entry of *nolle prosequi* in the court docket.

Sullivan characterized nineteen-year-old Timothy Drummond as "one of the most active in firing buildings" and smashing windows. Timothy's mother Abigail emigrated sometime prior to 1850. The fifth of seven children, Drummond spent much of his youth in Detroit and later Ypsilanti.[17]

A witness named John J. Bagley identified "the deaf and dumb boy Timothy Drummond" as one of Boyd's assailants. "I saw him kicking a negro who was lying in the gutter," Bagley said. "I spoke to him; he immediately stopped." The incident, according to Bagley, took place around 5 p.m., with the cooper shop engulfed by flames.[18]

14. Whitewash: The Trials of the Rioters (April–May 1863)

Drummond's alleged role in the riot put Lane in a delicate position. Drummond was repeatedly referred to in the court documents as well as contemporary newspapers as the "deaf and dumb boy," and his diminished mental capacity raised questions about his responsibility for his actions. He avoided any serious legal repercussions for his role in the riot.

The chief witness against fourteen-year-old Peter Doran was his twelve-year-old pal David M. Freeman, the son of saloonkeeper Bolivar Freeman and the nephew of constable David M. Freeman, after whom he was named. "[I] saw him take a picket from the fence," Freeman testified, "and break windows in the Cooper shop." He placed the time at 4:15 p.m. "I know that was [the] time," he insisted, "because school [Preston Union School] let out at that time." From a block away, Freeman saw a group of men, one carrying a revolver, swarm into the shop. Thomas Skillman verified the youngster's story.[19]

The jury found Peter Doran guilty as charged. Since he was only fourteen and too young for the Detroit House of Correction, the court sentenced him to the "State Reform School" in Lansing until he turned twenty-one, which amounted to a seven-year sentence for throwing rocks. This was the longest sentence for anyone found guilty of participating in the riot.

Sixteen-year-old William Carlow—the youngest child of shoemaker John Carlow—was convicted on the sayso of witness Robert Burley, who had seen him "breaking in the windows of Ben Singleton's house at the corner of Beaubien and Lafayette Streets." Burley lived across the street from Singleton and watched Carlow "throw at the windows with stones about 12 or 15 times." Then the defendant stoned his house. Burley, having bought wood from Carlow at the Gies wood yard the previous winter, said he knew him "well," so there was little doubt about the sanctity of his identification.

Deputy Charles Allen, who arrested Carlow, also testified. After Burley identified Carlow, Allen and Burley went to Geis wood yard where the teenager worked. Confronted by Burley, Carlow confessed to stoning the man's house. He said he had gone to the jail "to see what was going on" and "to stone niggers" but insisted that his targets consisted solely of houses.[20]

Burley and Allen were compelling witnesses. The jury convicted

Carlow, but unlike Peter Doran, his age did not save him from three months of hard labor in the House of Correction.

Despite hearing much of the same evidence that convicted William Carlow of vandalizing houses, however, the jury voted to acquit Edward Crosby of rioting. His penalty consisted of hefty fines and a lifetime reminder—a face pocked by shot—of his role in one of the city's most infamous events.

The last alleged "rioter" to go in front of a jury was twenty-two-year-old Charles Hall. His mother had emigrated from England, and he grew up in a Detroit neighborhood dominated by English and Irish immigrants and transplants from New York.[21]

Hall's trial began the following October. Despite the testimony of several eyewitnesses, Hall beat the rap with a hung jury.

PART 5
Rebuilding

15

Residual Effects and Legacy

> This brought the community plainly to see
> The danger in which all were likely to be;
> The rich and the poor, the black and the white,
> Stood a chance to be mobbed and burned out that night.
> —From "The Riot" by Benjamin Cutler Clark, Sr.

In the immediate aftermath of the riot, some Black residents left Detroit for Canada never to return. Others drifted back across the border, sifted what little they could find in the ashes of the Third Ward, and attempted to rebuild their lives from the smoldering ruins.[1]

In the waning months of the war, freed Blacks continued to settle in Detroit. By 1870, the population of "Free Colored" in Wayne County had risen to 2,683—over a 1,000 more than documented in the 1860 federal census.[2]

Their new home fell far short of the utopia they may have envisioned. Racial prejudice proved to be a resilient virus that survived the riot and its immediate aftermath. From time to time, the *Free Press* ran articles with racially-inflammatory language. The verbal barbs were particularly sharp in an article about a police raid of a Paton Alley establishment in 1869. The reporter described the "dusky spirits gathered there" as "the big deck-hand nigger, the fat and slim niggers, negro soldiers, negroes from coal cart and barber shop, and at about one o'clock in the morning Paton alley was just a-shaking with horse laughs and big heel stamping."

When the "blue coats" arrived, the reporter noted, "there was a time that exceeds description." He then proceeded to describe the indescribable with a smattering of racial epithets. "Niggers dove under the bed, niggers tried to get up the chimney, niggers jumped through windows...."

The reporter's description of the scene in police court was filled with vernacular as he attempted to recreate the drama for readers.

> One by one, they filed out before the Central Station Court yesterday morning to received sentence. First came Moses Jacob, having on a beautiful suit of second hand clothes, his hair fixed up like a hundred beautiful pine knots, his lips trembling with the weight of a sad, sweet smile. "Well, Moses?"
> "Fore hevin', boss, I clare to goodness I war just a shaking de foot a lit—"
> "Twenty dollars or four months!" and Moses fell back weak and exhausted, his legs shaking at the chairy prospect.
> "Rube Lewis," and Rube came up to the scratch looking lively, and getting around so as to have the reporters suppress his name in case the court let him off. "What's your case?"
> "Nuffin, sir—nuffin—we war jest up to Liz. Poin—"
> "Twenty dollars, or four months!" and Rube set sail for the other room, forgetting to make the request of the reporters, and the sole of one of his boots danced off, flapping as we went.[3]

Evidently, much of the reporter's article had been dramatized for effect, but the judge's reaction—interrupting the defendants in mid-sentence and passing summary judgements—if at all accurate, illustrates an undercurrent of racial prejudice in the court system of the era. This in turn suggests that the *Free Press* article reflected prevailing opinions among some of the city's residents.

The article was clearly an attempt to denigrate Black Detroiters by depicting them as dolts who spent all of their time dancing the night away, but the article inadvertently ridicules police court Judge Minot T. Lane, who is depicted as too swift with the gavel. This caricature is particularly ironic considering that Lane was a Democrat and thus in politics a kindred spirit of the *Free Press* editors.[4]

At least the news on the Paton Alley raid contained something newsworthy; another 1869 article titled "That Nigger" apparently had no other purpose than to attempt humor at the expense of the city's Black community. The use of the more offensive term in the title—not "colored" or "negro"—indicates that the piece was designed to lacerate as well as mock.

The article tells the story of a Black train conductor whom the writer does not name but describes as having a "complexion so dark that good looks are entirely out of the question." The anonymous conductor apparently ejected a Black passenger for riding without a ticket only to discover that the man climbed back on the train. Again, he put the man off at the next station.

15. Residual Effects and Legacy

Suspecting the troublesome passenger would try to sneak back on a third time, the conductor moved onto the platform, where he waited until the train began to move.

"As he entered the door of one of the coaches," the journalist wrote, "he saw his phiz reflected in the mirror at the opposite end. His brow clouded up in an instant, and with the exclamation, 'There's that d----d nigger again!' he clenched his knuckles and rushed down the aisle for the annihilation of the African. He discovered his error, of course, and more, so did all in the car; and he got unmercifully pickled during the balance of the trip."[5]

• • • •

With the suspected rioters identified and rounded up, Sullivan and his fellow officers spent the spring of 1863 resuming their war on the city's purveyors of sin. They busted up brothels, which the *Free Press* characterized as a "great source of evil."[6] Most of these small-scale Sodoms were located in the Third and Fourth wards.

Police court swelled with pimps who masqueraded as boarding house owners and madams who ran the businesses upstairs. Colorful characters with even more colorful names crowded into the small courtroom, where Justice Lane brought the gavel down on prostitution, usually with a fine or a sentence in Brockway's state-run boarding house. He referred more serious cases to recorder's court. The small case files, the paper browned from a century and a half of age, contain an interesting glimpse inside Detroit's seedy underbelly of vice during the Civil War.

On the evening of March 31, Sullivan led a four-man squad that busted up two notorious bordellos on Franklin Street along the Detroit River. They arrested thirty-five-year-old madam Christine Thede, also known as "Mother Thede" and "Mother Teddy," along with four of her prostitutes and an enigmatic figure known only as "the landlady." The same raid netted "Irish Lib"—Mary McKenzie—and four of her employees.[7] The *Advertiser and Tribune* writer had no love for "Irish Lib," describing her as a "woman of the lowest and most abandoned character."[8] The two madams each received six months in prison, but their lawyers managed to arrange an early release.

When Judge Witherell heard about the release, he ordered the madams rearrested. Sullivan walked "Irish Lib" back to the house for the duration of her sentence, but "Mother Teddy" managed to evade arrest until Sullivan tracked her down in December and dragged her back to her cell.[9]

Later that month, they arrested madam Adolphia Fields, who threw herself on the mercy of the court by pleading guilty. Justice Lane's mercy consisted of four months behind bars. Well-known madam Elisabeth Boyd was also arrested in the dragnet and sentenced to five months of hard labor following a guilty verdict.[10]

Dewitt Anderson, whom the *Free Press* described as "the negro who was recently indicted for keeping a house of ill fame" on Catherine Street, once again found himself on the wrong side of the law. He pled guilty and received eight months.[11]

The systematic attempt to break up the city's sex industry continued throughout April and May, bringing the three-month total to fifteen. The nymphs du pave received light sentences in police court while the proprietors faced more serious charges in recorder's court.

Catherine and Martin Blank, who ran the Blank "dance-house" at the corner of Macomb and St. Antoine, went before Lane in May. Sixty-year-old Martin Blank, a New York native, was the owner of the "dance-house" in name only; his forty-year-old wife Catherine ran the day-to-day operations of the brothel. The need to care for their five children—the oldest at ten years of age—kept the Blanks out of prison. Instead, Lane hit them with a collective fine of $525.[12]

Not all of the prostitutes, often called "inmates," were longstanding members of the oldest profession. Some were very young girls pulled into the dark web of prostitution. The tragic story of fourteen-year-old Sarah Higgins is a good example of why the *Free Press* condemned brothels as the root of all evil.

Arrested as a "disorderly person" at her mother's request, Sarah vowed to stay out of trouble, but she ran away after spending just one night under her mother's roof. Found in a brothel, she was re-arrested.[13]

Sarah Higgins was by no means the only teenager drawn into the underworld. Considered a valuable commodity, young girls became targets for unscrupulous, money-hungry purveyors who plied them pomegranate seeds in the form of alcohol, narcotics, and cash.

One of the more interesting cases came before recorder's court in May when Mary Shepard answered the charges of "keeping a house of ill fame." Shepard ran a two-bedroom bordello out of a house in an alley between Brush and Beaubien streets. The case illustrates the far-reaching extent of prostitution in Civil War–era Detroit and why authorities struggled to control it. It also illustrates how economic hardship lured young girls to enter the oldest profession.

Officers John Esser and James Love testified that Shepard's house was well known as a bordello that catered to both Black and white customers. "When I was near her house shortly after the riot on special police duty," Esser said, "a young man with me said that there is no use of watching that house as it is a whorehouse."

One of Shepard's flock was a thirteen-year-old named Julia Davis, an orphan who lived with her aunt's family in a multigenerational house owned by her grandfather Louis Fontaine and his wife Catherine.[14]

In April 1863, Julia ran away. "The reason I left my Aunt is," she later explained, "my aunt told me she had a large family + I should work somewhere." The teenager eventually found her way into one of Mary Shepard's two bedrooms.

Apparently, Catherine Fontaine suspected her granddaughter's whereabouts and confronted Shepard, who denied even knowing the girl. Something about Shepard's demeanor deepened Fontaine's suspicions, so she asked Officer James Love to investigate.

Warrant in hand, Esser and Love searched the property and found Julia Davis in the back room. Responding to Love's questions, the girl admitted to receiving payment for having sex with a man at Shepard's request.

Julia Davis testified to her short career as a prostitute, which began in a saloon on Russell Street. "[I] was in a saloon there and a woman asked me if I would sleep with a man, I said yes. I slept with him, but not all night. [I] never had anything to do with anybody either boys or men before that. Another girl sent me to Miss Shepard—went to Deft's [defendant's] house to have a place to live. Don't know how many boys were in the house. I went to bed first then Miss Shepard sent a man to me in bed. Miss Shepard asked me to sleep with a man, I said no I would not. She then said he would give me money."

Julia received $3 for having sex with the unnamed man Shepard sent to her room. She said that she kept half of the money and gave the other half to Shepard.

Shepard knew that coercing a thirteen-year-old into prostitution could cause her serious trouble. According to Julia Davis, "whenever anyone would come to the door, Miss Shepard would tell me to hide."[15]

Shepard pled not guilty and was sentenced to hard time in the House of Correction, but for reasons that have escaped the historical record, prosecuting attorney J. Knox Gavin motioned the court for a suspended sentence and Mary walked out of the county jail a free woman.

A New Order

The Detroit Metropolitan Police force was born out of the assumption that a larger group of officers would have been more effective in keeping the 1863 rioters in check. While the number of active rioters was relatively small, and Sullivan was able to single-handedly stop an attempt to set fire to the A.M.E. Church with nothing more than poise and a pistol, the perception that Detroit needed a greater presence of law enforcement led to the Metropolitan Police Act of 1865. Although Michigan legislators approved the law on February 28, 1865—almost two years after the Third Ward burned—prominent Detroit historians Clarence Burton and Silas Farmer both characterized the act as a direct result of the 1863 riot.[16]

The new act, brought about by efforts from Third Ward alderman John J. Bagley, improved on a similar act passed in 1861. Four police commissioners would oversee all department business. Because they were directly appointed by the governor, the four commissioners, in theory, would make decisions based on the welfare of the citizens and not based on the welfare of political patrons.

The new order met with fierce resistance, particularly among members of the old order. The city marshal and ward constables railed against the law that would make them virtually obsolete. Politicians likewise despised the law that would reduce their ability to influence the city's law enforcement arm with patronage or cronyism. And some Detroiters bemoaned the tax hike needed to pay for the police.

While questions about the legality of the act would linger until the Michigan supreme court deemed it constitutional in October 1865, the four-person commission moved forward and organized the first rendition of the Detroit Metropolitan Police. That year, the force consisted of a captain, three sergeants and forty-seven patrolmen. This fifty-one-man squad made more than 3,000 arrests in its first year of operation alone.[17]

To bolster the nascent department's respect among citizens, the earliest officers worked under strict guidelines. While on the beat, they were not permitted to use profane language or enter any establishment that served alcohol unless duty required it. Gone were the days when constables moonlighted as private detectives; they were forbidden from holding down second jobs, extra gigs, and side hustles.[18]

As the city grew, so too did its police force. By 1880, the force had more than tripled in size to 178, which included seven detectives.[19]

Villains: Mary Brown and Ellen Hoover

As difficult as Mary Brown is to track through the historical record, her partner in crime is even more difficult to find. News reports of the "Faulkner Outrage" refer to her as Ellen Hoover, although at least one later account names her Harriet Hoover.[20]

Less than two weeks after the riot, Brown and Hoover ended up reappearing in newsprint. Their further exploits led to a great deal of head-scratching and second-guessing about their character and the truthfulness of their ever-evolving story about the "Faulkner Outrage." The sticky-fingered pair robbed the cash drawer of a local butcher on Congress Street in mid–May and ended up facing larceny charges in Minot T. Lane's police court.

"These are the identical girls, it will be recollected," noted a *Free Press* reporter, "on whose testimony the negro Faulkner was convicted and sentenced to State prison for life. The girls have been constant playmates and companions ever since that affair, and many allege that they were before. Their present appearance indicates a hardened state of depravity shocking to behold in girls of their tender years. They do not appear to care anything about being locked up in jail, but, on the contrary, immediately commenced a series of amusements in the shape of pulling the bedding out and exercising themselves by tumbling and jumping upon the straw ticks."[21]

These slumber-party antics vexed the aged jail turnkey, the sheriff, the prosecuting attorney, and Detroiters who began to wonder if the

Detroit street scene in 1870 on a stereoview published by J.A. Jenney (Library of Congress).

girls had broken the ninth commandment, using their words as proverbial weapons against William Faulkner.

Both Brown and Hoover pled guilty to a single charge of larceny, which landed them inside the Detroit House of Correction for a three-month stint.[22] The story merited a significant column in the May 22, 1863, edition of the *Free Press*. The writer was less than complementary when he wrote, "The actions of these girls since their arrest has been such as to stamp them as the most hardened and depraved creatures of their age which have ever yet been developed in the police annuals of Detroit."[23]

15. Residual Effects and Legacy

The unnamed *Free Press* reporter, apparently present when Justice Lane sentenced the pair to three months, captured their reaction.

"Instead of lamenting the occurrence as most girls would," the reporter wrote with a hint of disgust evident in his word choice, "they actually grew jubilant over the fact of being in jail, and were as expert in the use of low and obscene slang and songs as any of the older depraved ones with whom they were thrown in contact in the jail. The sentence to the House of Correction did not disconcert them in the least, the little one declaring afterwards that she would have a 'bully' ride to the institution, as all of the constables in Detroit couldn't make her walk."

The writer ended with a cogent note. "When it is remembered that she is less than ten years of age, this behavior will strike the public as being unparalleled in youthful depravity."[24] According to contemporary news accounts of the Faulkner trial, Ellen Hoover was twelve in 1863, which meant that the little one with the adult vocabulary was Mary Brown, who apparently went to the big girl's wing of the penitentiary before she became a tween.

No police court or recorder's court documents have survived to tell the particulars of this story (the court docket does not contain an entry, either), but the reporter's description suggests that the pair had by this time acquired a reputation and perhaps a rap sheet to go along with it.

After the larceny case, Ellen Hoover disappears into the historical ether. Most of the subsequent news coverage focused on Mary Brown, Faulkner's white victim, who also happened to be the naughtier of the two.

During the Faulkner trial in March, the *Free Press* described Brown as "of extraordinary intelligence, of a good moral character, and trained from infancy, by a Christian adopted mother, to do that which is right, and abhor and abstain from anything wrong."[25] Three months later, their journalists sang a different tune when it became clear that Brown could do no right.

While Ellen Hoover faded into obscurity after the Faulkner trial, Mary Brown continued to find her way into the limelight, and newsprint, due to a string of court appearances. The ten-year-old could not escape her connection with the infamous Faulkner case or the subsequent riot; whenever her name appeared in print, it almost always came with a notation about the riot, usually vilifying Brown as the cause or indirect cause of the March 6 fiasco.

A small blurb in the Detroit *Free Press* noted Mary's second significant brush with the law a few years later, in June 1869, when she was fourteen years old. Once again, the reporter linked Brown with the Faulkner case and the riot. "Mary Brown, whose rape by a negro in 1863 caused the riot in this city, was arrested at the instance of her mother, on Sunday, and yesterday morning sentenced by Justice Julius Stoll to three months in jail."[26] Charged and found guilty of "vagrancy," Brown did her second stint in the Detroit House of Correction.[27]

The term "vagrancy" was often used as a pretext to punish those who engaged in "lewd" sexual behavior. For example, in August 1863, the *Free Press* reported on a police raid during which constables found "men and women of all shades and complexions … piled promiscuously in one bed. The parties were arrested and taken before the Police court, on Monday as vagrants." The orgy landed each of the "vagrants" in the House of Correction for a year.[28]

Coincidentally, one of the orgy "vagrants" was named Mary Brown—a twenty-year-old Black Detroiter from the Fourth Ward who wore a groove in the steps of police headquarters in the mid to late 1860s.[29] This was not the Mary Brown of Faulkner infamy, but the use of the term "vagrancy" suggests that Brown's mother Rosa may have found her in some type of compromising position, perhaps in the act of "amalgamation" or *in flagrante delicto* with a Black man or woman.

In fact, numerous sources depict Mary Brown of Faulkner infamy as a prostitute. In a rehash of the case published in an 1870 edition of the *Detroit Daily Post*, the writer described Brown as "a large and coarse girl" who was "of doubtful character and has since become a prostitute and a common thief."[30] This was most likely a reference to Mary's arrest for "vagrancy."

Brown's third major brush with the law occurred less than two months after her release from the House of Correction. In November 1869, Catherine Cramer accused Mary of picking her pocket on the steps of St. Mary's Church. Testifying in recorder's court, Cramer described the incident. "She crushed against me at the door," she said. About fifteen minutes later, she discovered that Mary had taken $3 and her pocket book. A hung jury gave Brown a temporary reprieve.[31]

Once again, the press linked Brown with the events of March 6, 1863. In a short piece about the St. Mary's pickpocketing incident, a *Free Press* correspondent described her as "Mary Brown, the indirect cause of the negro riot in this city."[32]

That same month, Elizabeth Siegle accused Mary of stealing $79.50 from her at the Stadt Theater. "She and another girl came in and took the front seat," Siegle testified. "After the theater was out I got up. I went to the door keeping my hand in my pocket till I reached the door. As I was going down [I] met defendant coming up again and I felt a pull on my dress when I got down, I found I was robbed."[33]

When reporting on Mary's second arrest in a span of two months, a *Free Press* reporter intensified his description of her role in 1863, referring to Brown as "the incipient cause of the negro riot in this city."[34] Brown's role as catalyst had evolved from "indirect" to "incipient."

By this time, Mary Brown's reputation for sticky fingers had become public knowledge. The police clerk, writing the entry for Brown in the Metropolitan Police Register of Arrests, included the notation "one of the sharpest little pickpockets in the west."[35]

The not-so-petty theft landed Brown in the House of Correction for two years and six months of hard labor, which she completed by working in one of the prison industries.[36]

These legal troubles eroded Brown's credibility, and since Faulkner was convicted largely on her word, people began to wonder about the righteousness of William Faulkner's conviction. Writing in January 1870, just after Brown's conviction and imprisonment, a journalist wrote, "The main witness [against Faulkner] hardly told a consistent story, has ever since been of depraved and dissolute character, and has been sent to prison for a term of years for larceny."[37]

The "depraved and dissolute character" emerged from the House of Correction two years later, in February 1872, her sentence reduced by six months for "good time." Mary Brown, the cherubic face that launched a thousand rioters, faded into obscurity after her third stint behind bars.

Unlike Mary Brown, Ellen Hoover managed to stay out of the limelight, which meant that after 1863, she kept her nose clean. It is unknown what, if any, relationship she maintained with Mary Brown after that date. In 1865, at the age of sixteen, Hoover married twenty-one-year-old Fletcher Young at the 2nd Baptist Church. Pastor Supply Chase performed the nuptials. She apparently outlived her husband and may have married a second time. The widowed housekeeper died of consumption in November 1874 at the age of twenty-three.[38]

Numerous contemporary newspaper accounts allege that Brown and Hoover admitted to fabricating their testimony against Faulkner, although exactly what they admitted and to whom remains obscure. No official documentation in the historical record has survived to verify this claim, and neither the *Free Press* nor the *Advertiser and Tribune* mentioned this confession when they reported on Faulkner's release—a curious omission given such a bombshell. It's not hard to imagine why the *Free Press* would not want to air this piece of dirty laundry, but one would expect the *Advertiser and Tribune* to seize on a smoking gun piece of evidence further underscoring the *Free Press*' role in inflaming public opinion against Faulkner.

Nevertheless, this alleged confession became part of the story, repeated by numerous secondary sources and seemingly cemented by the accuser's checkered reputation. "Mary Brown was constantly furnishing evidence in her vicious and depraved life," wrote a *Detroit Daily Post* reporter in 1870, "that she was quite capable of having made a false charge, for the sake of notoriety, or from malice." The reporter did not mention a specific admission to perjury, but he added the enigmatic line "Very damaging incidents of her history came to light."

Ellen Hoover, on the other hand, became "sick with remorse. She declared that she never would have sworn as she did if she had known the consequences."[39]

Henry Utley, one of the *Free Press*' men on the ground in 1863, witnessed the riot, which he later characterized as "possibly the biggest story with which I had anything to do in those early days." In his own rag's 1908 profile of the ancient journalist, Utley reminisced, "There were only a few of us to cover developments, but I remember we played it [the riot] good and strong, writing what in that day was considered a marvelous amount of copy."

"Many believed in the innocence of Faulkner," Utley continued, "and after he had served several years the girl confessed that her story was false from start to finish." The "girl" was Mary Brown.[40]

The Faulkner "Outrage," the Faulkner Miscarriage

In the years following the "Faulkner Outrage," Detroiters developed a nearsightedness that allowed them to see the myopic circumstances surrounding Faulkner's trial and conviction. By the end of the decade, prevailing opinion in Detroit favored Faulkner's innocence. Fingers of blame inevitably pointed to the *Free Press*. "During the progress of his trial," wrote one journalist, "the *Free Press*, of course, kept up its stock of 'nigger' editorials, clothed in all the choice billingsgate which that paper was always master of when speaking of the blacks—for Faulkner was really guilty of one crime which the *Free Press* was never known to forgive: the crime of having a little negro blood in his veins. A 'nigger' was on trial, and that was text enough for the purposes of a Democratic paper of the orthodox kind."[41]

The *Advertiser and Tribune*, while not guilty of fomenting unrest, was not entirely blameless, either. If the *Free Press* was too harsh in its condemnation of Faulkner, the *Advertiser and Tribune* was too meek in its condemnation of the Faulkner miscarriage. The *Daily Post* later criticized the Republican rag for being "so exceedingly prudent that it opposed a mere barrier of straw to the rising torrent of the mob spirit."[42]

Recapping the Faulkner case seven years later, a *Daily Post* writer concluded that the trial could never have been considered "fair" given the political climate in the city. "The crime charged was the very one best calculated to arouse the ferocity of the mob, acting upon prejudices previously intensely stimulated by political appeals. It was, nevertheless, that particular crime which the greatest of English and American jurists have concurred in pronouncing the most easy to charge and the most difficult to disprove; and, therefore, it requires the calmest, most searching, and most impartial of trials in order to arrive at the truth."[43]

No twelve men could be considered unbiased, and Faulkner's conviction came amid rumors of jury intimidation by the mob. And when Witherell denied Chipman's request for a continuance to summon witnesses, he limited the defense to a cross-examination of prosecution witnesses. The whole proceeding was a rush to judgment apparently in an effort to appease the angry mob outside city hall. "The Court," the *Post* writer concluded, "was evidently impressed by the prevailing excitement."[44] The "Court" was an oblique reference to Judge Witherell.

Even the key figures involved in Faulkner's arrest and conviction—Judge Witherell, prosecuting attorney J. Knox Gavin, defense attorney Chipman, and Sheriff Fralick—questioned the verdict.

Witherell and Gavin both expressed their belief in Faulkner's innocence. Chipman went one step farther when he claimed that he could have proved his client's innocence if given adequate time to prepare a defense.

Several influential Detroiters joined Witherell and Gavin in signing a petition asking Governor Henry P. Baldwin to investigate the case. Among the signers was the editor of the *Free Press*.[45]

A short article in the *Jackson Citizen Patriot* about Baldwin's review of the case characterized Faulkner as a victim of racial hatred. The writer alluded to powerful men of Detroit who bent the governor's ear with talk about a miscarriage of justice. Baldwin launched an investigation and "became so well convinced in Faulkner's innocence" that he freed him with one swipe of his pen. The writer leaves no doubt when he describes Faulkner as "having been immured for seven long and weary years, as punishment for a crime of which he was innocent."[46]

On the afternoon of Thursday, December 30, 1869, the governor's emissary delivered the pardon to Warden Henry H. Bingham, who sent a guard to bring Faulkner from the workshop, where he was busy working off the "hard labor" portion of his life sentence, to his office. Bingham and the prison chaplain posed a series of questions to the prisoner. The brief interview ended with a perplexing query: what would he do if suddenly set free?

Unaware of the attempts to free him, Faulkner said that he had no hope of seeing the world outside the prison's walls. Even if the impossible were to happen, he had no one on the outside—no friends, no family—waiting for him. He did have a brother, but he heard that his brother had died in Canada. When Bingham handed Faulkner the pardon, he broke down and began weeping.

Most of the key figures in Faulkner's 1863 conviction never had the chance to see the wrong righted by Baldwin. By the time Faulkner emerged from prison a free man in January 1870, Witherell, Gavin, Cicotte, and Fralick were all dead (see Epilogue).

Faulkner returned to Detroit in time to be counted for the 1870 federal census, which describes him as a fifty-seven-year-old North Carolina native who "keeps eating house." Under the column "color," he is given the designation "B" for Black. Later that year, he married saloon-keeper Arneta Thomas.[47]

The 1863 trial left Faulkner penniless, so a year after gaining his freedom, he petitioned the state for remuneration—a request immediately rejected by legislators. Giving Faulkner reparations would, they reasoned, open the door for others to make similar claims.

"It would seem as if an innocent person should be in some way remunerated for the mistakes of judges and jurors," wrote a *Free Press* reporter in 1871, "but, in most cases, the pardoned person should feel that getting pardoned out at all was worth a round sum, for it is only now and then that an innocent person sent to State Prison can establish the fact that he is unlawfully incarcerated."[48]

In the ensuing years, Faulkner supported his family—he and Arneta would have two children together—by working as a "huckster" or peddler of fruits and vegetables in Detroit's Central Market. He also became an active member in the Zion Baptist Church located on Calhoun Street.

Faulkner died in Detroit on May 30, 1877. Even in death, he could not escape the role that made him infamous. The *Detroit Advertiser and Tribune* provided a succinct, one-line blurb: "Thomas Faulkner, the colored man who was the indirect cause of the terrible riot in Detroit in 1863, died at his home in this city on May 30."

The *Free Press* offered a short, one-paragraph obituary under the heading "Riot of 1863." The writer presented a post-mortem pardon of sorts by noting, "After serving eight years in prison it was found that Faulkner was innocent of the crime and he was pardoned."[49]

He was fifty-one or fifty-two years old given an uncertain birth date of 1825.[50] The man whose alleged crime sparked Detroit's 1863 race riot is buried in Section C of Detroit's Woodmere Cemetery.

16

Lessons: The Children's Crusade

> Humanity wept, she lamented the sight,
> The groans, blood and tears of that terrible night;
> Yet, oh, may the town of Detroit never see
> Such a day as the sixth of March, sixty-three.
> —From "The Riot" by Benjamin Cutler Clark, Sr.

The Wild Boys: Who Were They?

Almost all contemporary sources agree that the active elements of the riot consisted of boys ranging in age from ten to eighteen. The most direct evidence came from Dennis K. Sullivan, who characterized the mob as consisting mostly of teenagers when he testified in the case against the alleged rioters.

In criticizing the authorities' inability to control the rioters, the *Free Press* capitalized on the youth of the rioters and repeatedly emphasized that a small group of "boys from ten to eighteen years of age" had run riot in the Third Ward.

The *Advertiser and Tribune* likewise seized on this theme, even using the rival paper's words in emphasizing the youth of the malcontents. "The security of a city is in poor hands when a small lot of 'boys from ten to eighteen years of age' can thus drive and put to shame ALL its officers," noted a journalist.[1]

In its day-after coverage of the riot, the *Advertiser and Tribune* described a harrowing incident during which the tiger cubs attacked a Black man. "Boys from eight to ten years of age, seized bricks and stones, and with the most fearful imprecations, such as 'pray, you d—d nigger, we will kill you!' rushed upon him. A citizen stepped in and attempted to shield the negro, who in piteous tones appealed to the excited mob to spare his life, when a dirk knife was plunged into his side, passing through the vest, several layers of papers, and lodged in his watch case."[2] The account did not name the victim, the Good Samaritan protected from a knife wound by a pocket watch, or the tween assailants.

These malignant children would escape any consequences for their actions. None of the court documents or news articles in either paper suggest that any rioter younger than the fourteen-year-old Peter Doran was arrested—likely a purposeful oversight due to their age.

Their names have likewise escaped the historical record, but it appears that a majority were anchorless, Dickensian street toughs who resided on the mean streets of East Detroit. "The mob was composed, to large extent, of young fellows brought up in the 'street school,'" noted an *Advertiser and Tribune* journalist, "rowdies and vagabonds, ignorant, unreasoning, and crazy with whisky and prejudice. Their spirit and their shouts were full of bitter and violent hatred for the negro."[3]

It bears noting that the same edition of the same paper contained a contradiction when it hinted that at least some of the boys came from "respectable" families: "The acts of brutality of these rowdies are only equaled by the Sepoys of India. Well may respectable citizens blush, when boys, the sons of respectable men, are seen taking an active part in a riot so malignant in its nature."[4]

While some of the rioters may indeed have come from "respectable" families, that wasn't as popular a narrative, and so the rioters were labeled "vagabonds." This was apparently a widespread belief. When the *Advertiser and Tribune* editors suggested that Faulkner needed to be transported in the wee hours of the morning to avoid a lynching in Jackson, a *Jackson Citizen Patriot* journalist retorted that this was never a threat because unlike Detroit, Jackson did not host a "floating" population of vagabonds.

That the riot was perpetrated by a group of teens leading tweens would become a dirty little secret of Civil War Detroit. Perhaps attempting to avoid the ignominy, later journalists would steer clear of the topic and spilled little ink in attempting to identify the guilty parties.

The sheer difficulty in pinpointing the rioters in federal census records tends to support the idea that they came from Detroit's "floating" population. Such nomads are difficult to find.

It Takes a Village to Raze a Ward

The *Advertiser and Tribune* and the *Free Press*, rival papers whose editors loved to punch and counter-punch, to parry and thrust, nevertheless managed to agree on one point about the riot: lawlessness ensued on the streets of Detroit in part because good, law-abiding Detroiters allowed it to happen.

In a guest editorial published a few days after the riot, "A Tax Payer" indicted city officials for failing to stop the three dozen rioters who led the charge in the Third Ward. The anonymous citizen pointed out that "the rioters had the warm sympathy of many of those that are connected with the city government."[5]

"A Tax Payer" limited his ire to city officials, but in making the point that so many failed to stop so few, he also indicted the hundreds if not thousands of spectators who stood by and did nothing.

The *Free Press* went beyond insinuation when defending the city's outnumbered police force. "The rioters on Friday, therefore, had only this small force to oppose them, for the reason that, while hundreds of citizens gazed upon the work of destruction, they made no hearty effort to arrest its progress."[6]

While both newspapers suggested that the good people of Detroit did too little, the *Tribune* offered a justification of sorts when it blamed acting mayor Phelps. "It was the duty of the acting Mayor to call upon the citizens for such help as he needed, and confer upon them police powers. If he had made the call there would have been no lack of responses. His astounding incompetence and indifference never suggested to him this plain duty. For single citizens to interfere simply subjected them to the rage of the mob as 'abolitionists.'"[7]

For this argument to hold water in a court of law, say, twelve reasonable citizens would have to accept the notion that hundreds (and possibly thousands) of adult onlookers feared violent retribution by perhaps two dozen teenagers whom the *Advertiser and Tribune* writers dubbed "floating vagabonds."[8] The *Advertiser and Tribune* suggested that Phelps would have found no shortage of volunteers if he had given them "police powers," but the fact that so few stepped forward to prevent violence indicates a different and perhaps more disturbing conclusion: they did not help because they did not want to help.

It is reasonable to conclude that the riot would not have, could not have, gone as far as it did without the tacit support of the audience. The teenagers who terrorized Black Detroiters that day became weapons used by the adult population to wage a war against change personified by the unfortunate victims. Given the influence that adults can wield over children, their use as a proxy tool adds a sinister and perhaps even sadistic twist to the riot. It could be said that the Detroiters who watched the riot unfold had in essence weaponized these kids. It's hard not to see fourteen-year-old Peter Doran as a puppet manipulated by a faceless, malevolent puppet master.

Doran could very well have been the "mere boy" referenced in a March 10 *Advertiser and Tribune* editorial. "Another, a mere boy, who saw an aged negro lying helpless in the gutter, and as was thought at the time, dead, exclaimed with a fiendish chuckle, horrible in one so young, 'There goes another Lincoln voter.'"[9] This statement, one could conclude, emanated from ideas promoted by the adults in his life.

As to why otherwise law-abiding citizens would allow the systematic targeting of the city's Black community, motives were many and varied: angst for the draft, fear about a new future of racial equality, disgust with the war, unabated racism, or a combination of these things.

Many sources depict the riot as a result of angst over the Conscription Act and cite the timeframe as evidence: news of the draft hit the streets at the same time as the Faulkner trial took place. Most of the actual rioters, however, weren't old enough to be drafted or serve in the army unless they lied about their ages.[10]

Yet when the rioters went to trial, they became scapegoats for the larger community. Acknowledgment of this fact certainly led the court to hand down more lenient sentences.

Whereas misplaced and misguided passions were behind the more violent acts, the motives of some puppet masters were purely mercenary. Catherine Prusher, for instance, saw a gleam of gold and silver in the smoldering ruins of the Third Ward and enlisted two boys—Michael Hider and Francis Carr—to help her make money off of misery. The *Advertiser and Tribune* described Prusher's strategy: "While the fires were raging in several parts of the city, she called small boys into a wretched looking saloon, which she kept, and hired them, for liquor, to purloin all the articles they could, and to incite others to engage in the same nefarious business."[11]

Prusher plied the boys with liquor, coerced them into looting, and attempted to sell the purloined merchandise. At the outset of Prusher's trial, the *Advertiser and Tribune* commented on her turning the teenagers into tools for profiteering: "It is gratifying to know that severe punishment will be visited upon the heads of those who teach children to defy the law and to abhor peace." Prusher sidestepped "severe punishment" when a jury found her innocent of "stealing stolen property." The boys, who pled guilty, received six months of hard labor in the House of Correction.[12] Hider was seventeen years old.

Like Prusher, the other puppet masters evaded legal trouble and exist in the historical record only as the silhouettes standing by and watching the teenagers wreak havoc in the Third Ward.

One of the silhouettes cast a shadow long enough to be seen a hundred and sixty years later in microfilm of Civil War–era newspapers. Watching the scene unfold outside of Whitney Reynolds' house, Morris Horan—a twenty-seven-year-old blacksmith—was struck by a wayward load of shot fired by someone inside the residence.

In its initial coverage of the event, published in the morning edition of March 7, the *Advertiser and Tribune* portrayed Horan as an innocent bystander accidentally strafed by a wayward cluster of shot.[13] In the afternoon edition, however, they changed their tune.

"In our account in this morning's paper it was intimated that the man Horan, one of those shot, did not belong to the mob. This is erroneous," the *Tribune* writer admitted. "A respectable citizen who observed Horan's movements says he had a bludgeon raised in the very act of bringing it down to smash in a window when he received a gunshot charge in his left shoulder and left cheek." This was, however, an error. The retraction ascribed Edward Crosby's wounds to Horan.[14]

A few days later, they further muddied the waters when they attempted to correct their correction. In the March 11 edition, they described Horan as "an industrious mechanic" who "through misapprehension … has been represented as sympathizing with the tumultuous proceedings. He was badly injured, but is recovering."[15]

The *Advertiser and Tribune*'s ambivalence toward Horan, who was never charged, is significant and suggests that the editors believed that even though he may or may not have waved a club alongside the other rioters, he was at least guilty of tacitly supporting the mob by standing by and watching, perhaps even urging them on.

Like hundreds if not thousands milling about and watching the scrum in the Third Ward that fateful afternoon, Morris Horan was guilty of inaction.

"Us vs. Us"

Newspapers of the era tended to cast the "Great Riot" as an "us-vs.-them" conflict between Democrats and Republicans. This was in large part because the papers catered to the extreme elements of their respective political parties. The uncomfortable reality, however, is that it was really more of an "us-vs.-us" conflict in which neighbors turned on one another.

Lost in the historical blame game is the simple fact that at least some perpetrators had known their victims beforehand. Census records indicate that many of those taken to court for rioting lived in the Third Ward or frequented it enough to have become at least somewhat acquainted with the residents. Marcus Dale, Robert Bennette, and Lewis Pierce all identified at least one of their assailants in court. Pierce fingered John Davis as one of the bunch to throw stones at the cooper shop. More significantly, he testified to having known Davis for more than a year.

Under the topsoil of excuses, explanations, and justifications that have been offered since that fateful Friday in Detroit lies the fact that these boys attacked their neighbors—people known throughout the community as law-abiding, industrious individuals. Teenagers hurled stones and swung axes at people they knew to be mothers and fathers and husbands and wives while their mothers and fathers watched.

And did nothing.

Perhaps that is the most significant lesson to be learned from this tragic episode.

Prosecutable Cases: Whitewash?

Among the adults who could be considered guilty of inaction were prosecutor J. Knox Gavin and fire marshal William Champ. Days elapsed before authorities managed to find any of the rioters, which caused some to question whether Champ—considered a gifted investigator—had stonewalled his own investigation. The same might be said for the ward constables and sheriff's deputies. The riot occurred in front of an audience, many of whom knew the perpetrators, yet only Conrad Kalb faced charges for a violent crime. Solomon Houston identified him as his assailant, but Kalb beat the attempted murder rap and was given a judicial hand slap for assault and battery instead.

No one faced charges for the murder of Joshua Boyd. The savage beating that led to his death occurred offstage—behind the cooperage—but given the sheer number of people watching the tragedy unfold, someone saw something.

The apparent lack of witnesses to this violent crime goes to further indict the "good" citizens who stood by and did nothing while it occurred. The absence of murder charges suggests a few additional possibilities: Gavin either possessed credible information to identify one or more of Boyd's assailants and chose not to indict; he did not press witnesses; or he suspected that the kids were hand puppets and could not make a case against their puppeteers.

Consider the case against John H. Davis. Lewis Pierce testified that Davis hit him with a stone when he darted through the back door of Whitney Reynolds' house. August Sprege swore that during the riot, Davis (who lived half a block away) came to his house with blood on his hands and bragged that it was "nigger blood." Yet Gavin elected not to charge Davis with anything more than burning houses (of Whitney Reynolds and Benjamin Singleton) and "rioting." This is an odd omission given Pierce's statements, which suggests that the courts did not entirely accept his testimony at face value and hints at a degree of institutional racism in the justice system at the time. Found not guilty of the first charge, Davis evaded any punishment whatsoever when Gavin later dropped the charge of "riot."

In 1863, courts throughout the South did not allow the testimony of Blacks against white defendants, which meant that white suspects could literally get away with murder if the only witnesses to the crime were Black. Michigan courts, like other courts throughout the North, in theory made no such racial distinctions.

That is, in theory.

In fact, the juries consisted of the same citizens who watched the riot and did nothing to stop it. There is very little doubt that their sympathies played a role in both Faulkner's conviction and the hand-slapping of the rioters.

Anatomy of the News: The Free Press and the Riot

Advertiser and Tribune editors did not shy away from accusing the *Free Press* for inciting the mob. On the contrary, they reiterated this claim several times in the immediate aftermath of the riot. In the March 9, 1863, issue, they posed a question. "Such being the ferocious and destructive character of the mob, where did it come from?"

Then, they supplied the answer. "We all know. The conversation of the vast crowd that lined the streets last evening, declared with unerring certainty, *this is a Free Press mob*! And so it was. All this terrible assault upon life, and destruction of property—these scenes that disgrace civilization, and made strong men weep for pity, indignation or disgrace, have for months been studiously fomented for exclusively political objects. The case of Faulkner was only a pretext."[16]

The attack continued in a March 10 editorial. "We have charged that the riot on Friday was a *Free Press* riot, and endeavored to show by what process it had educated the ignorant mob up to the necessary ferocity."

This finger-pointing radiated out of Detroit. The *Advertiser and Tribune* ended their March 10 diatribe with a quote from the Republican-leaning *Cincinnati Commercial*. "The *Daily Free Press* has, since then, daily indulged in tirades against the negroes, and, if such a thing is possible, exaggerated the character of the crime committed, and deplored the inadequacy of the law to punish the reprobate as he deserved. The object was to stir up disorder, and that result was brought about yesterday."[17]

The *Tribune*'s finger-pointing climaxed in the March 14 edition when they accused the *Free Press* of trying to deflect blame onto German and Irish immigrants. "If anyone is to be punished for these crimes, they prefer it to be some ignorant American or poor Irishman or German, who they have advised to the acts. *They* ought to stand by the mob *they* stimulated—*their* mob, and defend them as they do, in their man-killing, woman-roasting, baby-beating, house-burning atrocities."[18]

The *Advertiser and Tribune* editors attempted to try their *Free Press* adversaries in the court of public opinion. The witnesses for the prosecution consisted of editorials, in which they presented evidence in the form of excerpted *Free Press* articles and attempted to make their case through logical and emotional appeals. The politics and rhetoric of feuding editors has muddied the waters, but a close look at the tone and content of the news coverage leading up to the riot reveals a few thought-provoking conclusions.

1. The *Free Press* committed more ink to the Faulkner case than to any other similar crime. The Wineman rape case, the only other rape case on the recorder's court docket in the first few months of 1863 (January), came and went with little more than a mention in the section devoted to court matters. The Faulkner case, on the other hand, consumed entire columns.

2. In the months leading up to March 6, 1863, the *Free Press* emphasized coverage of stories about raids on "amalgamation dens." These sensationalized stories, which were featured in lengthy page one write-ups, invariably condemned the sexual mingling of Blacks and whites. The gravity given to these cases was greatly exaggerated; none of them were considered serious enough offenses to warrant full jury trials in recorder's court, yet they received more coverage than homicide cases. The *Advertiser and Tribune* did not cover these raids at all.

3. *Free Press* reporters committed a character assassination of William Faulkner by presenting the "outrage" as a good versus evil dichotomy between the demonic Faulkner and the angelic Mary Brown. Almost fifty years later, *Free Press* scribe Henry Utley admitted as much when he wrote, "We had a man on the *Free Press* whose name has escaped me, but who wrote the case up in a vigorous style, calculated to create sentiment for the girl. It had the desired effect."[19]

A brief comparison of articles about Faulkner's arraignment and examination illustrates the differences in the tone and content of the coverage and what Utley meant by "vigorous style, calculated to create sentiment for the girl."

◄ *Advertiser and Tribune*, March 6, 1863, p. 1
GREAT EXCITEMENT.—Faulkner, the negro who is charged with committing a gross outrage upon a little girl a few days ago, was arraigned before the Recorder yesterday for trial. The evidence disclosed a state of facts that greatly incensed the large crowd that had assembled in and around the City Hall. The trial not being concluded, the prisoner was remanded to the jail, and on his way thither, under charge of an officer, he was followed by a mob and threatened with summary vengeance, and barely escaped with this life. He was safely locked up, and will be again brought before the Court this (Friday) morning, when it is apprehended, efforts will be made to wrest him from the officer, for the purpose of administering summary punishment.

◄ *Free Press*, March 2, 1863, p. 1
The examination of Faulkner, the negro charged with committing the outrage upon little Mary Brown, took place at the private office of Justice Lane Saturday morning. Long before the hour appointed for the examination arrived, a dense crowd of excited people congregated in and around the court-room, to witness the proceedings. So numerous and excited were the rabble, that it was with great difficulty that sufficient order could be preserved to proceed with the other business which preceded the case which had drawn together the large gathering. For the purpose of saving the child the embarrassment of telling her story before so many persons, the Judge very properly held the examination, as above stated, in his private office.

The victim of the outrage was first sworn. She appeared to understand perfectly well the nature of the obligations of an oath, answering, with the simplicity of childhood, the questions usually put to children previous to taking the stand. Her statement was substantially the same as the account continued in *The Free Press* of Friday morning. It could not, of course, be expected that a mere child, like her, would be as precise in all her statements as a person of maturity; but to all intents and purposes there was nothing contradictory in her statement, though her diffidence may have prevented her telling the whole villainous transaction. The evidence was taken down by our reporter, but, from the nature of the offense was totally unfit for publication. It is sufficient to say that, if the story of this child is entitled to any credit, the crime was one of the most aggravated and fiendish ones ever recorded.

Dr. Charles H. Barrett, who had been employed to make an examination of the person of the girl, testified as to the results of his investigations. His testimony concurred in every respect with that of the girl, showing conclusively that her statement was not in the least exaggerated.

Mrs. Rose Brown, the adopted mother of the child, was also sworn. Her testimony was in all respects the same as the time of making the complaint, which was given in Friday's *Free Press*.

The counsel for the prisoner, in behalf of his client, waived the right of putting in a defense at the examination, stating, however, that "a full and ample defense" would be made at the trial, before His Honor, Judge Witherell.

In this place it is proper to correct an erroneous impression contained in the account given in our former article. The colored girl who went with little Mary to the saloon of Faulkner is not in any manner implicated in the foul transaction. It appears she was slightly acquainted with the prisoner, and went into his saloon merely for the purpose of warming her feet, without having any knowledge of his intentions and subsequent acts.

At the conclusion of the evidence on the part of the people the prisoner was remanded to jail to await his trial at the Recorder's Court, which will probably take place sometime during the present week.

The defense intimated that the witness on whom they relied to acquit the prisoner was the colored girl who went with her to Faulkner's saloon, who, they claimed, would entirely controvert the statement of Mary Brown, the victim. How far the testimony will go to shield the monster from justice may be inferred from a circumstance which transpired after the examination. Prosecuting Attorney Gavin requested that the Court hold the girl in question, to insure her appearance at the trial. She was accordingly required to give bail in the sum of $300, failing to obtain which she was temporarily detained. On the way to the jail the girl burst into tears, and, clinging to the officer for protection, asked, amid choking sobs, the following question: "Will he kill me if I tell the truth?" Her fears being put at rest on that point, she voluntarily admitted her knowledge of all the material facts alleged by Mary Brown; stated that she was in the room at the time the outrage was committed; that Faulkner locked the door, and would not let either one of them out; and that she would testify to the whole proceeding, exactly as she saw it. These confessions of the only witness for the prisoner were made in the presence of officer Sullivan and our reporter, and there is no room for doubt that they are strictly true. That this girl had been tampered with, and either bribed or intimidated to swear falsely to screen the villain Faulkner, is beyond a doubt. The only

16. Lessons: The Children's Crusade

difference in their stories is that part relating to the colored girl's being present in the room. This, however, is of no earthly consequence; both the girls were, as they had reason to be, in a terrible condition of fright, and the younger one did not probably notice at the time the presence of the other. The evidence of the negro's guilt is overwhelming, and cannot be controverted. The only thing to be regretted is that there is no law sufficiently severe to punish him as the damnable crime which he has committed so richly merits. The gibbet or the guillotine alone would subserve the ends of justice in the case of the ten-fold worse than murderer, the black fiend, the monster Faulkner.

On his emerging from the place of examination loud threats of violence were made, and, had he not been hurried into the jail before it was generally known, it is thought that an excited and indignant mob would have attempted to wreak summary vengeance upon him within the very walls of the court-room. There was, happily, no other demonstration than the fierce threats, and he was safely lodged in jail to await conviction at the Recorder's Court.

While the *Advertiser and Tribune*'s treatment of Faulkner's arraignment was little more than a blurb, the *Free Press* article about the same event occupied two-thirds of an entire column. Since the Faulkner files are missing, this extensive coverage is invaluable as the only extant record of what occurred during the hearing, but the difference in article length suggests that the *Advertiser and Tribune* editors either did not consider the story as newsworthy as their *Free Press* counterparts or chose not to emphasize it. It is possible that since the *Tribune* did not publish a single word about the arraignment until four days after the *Free Press*, this relatively muted treatment was because they had been "scooped" or because the Faulkner arraignment was yesterday's news. However, this postponement in coverage may also provide further evidence that they did not consider the case as noteworthy as the *Free Press*.

The juxtaposition of language used to describe Faulkner and Mary Brown illustrates what Utley meant by creating "sentiment for the girl." Whereas Brown is depicted as an angelic, virginal youth above reproach, Faulkner is demonized with blatant name-calling. This is perhaps most evident at the end of the article, when the author drops any pretense of unbiased reporting and morphs into editorializing about "the black fiend, the monster Faulkner."

The writer emphasizes the "Faulkner outrage" with a subtle and ingenious device. Rather than using terms such as "indecent outrage" or "rape," he engages the reader's imagination through suggestion when he states, "The evidence was taken down by our reporter, but, from the nature of the offense was totally unfit for publication." This prompts the reader to wonder what constitutes "unfit for publication," and the mind can wander into some very dark places—places perhaps darker and more sinister than those presented by any combination of words.

This juxtaposition of the pure, innocent Brown with "the monster Faulkner" was designed to push the reader toward convicting Faulkner before the trial—an outcome the writer nudges along with word choice. In the final line, he writes that Faulkner "was safely lodged in jail to await conviction at the Recorder's Court." For the writer, Faulkner's guilt was a foregone conclusion and not a matter of "if" but "when."

4. *Free Press* writers promoted vigilantism in the Faulkner case. The initial report about the alleged rape of Mary Brown contained the assertion "There is no punishment on the statute books of Michigan which would, in a hundredth part, atone for the heinous crime." The writer added, "Let a fair examination be had, and justice, though it be utterly inadequate, take its proper course." The message was clear: life in prison—the maximum penalty in Michigan—would be "utterly inadequate."

A week later, the writer reiterated this message in even stronger terms, leaving no doubt about what would constitute "justice" in the Faulkner case: "The gibbet or the guillotine alone would subserve the ends of justice in the case of the ten-fold worse than murderer, the black fiend, the monster Faulkner." According to *Tribune* editors, this statement was equivalent to throwing gun powder into a fire.

5. *Free Press* writers emphasized the Black-white angle of Faulkner's crime. They accomplished this by repeatedly prefacing Faulkner's name with a racially-charged descriptive term. He wasn't just a "fiend" but a "black fiend." He wasn't just William Faulkner but "the Negro Faulkner."

· · · ·

It is impossible to prove a causal connection between *Free Press* articles and events of March 6, 1863, but a close examination of *Free Press* coverage of the Faulkner case suggests an agenda that helped to create a charged atmosphere.

The role of the *Free Press* in the riot of 1863 may be summarized with a slight addition to an old adage:

>You can lead a horse to water, but you can't make him drink.
>You can, however, salt the oats.

Free Press articles were very salty.

One final note: another adage—one involving sticks, stones, and words—may apply. Free Press writers wielded words, but it was the rioters, and the rioters alone, with the sticks and stones.

History Repeated

Lured by Henry Ford's offer of a $5-a-day wage, workers from all over the United States came to Detroit, including thousands of Blacks fleeing the Jim Crow South for what they hoped would be a more welcoming environment in the North.

When a Black physician named Dr. Ossian Sweet relocated to Detroit in 1921, he moved into a city characterized by racially-segregated housing, an active KKK, and an alarmingly high number of Blacks killed by police officers. Black Detroiters were confined to old, deteriorating neighborhoods (sixty square blocks were nicknamed "Black Bottom") and kept there by a 1923 Michigan Supreme Court decision that cemented *de jure* discrimination in housing.

In 1925, Dr. Sweet moved into an all-white neighborhood, which triggered angry protests from his white neighbors who gathered outside his door at 2905 Garland and pelted the home with stones. Acutely aware of the danger, Sweet had asked his brother and a few friends to join him and brought several guns for self-protection. On the evening of September 9, 1925—a day after the Sweets moved into the neighborhood—shots fired from the upper story struck and killed a man standing on the porch of a neighboring house.

All eleven in the house at the time, including Dr. Sweet and his wife, were arrested and charged with murder. No less a personage than Clarence Darrow, who had represented Tennessee teacher John Scopes during the infamous "Monkey Trial" a few months earlier, defended the Detroit eleven. The first jury could not decide on a verdict. When Dr. Sweet's brother Henry was acquitted in a subsequent trial, the prosecutor dropped all charges against the others.

During his testimony, Dr. Sweet said, "When I opened the door, I saw the mob and realized I was facing the same mob that had hounded my people throughout our entire history."

Part of that history took place on March 6, 1863.

• • • •

On June 21, 1943, a melee between Black and white youths broke out on Belle Isle. Police managed to quell the incident but fictitious stories of savage violence quickly spread throughout Detroit. Black Detroiters heard the tale that white youths waylaid a Black mother and tossed her and her baby from the Belle Isle Bridge. White Detroiters heard a lascivious story of a white woman raped by a Black man in the same vicinity.

Violence erupted throughout the city and lasted until officials called in the troops. When the dust settled, 34 Detroiters were dead.

• • • •

Another, even deadlier riot occurred in 1967 after police raided a party for two veterans of the Vietnam War. They arrested everyone present, which included 82 Black party-goers. Long-smoldering resentment, based on a variety of factors including segregated housing and racism, turned into a conflagration. Violent protests resulted in the deaths of forty-three and continued until Governor George Romney ordered in the National Guard.

Epilogue

Dennis K. Sullivan continued to police Detroit after the riot and became a fixture on the witness stand in Judge Witherell's recorder's court. In 1865, twenty-four-year-old "Denny" joined the newly-formed metropolitan police force and served until 1870, when he went to work for Uncle Sam as a U.S. government detective. He worked his way up the ranks, eventually ascending to the position of "chief United States Treasury Detective for Michigan and Ohio."[1] From his headquarters in Detroit, he hunted counterfeiters and forgers, who ended up as federal prisoners in the Detroit House of Correction.

Sullivan rejoined the Detroit police in 1875, where he earned a reputation as a shrewd investigator and an incorruptible cop. "During his long and successful career as a detective," noted a *Free Press* writer, "he has unraveled numerous mysteries enveloping crime in the city and county.... No suspicions were cast on his official doings during his long and successful career."[2] Detective Sullivan died of heart disease on January 14, 1883, at the age of fifty-two.[3]

Like Sullivan, David M. Freeman continued to prowl the streets of the Third Ward as a constable and deputy sheriff until he also joined the Detroit metropolitan police force. He died of stomach cancer on December 6, 1892, at the age of seventy-eight.[4]

Fire Marshal William Champ resigned in 1866 and returned to private detective work. A lifelong sufferer of various pulmonary ailments, Champ died of consumption at the age of forty-nine in 1867.[5]

The Curse of Faulkner

The key courtroom figures involved with the Faulkner trial, except defense attorney J. Logan Chipman and his co-counsel A.W. Henssler, all died premature deaths.

Both Francis B. Phelps, the much-maligned acting mayor during the riot, and Francis X. Cicotte, the acting sheriff during the riot, both died in 1865. The fifty-three-year-old lawman died on September 6.

Judge Benjamin Franklin Hawkins Witherell suffered a catastrophic heart event and died on June 26, 1867. The seventy-year-old judge had outlived three wives (his third wife, Cassandra, died in March 1863) and two of his five children.[6]

A day after the death of Judge Witherell, former Wayne County sheriff Peter Fralick died of inflammatory rheumatism at the age of fifty-eight.[7]

James Knox Gavin, the Wayne County prosecuting attorney, did not live long after Judge Witherell's gavel came down on the rioters. He died of liver failure on July 22, 1865, at the age of thirty-six. A confirmed bachelor, Gavin never married. Instead, he dedicated his time to the prosecution of Detroit's miscreants, a task for which he had a singular talent. "As Prosecuting Attorney," noted a *Free Press* reporter, "he showed great ability—proving himself a match for the many able gentlemen who practice criminal law in this city."[8]

One of the "many able gentlemen" was J. Logan Chipman.

Chipman, the young attorney who defended just about everyone who appeared in recorder's court in 1863, won a seat in the Michigan state legislature that fall. Losing his bid for reelection in 1866, he spent the next thirteen years in private practice until he won election as a superior court judge. Upon retiring from the bench, he won a seat in the United States House of Representatives. He died of pneumonia on August 17, 1893, at the age of sixty-three.

In Detroit, the *Free Press* ran a special edition with news about Chipman's passing, and all of the justice courts except one closed in deference to the tireless litigator known for his encyclopedic knowledge of the law.[9]

Attorney A.W. Henssler's health continued to erode in the years following the Faulkner trial, and he became reliant on opium to control his coughing fits. He kept a bottle of "Dover's Powders," an opiate-laced patent medicine, by his side at all times, which is where police found it when they discovered Henssler lying unconscious on Belle Isle on August 30, 1891. He died later that day, prompting suspicions that the former defense attorney had committed suicide.

His son Edward insisted his father would never have killed himself. "He would not have done such a thing without leaving me some word," Edward W. Henssler said. "He was getting old and absent-minded, and, I believe, took the powders while in a fit of abstraction without knowing what he did. He had for many years made a practice of carrying Dover's powders in his pocket, using them for a bronchial trouble."[10]

Justice Minot T. Lane hung up his gavel and retired from the bench in July 1866. He remained an active and high-ranking member of the Independent Order of Odd Fellows until his death of pneumonia on February 23, 1875, at the age sixty-seven. At the time of his death, Lane's only child George was the commercial editor of the *Advertiser and Tribune*.[11]

Lt. John Van Stan served until the end of the conflict, mustering out with the 14th Regiment Michigan Infantry in July 1865. After the war, he ran for (and won) the position of Third Ward constable on the Democratic ticket, but on multiple occasions Constable Van Stan found himself on the wrong side of the law. He was suspended from duty in May 1866 when he faced a charge of attempting to murder his wife; he subsequently pled guilty to assault and battery.[12] A year later, Van Stan became entangled in a curious episode. Accused of stealing a dog, he landed in police court on a charge of larceny but beat the rap when it became evident that he had seized the dog "by virtue of a writ of replevin issued by Justice McCarthy."[13]

Whitney Reynolds, whose cooper shop became the epicenter of the 1863 Detroit riot, remained a resident of Detroit, where he died on March 8, 1889, at the age of seventy-three. He is a neighbor to fellow Tar Heel William Faulkner in Section C at Woodmere Cemetery.[14]

It is possible that Whitney Reynolds knew Faulkner. Both apparently came from North Carolina, and Detroit's Third Ward population of former Tar Heels was not a large one, which suggests that at some point they may have come into contact with one another and may have even had some type of association. This possibility raises the interesting yet unprovable thesis that the mob targeted Reynolds' cooper shop because of his association with Faulkner.

Marcus Dale enlisted with the newly formed 1st U.S. Colored Infantry in August 1863, an outfit originally commanded by *Advertiser and Tribune* editor Henry Barns. Unhappy that the soldiers of his regiment received half the pay of white soldiers, Private Dale refused to accept any payment, and he encouraged his fellow soldiers do the same, until they received equal pay. Dale's protest eventually worked. When the war ended, Dale mustered out of service as a commissary sergeant.

In 1867, Dale relocated to New Orleans, where he organized a school and church for freed slaves. His business acumen went on display when he brokered a deal with a local planter to acquire the bricks needed to build his church.

"Learning that a white man in the neighborhood intended to have 100,000 bricks made at eight dollars per thousand and furnish everything," a biographer later wrote of the scheme, "he proposed to him this plan: the minister would furnish the labor, and the white gentlemen the mules, land, lumber, etc. The colored people would make a kiln of 220,000 bricks, the church to have 120,00 bricks and give the other 100,000 to him for two hundred dollars less than he intended to pay. As he would have furnished everything to others he agreed to do this, and the colored laborers got their pay, built the church, and the benefactor was gratified as well, and was two hundred dollars better off."

Despite constant harassment from white supremacist groups, Dale continued teaching and played a prominent role in the Methodist Episcopal Church. The Rev. Marcus Dale died in 1892 at the age of sixty.[15]

Solomon Houston remained in Detroit. He would father seven children by his wife Sally, thirty years his junior. He died of "old age" on February 18, 1877, at the age of seventy.

Bernard Groghan's ploy of joining the army to sidestep criminal charges worked. He never answered for his alleged role in the 1863 riot.

Returning to Detroit after the war, twenty-two-year-old Groghan married nineteen-year-old Mary Engels.

Timothy Drummond, whom Dennis K. Sullivan described as one of the more "active" of the March 6 rioters, did not stay on the right side of the law. In November 1865, a larceny sent him to the House of Correction for a year. A few months later, "public drunkenness" landed him back in the House for a thirty-day stint. Drummond was an ornery drunk. After one binge, he and another "deaf mute" assaulted a night watchman at the Central Police Station.

When not working off his sentence in the House of Correction or sleeping off a binge in the police station, Drummond worked as an on-again, off-again laborer until he died of a freak accident in 1873.

The weird incident led to a page-one item in the December 27, 1873, edition of the *Free Press*. The writer described Drummond as a constant thorn in the side of Detroit police officers. "The reporters, police and many other people have long been acquainted with a deaf and dumb young man named Timothy Drummond, who lives with his mother and brother on Congress street east, and his peculiar habits have several times caused him to appear before the courts. His vice was drunkenness, and when about half-drunk he was ready to fight anything or anybody."

One such occasion led to his demise in December 1873. Drummond wobbled into Joe Conrad's saloon and attempted to pawn a pistol. The barkeep didn't want it, so Drummond turned to Jim McGuire, who made an offhand remark about the gun being hot. Drummond erupted in anger, wildly waved his fists in the air, and charged out of the saloon.

A few minutes later, he returned for a drink, but Conrad refused to serve him. Gripping Drummond's arm, Jim McGuire tugged him out of the tavern and took him to "the little house occupied by the flagman at the crossing," most likely on the pretense of a free drink or two.

McGuire and several of his friends proceeded to mock Drummond, who lost his cool. He palmed the pistol and began pointing it at his tormentors, but McGuire told his friends that Drummond's pistol wasn't loaded. They howled with laughter.

In the ultimate gesture of defiance, Drummond pressed the barrel against his stomach and "snapped it nine or ten times." On the tenth squeeze, the gun went off. The laughing stopped as Drummond crumpled to the floor. He died the next day at the age of twenty-eight.

The rumor mill in Detroit began churning out stories of a quarrel that had turned violent, but after listening to the testimony of four of McGuire's friends who witnessed the incident, the coroner's jury ruled that Drummond died "from a pistol shot fired by himself."[16]

Despite the jury's finding, some questions remained, particularly among Drummond's family. An *Evening News* correspondent noted an interesting discrepancy that convinced the Drummonds that McGuire shot their boy. "They call attention to the circumstances (not developed in the testimony before the coroner), that the charge, by whomsoever it was fired, made but a small bullet hole in the clothing and skin of the dummy, whereas if the pistol had been held close to his person by the unfortunate man himself, the powder would certainly have burned the clothing and skin, at least enough to be noticed on close examination."

McGuire and his cronies, the reporter noted, all lived in the worst section of "The Potomac," a low-rent, high-crime district. Suspected of numerous crimes, McGuire and his brother "never failed to find plenty of witnesses in the 'Potomac' to 'swear them free.'"[17]

Henry Munson Utley continued to write for the *Free Press* until he took a job as the city librarian, a post he held for twenty-seven years. Shortly after he retired he suffered a nervous breakdown and died in 1917 at the age of seventy-nine.[18]

Henry Barns continued as an editor of the *Advertiser and Tribune*. Following the riot, he authored a series of articles promoting the formation of a Black regiment, which sparked a war of words with his counterparts at the *Free Press*. In no small part due to Barns' efforts, the 1st Michigan Colored Infantry formed in August 1863. Commissioned as a colonel, Barns commanded a group of more than eight hundred soldiers that included Private Marcus Dale.

After the war, Henry Barns was victimized by a series of disastrous business decisions. Failed speculation and a crooked business partner who skipped town with Barns' stake left him penniless. He committed suicide in 1871 at the age of fifty-six.[19]

Appendix 1: "The Riot"

The following poem, written by Benjamin Cutler Clark, Sr., originally appeared as a postscript in the 1863 publication *A Thrilling Narrative from the Lips of the Sufferers of the Late Detroit Riot, March 6, 1863, with the Hair Breath Escapes of Men, Women and Children, and Destruction of Colored Men's Property, Not Less Than $15,000*.

The son of slaves who earned their freedom, Benjamin Cutler Clark, Sr., was a native of Maryland who prospered as a "blue dyer." Suffering from a lung ailment, Clark moved to Detroit, where he became an active member of the African Methodist Episcopal Church, in 1861. He died on March 12, 1864, at the age of sixty-three.

Clark frequently wrote verse about social and political issues, many of his poems appearing in periodicals. A collection of his writings, *The Past, Present, and Future in Prose and Poetry*, was published posthumously in 1867.[1]

THE RIOT.

BY B. CLARK, SEN., A COLORED MAN.

'Twas in Detroit city, the State of Michigan,
Where mob law reigned rampant, disgraceful to man,
In killing and beating both women and men,
And sacking and burning beyond human ken.

The crowd ran collected and beat every one,
Whose skin were not colored exact like their own,
And swore they'd have "Falkner," [sic][2] and hang him that day,
Or kill every "nigger" that came in their way.

The only pretext for this outbreak in fact,
Was "Falkner" [sic] committed an now nameless act,
Although given up to the law right away,
The mob sought to lynch him in broad open day.

Now be it remember'd that Falkner [sic] at right,
Although call'd a "nigger," had always been white,
Had voted, and always declared in his shop,
He never would sell colored people a drop.

He's what is call'd white, though I must confess,
So mixed are the folks now, we oft have to guess,
Their hair is curl'd and their skins are so brown,
If they're white in the country, they're niggers in town.

To keep from a rescue, and take him to jail,
The soldiers were ordered to come without fail,
But they were insulted and stoned at—pell mell—
Till some of them fired and down a man fell.

The mob, disappointed, now hied to a place
Where some humble coopers, of the sable race,
Were honestly working to earn their own bread,
By rowdies were set on and left almost dead.

They enter'd, and beat them with billets of wood,
Then fired the cooper shop just as it stood,
And as they attempted to rush from the flames,
They met them with bludgeons to dash out their brains.

Then they took the city without more delay,
And fired each building that stood in their way,
Until the red glare had ascended on high,
And lit up the great azure vault of the sky.

The sight was most awful indeed to behold,
See women and babes driven out in the cold,
And old aged sires, that fought for the land,
Beat almost to death by a desperate band.

Whilst females were heard crying, "kill them"—Oh; shame,
They urged on the mob, yet there's no one to blame,
'Twas got up to please our friends of the South,
Now don't say a word—nay, don't open your mouth.

We go in for the Union just as it was.
And slavery also, and all the slave laws;
Now do not think hard if we do behave rash,
By burning those houses we pocket some cash.

'Tis said that those houses and inmates were bad,
And hence the excuse that the outragers had,
Yet was it the true love of virtue alone,
That made the mob anxious to pull a church down?

Strange as it may be, yet 'tis true without doubt,
Mobs do not discriminate if once let out;
So when they had fired the huts of the poor,
They ran with the torch to their rich neighbor's door.

Appendix 1: "The Riot"

This brought the community plainly to see
The danger in which all were likely to be;
The rich and the poor, the black and the white,
Stood a chance to be mobbed and burned out that night.

I blush when I think that such deeds should take place,
Not heathens or Turks, a civilized race,
Not where savage nations alone have the rule,
But here amidst churches, the Bible and school.

Humanity wept, she lamented the sight,
The groans, blood and tears of that terrible night;
Yet, oh, may the town of Detroit never see
Such a day as the sixth of March, sixty-three.

Appendix 2: Kids in the Big House, Juveniles in the Detroit House of Correction

When she was sentenced for disorderly conduct in 1863, ten-year-old Mary Brown became the youngest prisoner admitted to the House of Correction since the facility began registering inmates on December 18, 1861. She was not the only youngster incarcerated in Detroit's big house in 1863. Of the 374 prisoners admitted in 1863, forty-five were under the age of seventeen.[1] By posting bail, it appears that several of these juvenile offenders spent little or no time behind bars in the House of Correction.

In theory, juvenile offenders were transferred to the House of Correction for Juvenile Offenders, which opened in 1856 for the express purpose of separating the youth from hardened offenders. The Lansing facility functioned as a reform school. When prisoners reached the age of consent, they were transferred to one of Michigan's prisons. Some of Detroit's youngsters sentenced to lengthy incarceration may have been transferred to the Lansing facility, but the Detroit House of Correction records indicate that—rules, procedures, tradition, and logic aside—many underage prisoners served their time in the big house. This may have been particularly true for kids sentenced to short terms for crimes such as petty larceny. Peter Doran, who was sent to the Lansing reform school because of his age, does not appear in the prison registry, so the names of other kids in the registry probably remained in Detroit.

A log of punishments for 1872 provides evidence that even fifteen years after the Lansing facility opened, young prisoners still served time at the Detroit prison (see discussion below).

Appendix 2: The Big House and Detroit House of Correction

The prison records underline the arbitrary nature of shipping juveniles to other facilities. In 1869, for instance, an eleven-year-old girl convicted of larceny was transferred to the House of Shelter "by order of inspectors"; fourteen-year-old Mary Rose and fifteen-year-old Nellie Stevens—both also sentenced for larceny—remained in the House of Correction.

The problem of keeping juveniles in the Detroit House of Correction persisted for years, prompting Michigan legislators to propose a bill in 1903 "to regulate the treatment and control of dependent, neglected and delinquent children under the age of sixteen years within the city of Detroit; to regulate the practice in such court; to provide for the appointment of probation officers; to prohibit the commitment to any jail or police station within the city of Detroit of any child under the age of fourteen years."[2]

The following list contains the names of all perpetrators under the age of seventeen that appear in the Detroit House of Correction commitment records for 1863. If any of them were transferred to reform schools, it was not noted in the register. The maximum sentence is one year, which suggests that juveniles serving longer sentences were indeed transferred, while those short-timers remained behind.

Name	Age	Offense	Sentence	Sentencing Authority
Aller, Fannie or Mattie	15	disorderly	bail filed	Detroit Police Court*
Anderson, Cornelia Francis	16	disorderly	1 year	Kalamazoo County
Baker, Elizabeth	14	disorderly	90 days	Detroit Police Court
Bates, George V.	13	larceny	90 days	Detroit Police Court
Beaufort, Charles	14	disorderly	bail filed	Detroit Police Court
Beaufort, George	15	disorderly	bail filed	Detroit Police Court
Bradley, Josephine	16	disorderly	bail filed	Detroit Police Court
Brown, Mary	10	larceny	90 days	Detroit Police Court
Cavanaugh, James	16	disorderly	bail filed	Detroit Police Court
Commons, James	13	larceny	15 days	Detroit Police Court
Condon or Connolly, Kate	13	disorderly	bail filed	Detroit Police Court
Corcoran, Dennis	14	larceny	12 days	Detroit Police Court
David, Kittie	15	disorderly	bail filed	Detroit Police Court
Dewzel, Cornelius	16	larceny	25 days	Detroit Police Court
Downey, Patrick	12	larceny	15 days	Detroit Police Court

Appendix 2: The Big House and Detroit House of Correction

Name	Age	Offense	Sentence	Sentencing Authority
Dyver, Nancy	16	disorderly	1 year	Lenawee County
Eller, Mary	16	disorderly	bail filed	Detroit Police Court
Fitzgerald, Frank	10	disorderly	29 days	Detroit Police Court
Fork, Jacob	14	larceny	30 days	Detroit Police Court
Gray, Nicholas	16	larceny	20 days	Detroit Police Court
Haley, Michael	16	disorderly	90 days	Lenawee County
Harper, Enos	16	larceny	90 days	Detroit Police Court
Higgins, Sarah	16	disorderly	bail filed	Detroit Police Court
Homel, Josephine	15	disorderly	bail filed	Detroit Police Court
Hoover, Ellen	11	larceny	90 days	Detroit Police Court
Johnson, Leonard	11	larceny	90 days	Detroit Police Court
Malyn, Henry	14	disorderly	90 days	Lenawee County
Markham, James	14	larceny	25 days	Detroit Police Court
Minor, John	16	malicious trespass	15 days	Detroit Police Court
Nagel, Nancy	13	disorderly	1 year	Kalamazoo County
O'Hanan, Edward	15	disorderly	90 days	Lenawee County
O'Neil, John	12	disorderly	bail filed	Detroit Police Court
Preston, Charles	14	malicious trespass	bail filed	Detroit Police Court
Preston, William	10	malicious trespass	bail filed	Detroit Police Court
Rogers, William	12	larceny	50 days	Detroit Police Court
Rush, William	13	larceny	bail filed	Detroit Police Court
Sampson, Joseph	13	assault and battery	25 days	Detroit Police Court
Shepherd, W.T.	12	disorderly	bail filed	Detroit Police Court
Smith, Henry	12	disorderly	bail filed	Detroit Police Court
Solis, Charles	14	disorderly	bail filed	Detroit Police Court
Sweet, Wilson	16	larceny	50 days	Detroit Police Court
Taylor, Margaret	15	disorderly	9 months	Kalamazoo County
Turner, Sarah June	15	disorderly	bail filed	Detroit Police Court
Van Sickle, Sarah	16	disorderly	bail filed	Detroit Police Court
Wilson, Eliza Anne	15	disorderly	1 year	Lenawee County

*All cases in Detroit Police Court presided over by M.T. Lane.

Appendix 2: The Big House and Detroit House of Correction 231

The most common offense entered by the prison clerk was "disorderly [conduct]." This notation, however, evidently denoted more than one possible crime. In 1863, Minot T. Lane sentenced ten-year-old Mary Brown to ninety days for "vagrancy"—mid-nineteenth-century code for prostitution—but her entry in the prison register lists "disorderly" as her offense.[3] The "disorderly" notation in the House of Correction register suggests that in 1863 the clerk considered "vagrancy" one of a number of crimes under the umbrella of "disorderly," which also likely included inebriated teenagers whose conduct amounted to "disorderly." If Mary Brown's case was not unique, then at least some of the girls imprisoned in 1863 had entered into the oldest profession.

The entries for twenty-five-year-old Sarah Campbell, twenty-year-old Margaret Champagne, and twenty-year-old Mary Washington—Martin Washington's retinue of nymphs du pave—appear to confirm this possibility. Sentenced for "vagrancy" in Minot T. Lane's police court, their offense is listed as "disorderly" in the prison register.[4]

Over the next few years, prison clerks would begin to delineate specific offenses previously included under the "disorderly umbrella." Register entries in 1869 contain "drunkenness" and "vagrant" whereas entries from 1863 do not.

Some of the kids avoided hard time by filing bail, but the others completed sentences varying from twelve days to a full year. Judging by the prisoner records, some of them did very hard time.

While the index of inmates contains entries from the day the cell doors closed on the first inmates in December 1861, existent records detailing prisoners' specific records behind bars begin in 1871. Either the earlier volume is missing or the House authorities did not create individualized records during the first decade of the prison's existence. Either way, how the feisty Mary Brown behaved while behind bars is lost to history.

Two later records of teenage inmates, however, suggest that prison authorities took off the kid gloves when treating juvenile offenders who violated the rules and provide a pretty good glimpse of what Brown would have faced had she carried her attitude with her from Judge Minot T. Lane's courtroom.

Mary Rose was fourteen years old when she entered the House on December 27, 1869, following a larceny conviction. In 1872 alone, the teenager violated prison rules no fewer than twelve times for "disobedience," "bad work," and "talking" (prisoners were required to follow the "silence rule" and refrain from communicating with other prisoners).

"Standing" appears to have been the preferred method of punishing female juvenile rule-breakers, much like a teacher might punish a recalcitrant student by requiring her to stand in a corner and wear a dunce cap.

The instance of "disobedience" on January 12 cost Mary Rose her dinner. Instead of dining, she spent thirty minutes "standing in hall." The next two infractions led to sentences of "standing in hall two hours." The subsequent infraction landed Rose in solitary, where she was required to stand for four hours.

The punishment differed for boys. Like Mary Rose, fifteen-year-old Ray Reuben, serving a sentence for "vagrancy," struggled to follow prison rules. His record contains no fewer than seventeen infractions in the first four months of 1872 alone. The same offenses that left Mary Rose standing for hours on end instead cost Ray Reuben his supper, indicating that the punishment for unruly male inmates consisted of withholding food.[5]

Appendix 3: The Rev. Sylvan S. Hunting's Sermon of March 15, 1863

In the March 19, 1863, afternoon edition, the *Advertiser and Tribune* published extracts of Sylvan S. Hunting's sermon from Sunday, March 15, 1863, under the headline "The Protection of All Is the Only Security for Any." These excerpts were republished in *A Thrilling Narrative*. The pamphlet's anonymous author attributed the text to the *Advertiser and Tribune* but did not include a date or credit the Rev. Hunting as the author.

The original newspaper article contained a paragraph of explanation preceding the excerpts: "The principle that all peaceable and industrious members of society, however poor and humble, must be protected in their legal and natural rights, in order that any of us may be secure, is strongly presented in the following extracts from Rev. S.S. Hunting's sermon, in this city, last Sunday evening."

> But the threat is made, that "if the course of things," which I would do my utmost to help on; viz.: the elevation of the negro in moral, intellectual and social endowments, "shall not be arrested," the recent riot "is but premonitory of an uprising which will leave no resting place for the negro in the States of the Northwest."
> Now, let it be distinctly understood, that the attempt to exterminate the negro, will bring extermination to certain classes of their enemies, who are not yet prepared to die; indeed, that the persistent attempt to drive the negroes from this city, would lead to the utter destruction of it. It is not easy to root out a body of loyal, peaceful citizens from a community, who have their firm minds, without revolutionizing society and producing chaos. There are people here who would deem it as honorable to die defending the homes of the humblest citizen, as they would to die at the head of the army, in defense of the Government.

Appendix 3: The Rev. Hunting's Sermon of March 15, 1863

And what is defending the Government, but protecting the property of persons who are a legitimate part of the nation? That Government is of little value which does not hold the rights of its poorest subject as sacred as those of the richest. Indeed, who will show us the distinction to be made between the homes of the white and black, the rich and the poor? Is not your house protected from the fire by extinguishing the flames on that of your poor neighbor? If the houses of one class of citizens are not safe from the torch of the incendiary, is any body's safe? If we resort to mobs, where shall we stop?

The colored man is not wanting in muscular strength, nor in shrewdness; and does any one dare to encourage this plan of extermination? Do journalists know what fire-brands they are handling when they use such language, or make such threats? There is not the least possibility that an oppressed race, having caught the inspiration of a progressive age, will sink back into their former degradation, or stop in their progress. The negro may claim this as his native land; he is susceptible to social and political influences, and he must rise with the general progress of society and the advancement of civilization, and whoever lifts the brickbat or cudgel to beat him down,—or, which is the same thing, slanders him and talks of his extermination—is putting a torch to his own house, is fighting against the will of God, and will sooner or later be defeated. He who falls upon the "rejected stone, shall be broken," but "he upon whom it falls shall be ground to powder." Let all beware how they countenance this prejudice against a race, or give their sanction to it in the least. This negro hatred is what blinded the eyes of the nation, and threatens future calamity if it is not checked and overcome.

The destruction of the property of the poor man, all the goods he has, and taking from him every earthly comfort, is a sad and serious loss; but the attacks upon the rights of life and liberty of this people, by the mob and their abettors, is a much more alarming fact. The protection of property is one of the "social and relative" rights, and secondary to the absolute right of the protection of one's person; and it is upon this point that we witness a sad confusion of mind.

After so many families had been burnt out of their homes and brutally treated—men escaping murder only by their physical endurance, and women outraged,—we could hear people on the street saying: "What a pity it was to destroy so much property"; "Too bad to burn up so much property—too bad, indeed!" But these very exclamations show how we habitually lose sight of natural rights by our absorption in what ministers to cupidity or animal want. The "Almighty Dollar" is good in its place, but when it fills a larger place in the hearts of the people than mankind, the rights of property will be defended when personal rights will be forgotten. Then a suicidal policy may be adopted by the Government, for only by protecting the poorest and weakest members of the community in their rights, can we have any assurance of protection for the richest and the strongest.

Tax-payers open their eyes when they pay for the property which the mob destroyed; but to refuse to pay for the homes of the virtuous poor thus destroyed, is a kind of thieving which honorable men will not be guilty of. But this is not all the compensation which justice demands. She demands pay for

Appendix 3: The Rev. Hunting's Sermon of March 15, 1863

the days and weeks of suffering which those poor men must endure as the result of the attack upon their natural rights. Who pays for the attempt to kill the old Sexton who has been a peaceful citizen for fifty years? Who pays for the blow which laid him upon the sidewalk? Will the ruffian? Will the policemen who coldly looked on, not offering to protect him, nor to arrest the criminal when reminded of their duty? Justice requires that the city pay a fine for every blow inflicted by the mob upon industrious and sober citizens. Every person in the community, who is in any sense a citizen, is a member of the body-politic; and when, by the negligence, carelessness, imbecility, or complicity of the Government, through any of its agents, a single member of a society is injured in his person or property,—even the weakest member, himself not a criminal,—the corporation should pay all damages,—for every wound inflicted, every limb maimed;—and not until there is some such protection to natural rights will our liberties be secured. Individuals can give aid and comfort to the sufferers, but the whole city should be bled in the pocket for every drop of blood shed by that mob.

And let no one think of the distinction of races, but deal justly and mercifully with the German, the Irish and the Negro. All the innocent should be remembered. If it can be proved that any person injured in his property was using the house illegally—for instance, was keeping a house of ill-fame—we give him no sympathy for his losses, and only pity him for his depravity. But, yet, there is a legal way to break up these social hells. Let the wicked be punished and the virtuous be protected.

Appendix 4: Questions for Study and Contemplation

1. According to a quote often attributed to Edmund Burke, "The only thing necessary for the triumph of evil is for good men to do nothing." In what ways might this apply to the Detroit Riot of 1863?

2. "A mob's a monster," Ben Franklin once said. "Head's enough but no brains." Is this an accurate description of the "mob" that terrorized Detroit's Third Ward on March 6, 1863?

3. "Those who cannot remember the past," according to philosopher George Santayana, "are condemned to repeat it." Does this statement apply to residents of Detroit in 1863? It what ways has the history of the Detroit riot of 1863 repeated itself?

4. Are there any twenty-first-century parallels of the 1863 Detroit riot?

5. What would you say is the moral of this story or the key lesson this story teaches?

6. What one aspect of the riot did you find most interesting, shocking, or thought-provoking?

7. Several social and political tensions led to the Detroit riot of 1863. What do you think was the single biggest contributing factor?

8. Research another riot in an American city and compare it with the Detroit riot of 1863. Do any patterns emerge?

Chapter Notes

Preface

1. On February 24, 1863, the *Advertiser and Tribune* (afternoon edition) ran a piece under the headline "THE CONSCRIPTION ACT." "The telegraph rumors that a large number of men are to be called for under the Conscription Act. There will probably be no immediate call, but the rumor is suggestive."

2. *Detroit Free Press*, March 7, 1863 (all references are from the morning edition unless otherwise noted).

Introduction

1. *Advertiser and Tribune*, March 14, 1863 (afternoon edition).

Chapter 1

1. *The Detroit Daily Post*, January 1, 1870. Also, *The Colored People of Detroit: Their Trials, Persecutions and Escapes* (Detroit: The Detroit Daily Post, 1870), p. 11.

2. For a thorough discussion of how geography and ethnic diversity led to unrest in early Detroit, see John C. Schneider, *Detroit and the Problem of Order, 1830–1880: A Geography of Crime, Riot, and Policing* (Lincoln: University of Nebraska Press, 1980). This work explores the notion that as Detroit developed, the formation of neighborhoods led to conflicts over space during which majority groups targeted minority groups.

3. *The Detroit Daily Post*, February 7, 1870. Also, *The Colored People of Detroit: Their Trials, Persecutions and Escapes* (Detroit: The Detroit Daily Post, 1870), p. 3.

4. For a brief description of the Blackburn case, see George B. Catlin, *The Story of Detroit* (Detroit: Detroit News, 1923), pp. 345–346. A more detailed discussion can be found in the January 1, 1870, edition of the *Detroit Daily Post* and subsequent reprint titled *The Colored People of Detroit: Their Trials, Persecutions and Escapes* (Detroit: The Detroit Daily Post, 1870), pp. 3–5.

5. Of the aggregate population of 42,756, the federal census records a total of 724 "Free Colored" of all ages residing in Wayne County in 1850. By 1860, this number had risen to 1,673 out of a county-wide aggregate of 75,545. In 1850, "Detroit City" had a population of 587 "Free Colored," which rose to 1,403 in 1860. In 1860, four city wards contained a majority of Detroit's Black population. Third Ward: 326; Fourth Ward: 373; Sixth Ward: 192; Seventh Ward: 267. "Free Colored" Residents of Wayne County, Michigan. Population by Counties—Classification by ages and color—Aggregates. 1850 U.S. Census, pp. 886, 896. Residents of Wayne County, Michigan. Population by Counties—Classification by ages and color—Aggregates, 1860 U.S. Census, pp. 231, 233, 246.

6. According to Schneider, this positioning was strategic. Thus located on the outskirts of the city and along the railroad tacks, the brothels were within sight of arriving passengers but beyond the sight of the law. John C. Schneider, *Detroit and the Problem of Order, 1830–1880: A Geography of Crime, Riot, and Policing*, p. 21.

7. *Detroit Free Press*, July 6–7, 1855. The two successive news accounts give wildly

differing versions of this incident. The July 7 piece suggests that the riot ensued when police raided the brothel of a Black man named Whitfield. The July 6 article identifies Charles Lawrence as the proprietor of a "dance hall."

8. *Detroit Free Press*, June 14, 1856.
9. *Detroit Free Press*, June 21, 1857.
10. *Detroit Free Press*, August 4, 1857.
11. Van Stan et al. arrested twenty-four: eight women and sixteen men. The *Free Press* listed the individuals by name and sentence. James Walker (ten days); Charles Henry (ten days); George Butler (ten days); John Thomas (sixty days); Henry Dudley (ten days); James Branly (ten days); John Davis (ten days); William Bowles (ten days); James Lacy (ten days); James White (ten days); Walter Scott (ten days); William Glaze (ten days); Samuel Martin (ten days); Martin Fisher (ten days); Samuel Morin (ten days); William Turner (twenty days). The house cook, Eliza Taylor, was released. The other women were apparently Turner's prostitutes, each of who received a sentence of ten to twenty days: Eliza Fisher (ten days); Elmira Williams (ten days); Polly Sowers (twenty days); Eliza Chambers (twenty days); Maggy Champagne (twenty days); Mary Luke (ten days); and Livinia Brown (ten days). *Detroit Free Press*, June 4, 1858.
12. A.E. Parkins, *The Historical Geography of Detroit* (Lansing: Michigan Historical Commission, 1918), pp. 315–319.
13. 1860 U.S. Census, Wayne County, Michigan, population schedule, Third Ward in city of Detroit, pp. 170–171, NARA microfilm publication M653, Roll 653.
14. For a thorough discussion of this case, see L.L. Valentine, "Sue Mundy of Kentucky," *The Register of the Kentucky Historical Society*, vol. 62, no. 3 (July 1964): 175–205.
15. Clarence M. Burton, ed., *The City of Detroit Michigan, 1701–1922, Volume 1* (Detroit: S.J. Clarke, 1922), p. 804.
16. Silas Farmer, *The History of Detroit and Michigan, or the Metropolis Illustrated* (Detroit: Silas Farmer & Co., 1884), p. 1096. Catlin names Scripps as the editor of the *Advertiser and Tribune* in 1863: "In 1862 he became the business manager of the consolidated *Advertiser and Tribune* and a year later the editor." George B. Catlin, *The Story of Detroit* (Detroit: Detroit News, 1923), p. 564.
17. Silas Farmer, *The History of Detroit and Michigan, or the Metropolis Illustrated* (Detroit: Silas Farmer & Co., 1884), p. 683. Farmer names Henry Barns as editor and Scripps as business manager.
18. *Detroit Free Press*, April 22, 1902.
19. *Detroit Free Press*, July 23, 1894.
20. *Detroit Free Press*, May 26, 1894.
21. *Detroit Free Press*, August 9, 1908.
22. *Detroit Times*, June 9, 1908.
23. For an in-depth discussion of the role of the *Free Press* in the riot, see Matthew Kundiger, "Racial Rhetoric: The *Detroit Free Press* and Its Part in the Detroit Race Riot of 1863," *Michigan Journal of History* (Winter 2006): 1–29.
24. An editorial published in the March 10, 1863, edition of the *Advertiser and Tribune* included excerpts from the *Free Press* as a basis for their argument that the riot was "a *Free Press* mob." The excerpts come from editorials published in the *Free Press* on December 2, 1862; January 1, 1863; January 4, 1863; January 14, 1863; February 1, 1863; and February 6, 1863.
25. *Detroit Free Press*, January 24, 1860.
26. *Detroit Free Press*, February 19, 1860.
27. *Detroit Free Press*, March 3, 1860.
28. *Detroit Free Press*, March 6, 1860.
29. *Detroit Free Press*, March 15, 1860.
30. *Detroit Free Press*, December 24, 1862.
31. *Detroit Free Press*, December 30, 1862.
32. *Detroit Free Press*, May 20, 1859.
33. *Detroit Free Press*, December 24, 1862.

Chapter 2

1. Johnston's Detroit City Directory for 1861 lists 28 deputies: Charles T. Allen, Isaac Austin, Israel J. Beniteau, Julius S. Blodget, Jacob B. Bromfield, John Buckley, Theodore L. Campau, William Champ, David M. Freeman, Frederick Freyburger, John Fuller, Peter Gadway, Archilaus Green, William P. Griffin, James A. Gunning, Louis Heidt, Warham P. Isham, A.S. Johnson, Joseph O'Connell, William P. Johnson, Thomas Joyce, Eli Ladaroot, Daniel Mahoney, Charles Meyers, C. Neidermuller, James Riley, Dennis K.

Sullivan, John Van Stan, and W.J. Wilkinson. In 1863, Van Stan was a lieutenant with the provost guards, and William Champ was the city fire marshal. *Johnston's Detroit City Directory and Advertising Gazetteer of Michigan*, 1861 (Detroit: James Dale Johnston & Company, 1861), p. 25.

2. *Advertiser and Tribune*, February 26, 1863 (afternoon edition).

3. *Advertiser and Tribune*, March 3, 1863 (afternoon edition).

4. *Detroit Sunday News-Tribune*, March 10, 1895. For a brief biographical sketch of Champ, see *Detroit Free Press*, July 28, 1867.

5. The *Advertiser and Tribune* published monthy lists of those incarcerated in the county jail, usually in the first few days of the new month. The list for February 1863, for example, appeared in the March 2, 1863, afternoon edition. No attribution is given for the information, but it most likely originated with turnkey Charles C. Bird.

6. These lists appeared in the *Detroit Free Press* at the beginning of each month and each year. The January 1, 1862, edition contains Bird's tally for the year 1861. The December 2, 1862, edition contains Bird's tally for November 1862. Of the sixty-two crimes enumerated, the three most common offenses were drunk and disorderly (thirteen), assault and battery (nine), and larceny (nine).

7. *Detroit Free Press*, January 1, 1862.

8. An article in the February 2, 1863, edition of the *Detroit Free Press* enumerated the crimes of the ninety-eight prisoners lodged in the jail throughout the month of January.

9. Brockway's obituary in the October 20, 1920, edition of the *Elmira* [New York] *Star Gazette* contains a biographical sketch.

10. F.X. Cicotte lived at 226 Beaubien. *Johnston's Detroit City Directory and Advertising Gazetteer of Michigan*, 1861 (Detroit: James Dale Johnston & Company, 1861), p. 103.

11. 1860 U.S. Census, Wayne County, Michigan, population schedule, Third Ward in city of Detroit, p. 138, dwelling 846, family 897, NARA microfilm publication M653, Roll 653.

12. Johnson's City Directory gives the address as 111 Griswold St. *Johnston's Detroit City Directory and Advertising Gazetteer of Michigan*, 1861 (Detroit: James Dale Johnston & Company, 1861), p. 27.

13. In some cases, such as the trial of the rioters (file #450), the recorder's court file contains what appears to be a transcript of testimony given in police court but none from the subsequent trial in recorder's court. Testimony in this case comes under the heading "Police Court March 29, 1863." *The People vs. Edward Crosby, William Naylor, Peter Doran, Charles Hall, Con Dwyer, John H. Davis, Antoine Downer, William Carlow, Andrew Manning, William Krueger, John Dollar, Timothy Drummond, Conrad Kalb, and William Crosby* in the Recorder's Court in and for the City of Detroit, County of Wayne, case file 450, Box 2, Record Group 2011-37, Archives of Michigan, Lansing.

14. Biographical information from Lane's obituary, published in the *Detroit Free Press*, February 24, 1875.

15. Robert B. Ross, *Early Bench and Bar of Detroit: From 1805 to the End of 1850* (Detroit: Richard P. Joy and Clarence M. Burton, 1907), pp. 237–238.

16. Ross, *Early Bench and Bar of Detroit*, pp. 69–70.

17. For a biographical sketch of J. Logan Chipman, see *Compendium of History and Biography of the City of Detroit and Wayne County, Michigan* (Chicago: Henry Taylor & Co., 1908), pp. 331–334.

18. Charles F. Clark, *Charles F. Clark's Annual Directory of the Inhabitants, Incorporated Companies, Business Firms, Etc., in the City of Detroit for 1862–'63* (Detroit: Charles F. Clark 1862), p. 5.

19. *Detroit Free Press*, June 30, 1863.

20. Testimony of Flora Bell, *The People v. Joshua Coon* in the Recorder's Court in and for the City of Detroit, County of Wayne City of Detroit, County of Wayne, case file 421, Box 2, Record Group 2011-37, Archives of Michigan, Lansing.

21. According to the 1860 Census, "Cath Hoffman" and a Black servant named Esther Johns lived with the Thedes. 1860 U.S. Census, Wayne County, Michigan, population schedule, Fourth Ward in city of Detroit, p. 48, dwelling 324, family 382, NARA microfilm publication M653, Roll 653.

22. Testimony of Dennis K. Sullivan, *The People v. Joshua Coon* in the Recorder's Court in and for the City of Detroit, County of Wayne, case file 421, Box 2, Record Group 2011-37, Archives of Michigan, Lansing.

23. Testimony of James Hepburn, *The People v. Joshua Coon*.

24. Testimony of John Starkweather and William Ball, *The People v. Joshua Coon*.

25. Testimony of Valentine Lee, *The People v. Joshua Coon*.

26. *Detroit Free Press*, January 30, 1863.

27. *Detroit Free Press*, June 29, 1861.

28. *Detroit Free Press*, February 13, 1863.

29. *Detroit Free Press*, February 13, 1863.

30. *Detroit Free Press*, February 19, 1863.

31. *Detroit Free Press*, May 31, 1863. The article notes that Anderson had been arrested four months earlier and had spent the interim in the county lock-up. That put his arrest in February, at or even before the raid on the Washington brothel. It is possible that the writer used the name "Kitty Briggs" to further vilify the Washington "amalgamation den."

32. *Detroit Free Press*, February 20, 1863. The article's ran under the subtitle "Arrest of Three White Women with their Negro Paramours," but this is an error and possibly and intentional one. The article names six people arrested. The three women included Mary Washington, Kitty Briggs, and Sophia Graham, but in the 1870 U.S. Census, both Martin and Mary (Harriet) Washington are given the "M" designation for "mulatto." The article describes Martin Washington as a "mulatto," which suggests that Harriet might have had a light complexion, which is supported by the writer's description of her as "fair-looking," and an interesting detail on the census record: the census taker added a loop to make the "W" into an "M" (the ink is darker suggesting a later alteration). It is possible that the writer characterized Harriet as a white woman to exaggerate the "amalgamation" angle of the story. Could this be what Benjamin Clark meant by the quizzical lines "So mixed are the folks now, we oft have to guess / Their hair is curl'd and their skins are so brown, If they're white in the country, they're niggers in town"? Could the "white in the country" remark be a reference to Mary Washington? If so, it was an apt comparison to Faulkner, who was depicted as a Black man based on his swarthy complexion, in part because it fit the narrative of a "horrible outrage" committed by a Black man on a white girl. Mary Washington was depicted as a white woman because it fit the amalgamation angle developed by the *Free Press* writer throughout the article sequence and was designed for maximum shock value by suggesting that Martin Washington was involved with a fifteen-year-old white girl. 1870 U.S. Census, Wayne County, Michigan, population schedule, Fourth Ward in the City of Detroit, p. 93, dwelling 666, family 782, NARA microfilm publication M653, Roll 653.

33. *Advertiser and Tribune*, February 24, 1863 (afternoon edition).

Chapter 3

1. *A Thrilling Narrative from the Lips of the Sufferers of the Late Detroit Riot, March 6, 1863, with the Hair Breadth Escapes of Men, Women and Children, and Destruction of Colored Men's Property, Not Less Than $15,000* (Detroit: Published by the Author, 1863), p. 2.

2. *Detroit Daily Post*, January 1, 1870. Reprinted in *The Colored People of Detroit: Their Trials, Persecutions and Escapes, Containing Sketches of the Riots of 1833, 1839, 1850 and 1863, with a Full Account of the Loss of Life and Burning of Negro Tenements in the Latter Year, and the Conviciton, Imprisonment and Release of William Faulkner, Together with Some Information Concerning the Concoction of the John Brown Raid* (Detroit: The Detroit Daily Post, 1870).

3. During a visit to the Archives of Michigan, the author cross-referenced docket entries by defendant name and number with each of the case files.

4. *Detroit Daily Post*, February 7, 1870. Reprinted in *The Colored People of Detroit*.

5. Contemporary sources disagree as to Faulkner's age. Newspaper accounts give his age as forty-five; the prison register gives his age as forty-two. (Michigan) State Prison Register, vol. 23, p. 20, Record Group 64-50, Archives of Michigan, Lansing. His *Free Press* obituary of 1877 states

his age as forty-nine, which would have made him around thirty-five in 1863, but this is almost certainly an error. *Detroit Free Press*, June 3, 1877.

6. A March 4, 1863, piece in the *Detroit Free Press* refers to Mary Brown as Mary Moore: "Yesterday afternoon the colored girl [Hoover] who was detained as witness in the Faulkner outrage made complaint before the Police Justice against the prisoner for the same crime as that alleged to have been committed in the case of Mary Moore."

7. 1860 U.S. Census, Wayne County, Michigan, population schedule, Fourth Ward in city of Detroit, p. 39, dwelling 253, family 314, NARA microfilm publication M653, Roll 563. In Johnston's city directory of 1861, Rosa Brown is described as "Rose Brown, widow of James, washwoman" and given an address of 198 Lafayette E. *Johnston's Detroit City Directory and Advertising Gazetteer of Michigan*, 1861 (Detroit: James Dale Johnston & Company, 1861), p. 125.

8. Later accounts insinuate that at least one of the girls may have been involved in prostitution. This version, albeit biased, hints that Hoover may have exchanged sexual favors for food. The version has Hoover forcing her companion into a compromising position, but it is possible that Brown may also have engaged in a trade of sexual favors for money or "luxuries." Faulkner's statement of twice ejecting Mary Brown from his saloon, as reported in the February 27, 1863, edition of the *Free Press*, begs the question, what would a ten-year-old-girl be doing in a saloon?

9. *Detroit Free Press*, February 27, 1863.

10. *Detroit Free Press*, August 9, 1908.

11. This statement insinuates that Faulkner was a pimp as well as a saloon owner.

12. "A few days since he was recognized, a warrant issued for his arrest, and on Wednesday [March 11, 1863] he was apprehended and placed in jail to await an examination, where he remains.... If guilty, his offence is scarcely less loathsome than that of the villain who is now expiating his crime in the State Prison." *Detroit Free Press*, March 14, 1863.

13. *Detroit Free Press*, February 27, 1863.

14. *Advertiser and Tribune*, February 27, 1863.

15. Recorder's Court clerk Francis N. Hughes referred to him as "John Schoff," but contemporary newspaper accounts spelled his name "Schaaf."

16. Testimony of Mary Smith, *The People v. John Schoff* in the Recorder's Court in and for the City of Detroit, County of Wayne, case file 417, Box 2, Record Group 2011-37, Archives of Michigan, Lansing.

17. Testimony of John Tisler, *The People v. John Schoff*.

18. *Detroit Free Press*, June 17, 1863. The trial began on March 3, but due to delays concluded four months later, in June 1863.

19. Their surname is spelled "Shaff" in the 1870 census. 1870 U.S. Census, Wayne County, Michigan, population schedule, 5th Ward, City of Ypsilanti, p. 19 [handwritten], dwelling 128, family 153, NARA microfilm publication M593, Roll 708.

20. The *Free Press* account is the only extent record of this exchange. In its 1870 summary of the case, the *Detroit Daily Post* noted, "She [Hoover] said, according to the *Free Press* of that date, that she was in the room all the time, and saw the outrage." *Detroit Daily Post*, January 1, 1870. Also, *The Colored People of Detorit*, p. 12.

21. The "Faulkner Outrage" article first appeared in the March 1, 1863, edition of *Detroit Free Press*. The article was republished in the March 2, 1863, edition.

22. *Detroit Free Press*, March 4, 1863.

Chapter 4

1. *Advertiser and Tribune*, March 9, 1863.

2. *Detroit Free Press*, March 6, 1863.

3. *Detroit Free Press*, March 6, 1863. The *Detroit Daily Post*'s 1870 summation of the Faulkner case contains the following description of this scene: "Women appeared at windows of some of the houses on the streets, and waved handkerchiefs, cheering the mob in its effort to kill the bleeding prisoner." The similarities in wording and phrasing between this and the *Free Press* description of the same moment indicates that the *Post* writer drew source material from the earlier *Free Press* account. *Detroit Daily Post*, January 1, 1870.

4. *Advertiser and Tribune*, March 6, 1863 (afternoon edition).

5. When the U.S. government passed

a conscription act during World War I, the *Free Press* published a history of military drafts in Detroit. The article provides numbers for the 1863 draft: twenty Michigan counties whose volunteers did not meet federal quotas were required to send an aggregate of 6,383. Of the 6,383 called, 1019 did not show. Six hundred draftees sent substitute, but of these, forty-three deserted before they reached the front lines. The article notes that most of the deserters were later caught "and six of them were shot." Exemptions further depleted the field. In the end, the 1863 draft produced 261 recruits, and only 128 of them saw combat. These numbers suggest that, at least in Michigan, the 1863 Conscription Act was a colossal failure. *Detroit Free Press*, June 18, 1917.

6. *Detroit Free Press*, March 5, 1863.

7. *Detroit Free Press*, March 6, 1863.

8. *Advertiser and Tribune*, March 9, 1863.

9. *Advertiser and Tribune*, March 6, 1863 (afternoon edition).

Chapter 5

1. *Detroit Free Press*, March 14, 1863.

2. A short article about these supposed warnings appeared in the *Advertiser and Tribune* of March 12 (afternoon edition). Neither the "city officials" nor the source of the quote are identified, but the vague references were enough for the editors to proclaim, "THAT THE LATE RIOT WAS PRECONCERTED there is ample proof."

3. Champ's report for the month of February 1863 appeared in the March 2, 1863, edition of the *Detroit Free Press*. In his entry for February 1, Champ noted, "Afternoon was windy and intensely cold. There were some eight or ten chimneys burned out, all of them very dirty." In a notice dated February 2, 1863, Champ warned Detroiters about unclean chimneys. "Chimney's must be swept and kept clean. A Chimney Sweep, appointed by the Council, will at all times be found at the City Hall, ready to attend to his duties." *Advertiser and Tribune*, March 6, 1863.

4. *Detroit Free Press*, March 6, 1863.

5. According to the *Advertiser and Tribune* of March 7, 1863 (afternoon edition), Pierce owned and operated a clothing store out of his residence located at 69 Lafayette Street. "His house was burned to ashes, and his stock entirely consumed, valued at about $500." This may have been in error. The same article described Solomon Houston as "the proprietor of the cooper shop" when in fact he was an employee of Whitney Reynolds. *A Thrilling Narrative* does not list Pierce as one of Reynolds' workers but quotes Pierce as saying, "I was at the cooper shop and when the mob attacked us."

6. William J. Simmons and Henry McNeal Turner *Men of Mark: Eminent, Progressive, and Rising* (Cleveland: G.M. Rewell and Company, 1887), pp. 685–689.

7. *Detroit Free Press*, March 7, 1863.

8. Henssler's obituary in the September 1, 1891, edition of the *Detroit Free Press* contains a quote from his son Edward, who described his father's condition as "bronchial trouble."

9. The *Free Press* articles detailing Faulkner's trial did not include specifics about Faulkner's remarks to the court. Since the court records are missing (and likely did not contain Faulkner's pleas to Witherell), the *Advertiser and Tribune* is the only extent source that mentions Faulkner's belief in a possible conspiracy. *Advertiser and Tribune*, March 7, 1863 (afternoon edition).

10. Quoted in the *Detroit Free Press*, March 9, 1863. According to the *Advertiser and Tribune*, before handing down a sentence Witherell responded to Faulkner's conspiracy theory. The reporter paraphrased the judge's remarks: "His Honor, the Judge, replied that if his [Faulkner's] statements were true, or had been established in evidence during the trial, this would have mitigated his case to some extent." *Advertiser and Tribune*, March 7, 1863 (afternoon edition).

Chapter 6

1. Phelps later explained that he visited the courthouse three times that day: twice in the morning and once around 2 p.m. After studying the crowd during his two morning visits, he surmised that they posed no threat to law and order. On his third visit, however, he believed that they would devolve into a mob that would

attempt to snatch Faulkner. After consulting with Cicotte and the J. Knox Gavin, he issued Order No. 1, a request for troops. The text of the order was published in the March 12, 1863, afternoon edition of the *Advertiser and Tribune*.

> ORDER NO. 1
> MAYOR'S OFFICE
> Detroit March 6, 1863.
>
> Lieut. Col. Smith, Military Commandant, Detroit:
>
> DEAR SIR—In accordance with the directions of the acting Sheriff of the county of Wayne, I am requested to furnish sufficient military force to preserve good order at the City Hall, where a large assemblage of persons are now congregated with the ostensible object of disregarding the authority of the civil officers of the city of Detroit and the county of Wayne.
>
> Yours respectfully,
> FRANCIS B. PHELPS
> Acting Mayor of the city of Detroit

2. *Advertiser and Tribune*, March 14, 1863. By the time the article appeared, the barracks housed a fourth group consisting of two hundred draftees and replacements.

3. The March 14, 1863, *Advertiser and Tribune* offered this parenthetical: ("we believe only ten minutes elapsed from the moment the order was received up to the time they were on the march").

4. Testifying at the inquest into the death of Charles Langer, saloon owner John O'Keefe said he arrived at the courthouse at approximately 2:30 p.m. and waited about half an hour before Faulkner emerged from the building, fixing the approximate time the procession left the courthouse at 3 p.m. *Advertiser and Tribune*, March 11, 1863. Although there may have been more than two deputies escorting Faulkner, the only two who testified at the coroner's inquest were Charles Allen and William Close. Sheriff Cicotte also testified.

5. Deputy sheriff William Close recalled this moment when he testified at the coroner's inquest into the death of Charles Langer. Quoted in the *Advertiser and Tribune*, March 11, 1863. Provost guard member John H. Palmer testified to hearing a nearly identical statement. "Van Stan said, 'Why in God's name don't you proceed with the prisoner.'" *Advertiser and Tribune*, March 13, 1863.

6. Quoted in the *Advertiser and Tribune*, March 12, 1863.

7. The soldier, writing under the pseudonym "BANKER," wrote a short article describing his ordeal and offering a reward of an "even interest" in his fife or half of month's rations in exchange for information leading to the identity of his assailant on Clinton Street. *Advertiser and Tribune*, March 14, 1863; March 17, 1863 (afternoon edition).

8. *A Thrilling Narrative*, pp. 3-4. Buckner did not name those whom he witnessed shot, but the *Detroit Daily Post*'s 1870 recap of the riot identified the victims: "Henry Hufnagle was shot through the thigh; Maurice [Morris] Horan through the jaw; Edward Crosby through the face; Wm. Berridge in the throat." The *Detroit Daily Post* article does not indicate when these injuries occurred, but Buckner's account indicates that Hufnagle, and possibly Horan and Berridge as well, were shot during the assault on Van Stan's troops. Crosby received his injury during the assault on Whitney Reynolds' cooperage. However, it is more likely that Buckner is confusing the tumult on Clinton Street with the siege of the cooperage and that Horan and Hufnagle received their wounds at the cooperage. The *Advertiser and Tribune* reported that Horan (whom they called Morris) was struck in the jaw by buckshot, which would have occurred when the occupants of Reynolds' residence attempted to defend themselves. Van Stan's soldiers would have used rifles, not shotguns. *Advertiser and Tribune*, March 11, 1863 (afternoon edition); *Detroit Daily Post*, January 1, 1870. Also, *The Colored People of Detroit*, p. 14.

9. *Advertiser and Tribune*, March 11, 1863.

10. Warmsley's testimony from the *Advertiser and Tribune*, March 11, 1863; King's from March 12, 1863.

11. Both Timm and Wilson testified at the coroner's inquest into the death of Charles Langer. Timm's and Wilson's testimony from *Advertiser and Tribune*, March 11, 1863.

12. *Advertiser and Tribune*, March 11, 1863.

13. *Advertiser and Tribune*, March 11, 1863.

14. Phelp's explanation was published alongside verbatim copies of the orders to various military units that he issued on March 6. It bears noting that when the *Advertiser and Tribune* published the orders in the March 12 edition, Phelps had been heavily criticized for his inability in stopping the riot and was in full defensive mode. In the same edition, the *Advertiser and Tribune* characterized Phelps as an ineffectual leader. "The Acting Mayor fussed about like a disturbed setting hen, and either did not know his duty, or dare not do it—and the rest of the 'city authorities' followed his shameful example." *Advertiser and Tribune*, March 12, 1863 (afternoon edition). In the next afternoon's edition, the editors accused Phelps of cowardice when they said he had "barricaded himself in his own house and threw out pickets." *Advertiser and Tribune*, March 13, 1863 (afternoon edition).

15. Testimony of Edwin Jerome and Edwin Jerome, Jr., *The People vs. Edward Crosby, William Naylor, Peter Doran, Charles Hall, Con Dwyer, John H. Davis, Antoine Downer, William Carlow, Andrew Manning, William Krueger, John Dollar, Timothy Drummond, Conrad Kalb, and William Crosby* in the Recorder's Court in and for the City of Detroit, County of Wayne, case file 450, Box 2, Record Group 2011–37, Archives of Michigan, Lansing.

16. Statement of Thomas Buckner quoted in *A Thrilling Narrative*, p. 4.

Chapter 7

1. Pages 2–13 of *A Thrilling Narrative* contains a series of eyewitness accounts that present an anecdotal chronicle of the riot. These accounts, which apparently emanate from interviews conducted by the unnamed author, lack any sort of timeline or progression, but when pieced together into a sequence, they provide a chilling recreation of the assault on Whitney Reynolds' cooperage. Statement of Thomas Buckner quoted in *A Thrilling Narrative*, p. 5.

2. *Advertiser and Tribune*, March 10, 1863.

3. Statement of Frederick Wilson quoted in *A Thrilling Narrative*, p. 9.

4. Statement of Frederick Wilson quoted in *A Thrilling Narrative*, p. 9.

5. Statement of Thomas Buckner quoted in *A Thrilling Narrative*, p. 5.

6. The 1860 federal census lists Parker Bonn's occupation as saloonkeeper. 1860 U.S. Census, Wayne County, Michigan, population schedule, Third Ward in City of Detroit, p. 175, dwelling 1061, family 1144, NARA microfilm publication M653, Roll 563.

7. Statement of Louisa Bonn quoted in *A Thrilling Narrative*, page 5.

8. *Advertiser and Tribune*, March 10, 1863.

9. The *Advertiser and Tribune* of March 7, 1863 (afternoon edition), described Edward Crosby as "fireman on the Central Rail Road," although the writer likely confused him with William Crosby, who is listed in the 1863 Detroit City Directory as "brakesman" who lived on "Paton's Alley." William Crosby was also arrested and later tried for rioting. The trial documents suggest that there was some confusion between the two Crosbys. Answering a question from Edward Crosby's lawyer, Dennis K. Sullivan testified, "[I] am positive that the [one] I saw was Edward Crosby. I think the looks of William Cosgrove are different from those of Edward Cosgrove." The clerk erred by substituting the surname "Crosby" with "Cosgrove." Clark, Charles F. *Charles F. Clark's Annual Directory of the Inhabitants, Incorporated Companies, Business Firms, Etc., of the City of Detroit for 1863–'4* (Detroit: C.F. Clark, 1863). Testimony of Dennis K. Sullivan, *The People vs. Charles Hall, William Naylor, Edward Crosby and John H. Davis*, in the Recorder's Court in and for the City of Detroit, County of Wayne, case file 452, Box 2, Record Group 2011–37, Archives of Michigan, Lansing.

10. Louisa Bonn recalled hearing this statement shouted as the rioters surrounded the Reynolds' residence. *A Thrilling Narrative*, p. 5.

11. At the coroner's inquest into the death of Joshua Boyd, Dennis K. Sullivan identified this rioter as Edward Crosby: "saw Edward Crosby when he was shot; Crosby had thrown two stones into the windows of the shop on the alley, and then ran around and kicked the front door open. He then went around on the vacant

lot east of the shop, and, picking up two stones, he was fired at from the shop, and was hit in the face, on the left cheek—apparently by a discharge from a shot gun." Quoted in the *Advertiser and Tribune*, March 13, 1863 (afternoon edition), and *A Thrilling Narrative*, p. 19. The *Advertiser and Tribune* of March 7, 1863 (afternoon edition), characterized Crosby's wound as minor. "Twenty-seven shot were taken from his back and shoulders, and six out of his cheek. Not badly hurt." The description indicates that Crosby may have attempted to turn from the window when shot.

12. Ada R. Smith, who knew Crosby and later testified against him, said Crosby "had a stick in his left hand—he drew the stick up as if [he] was going to strike into the window [of the house]." Testimony of Ada R. Smith, *The People vs. Charles Hall, William Naylor, Edward Crosby and John H. Davis*. Further substantiation that the correspondent confused Horan with Edward Crosby is a clue buried in the March 7 afternoon edition. The article stated that shot struck Horan in the cheek and left shoulder, which was an identical injury sustained by Edward Crosby. The paper admitted the error in the March 11 edition. *Detroit Advertiser and Tribune*, March 7, 11 (afternoon editions). The March 7, 1863, afternoon edition names another gunshot victim. "Passing by a house near the corner of Beaubien and East Fort, some person inside fired a shot gun into the crowd, and one of the shot took effect in the head of a boy named Michael Donohue, living on Prospect street." The gunshot may have emanated from Whitney Reynolds' residence, which lends credence to the idea that several shots were fired into the crowd and accidentally struck bystanders, or it may have come from Thomas Buckner, who testified to keeping rioters at bay with a shotgun. Buckner, however, did not say whether or not he fired the weapon.

13. Quoted in *A Thrilling Narrative*, p. 17.

14. Testimony of William Sullivan and John Venn, *The People vs. Edward Crosby, William Naylor, Peter Doran, Charles Hall, Con Dwyer, John H. Davis, Antoine Downer, William Carlow, Andrew Manning, William Krueger, John Dollar, Timothy Drummond, Conrad Kalb, and William Crosby*. Also quoted in *The Detroit Free Press*, March 23, 1863.

15. Statement of Louisa Bonn quoted in *A Thrilling Narrative*, p. 5.

16. Statement of Mrs. Reynolds quoted in *A Thrilling Narrative*, p. 6.

17. Statement of Mrs. Reynolds quoted in *A Thrilling Narrative*, p. 6.

18. *A Thrilling Narrative*, p. 3.

19. Jones' story is told in *A Thrilling Narrative*, p. 13.

20. Two shots were fired during the siege of the cooper shop: one fired from the shop, and the other, which wounded Edward Crosby, from the residence. It is unclear from Houston's statement to the *Thrilling Narrative* author which shot the crowd accused him of making.

21. Houston refers to Lansing Thayer as "Mr. Thairs" and "Mr. T." Statement of Solomon Houston quoted in *A Thrilling Narrative*, p. 7.

22. Testimony of Dennis K. Sullivan, *The People vs. Edward Crosby, William Naylor, Peter Doran, Charles Hall, Con Dwyer, John H. Davis, Antoine Downer, William Carlow, Andrew Manning, William Krueger, John Dollar, Timothy Drummond, Conrad Kalb, and William Crosby*.

23. *Detroit Free Press*, March 8, 1863. *A Thrilling Narrative*, p. 17.

24. Testimony of Ebenezer W. Cutler, *The People vs. Edward Crosby, William Naylor, Peter Doran, Charles Hall, Con Dwyer, John H. Davis, Antoine Downer, William Carlow, Andrew Manning, William Krueger, John Dollar, Timothy Drummond, Conrad Kalb, and William Crosby*.

25. *A Thrilling Narrative*, p. 4.

Chapter 8

1. *Detroit Free Press*, August 9, 1908.

2. Ingersoll's shop was located at 66 Fort Street. *Johnston's Detroit City Directory and Advertising Gazetteer of Michigan*, 1861 (Detroit: James Dale Johnston & Company, 1861), p. 193. The *Advertiser and Tribune*'s coverage of the riot in the March 9 edition contains a paragraph about Lydia Ingersoll's heroism, but the *Free Press* did not discuss it in any of their after-action reporting.

3. Statement of William Jones quoted in *A Thrilling Narrative*, p. 13.

4. *Advertiser and Tribune*, March 7, 1863 (afternoon edition), and March 9, 1863.

5. Addresses from Charles F. Clark, Charles F. Clark's *Annual Directory of the Inhabitants, Incorporated Companies, Business Firms, Etc., in the City of Detroit, for 1862–'63* (Detroit: Charles F. Clark, 1862).

6. Statement of Louis Houston quoted in *A Thrilling Narrative*, p. 8.

7. Statement of Lewis Pierce quoted in *A Thrilling Narrative*, p. 9.

8. Statement of Lewis Pierce quoted in *A Thrilling Narrative*, p. 9.

9. Statement of Louisa Bonn quoted in *A Thrilling Narrative*, p. 5.

10. Statement of Whitney Reynolds quoted in *A Thrilling Narrative*, p. 6.

11. *Detroit Free Press*, April 1, 1863.

12. Addresses from Charles F. Clark, Charles F. Clark's *Annual Directory of the Inhabitants, Incorporated Companies, and Business Firms, Etc., in the City of Detroit for 1862–'63* (Detroit: Charles F. Clark, 1862).

13. Romulus Morton resided at 156 East Lafayette. *Johnston's Detroit City Directory and Advertising Gazetteer of Michigan*, 1861 (Detroit: James Dale Johnston & Company, 1861), p. 232.

14. Statement of Thomas Holton quoted in *A Thrilling Narrative*, p. 11. According to Clark's city directory of 1862–63, Holton lived at 61 East Lafayette, but in *A Thrilling Narrative*, he states that he lived on Fort between Beaubien and St. Antoine. Charles F. Clark, Charles F. Clark's *Annual Directory of the Inhabitants, Incorporated Companies, and Business Firms, Etc., in the City of Detroit for 1862–'63* (Detroit: Charles F. Clark, 1862), p. 220.

15. Statement of Benjamin Singleton quoted in *A Thrilling Narrative*, p. 11. Singleton lived at 119 Beaubien. *Johnston's Detroit City Directory and Advertising Gazetteer of Michigan*, 1861 (Detroit: James Dale Johnston & Company, 1861), p. 272. Singleton probably knew Ellen Hoover personally. According to the 1850 census, he lived with Dennis Hoover, Hoover's wife Winey, and their four children: Eunice, Ann, Margaret, and John. Ellen had not yet been born, but it is likely that he kept in touch with the Hoover family. 1850 U.S. Census, Wayne County, Michigan, population schedule, city of Detroit, p. 150, dwelling 228, family 228, NARA microfilm publication M432, roll 365. Singleton is described as a thirty-eight-year-old cook.

16. Burley lived at 37 Lafayette Street. *A Thrilling Narrative*, p. 12.

17. *Advertiser and Tribune*, March 9, 1863.

18. Evans lived at 55 Fort Street. *Johnston's Detroit City Directory and Advertising Gazetteer of Michigan*, 1861 (Detroit: James Dale Johnston & Company, 1861), p. 157.

19. The incident is recalled in *A Thrilling Narrative*, p. 8.

20. Mary Mathews' story is told in *A Thrilling Narrative*, p. 11. Her residence was located at 65 East Lafayette. *Johnston's Detroit City Directory and Advertising Gazetteer of Michigan*, 1861 (Detroit: James Dale Johnston & Company, 1861), p. 223. Clark's city directory, however, indicates that a peddler named Samuel Mathews also lived at 65 East Lafayette. It remains unclear what relation, if any, Samuel had to Mary or Charles. Addresses from Charles F. Clark, Charles F. Clark's *Annual Directory of the Inhabitants, Incorporated Companies, Business Firms, Etc., in the City of Detroit, for 1862–'63* (Detroit: Charles F. Clark, 1862), p. 251.

21. *Advertiser and Tribune*, March 7, 1863 (afternoon edition), and March 9, 1863. It is possible that the "young colored woman" was Whitney Reynolds' daughter Louisa Bonn, who was nearly attacked by rioters when she attempted to flee the burning house. None of the eyewitness statements in the extant trial records or in *A Thrilling Narrative* indicate that Louisa's child was beaten, so the reporter's anecdote most likely refers to a separate incident. It is also possible that it is a sensationalized rendition of Louisa Bonn's experience, as a *Free Press* writer suggested.

22. *Detroit Free Press*, March 8, 1863.

23. *Detroit Free Press*, March 7, 1863; *Advertiser and Tribune*, March 10, 1863, and March 11, 1863. The *Advertiser and Tribune* refers to him a "Bryan Groghan," while the *Free Press* refers to him as "Bernard Groghan."

24. Whiting's fifteen minutes of fame came at the hands of an *Advertiser and Tribune* writer, who documented the moment

of heroism in the March 7, 1863, afternoon edition.

25. According to Clark's city guide of 1862-63, Gies lived at 95 Congress Street. Charles F. Clark, *Charles F. Clark's Annual Directory of the Inhabitants, Incorporated Companies, Business Firms, Etc., in the City of Detroit, for 1862-'63* (Detroit: Charles F. Clark, 1862).

26. *Detroit Free Press*, March 7, 1863. According to an item in the *Advertiser and Tribune* of March 7 (afternoon edition), strong winds caused the flames to spread to nearby structures, destroying several that belonged to a man named August Werner at approximately 9 p.m.

27. The *Advertiser and Tribune* placed the time at 10 p.m. The barn belonged to Charles P. Crosby, a thirty-one-year-old lawyer who lived in the Fourth Ward. 1860 U.S. Census, Wayne County, Michigan, population schedule, Fourth Ward in the City of Detroit, p. 107, Entry for Ch. P. Crosby, Dwelling 720, Family 879, NARA microfilm publication M653, Roll 653.

28. The *Advertiser and Tribune* of March 7, 1863 (afternoon edition), and March 9, 1863, published a list of the first group arrested in the dragnet under the headline "ARREST OF SOME OF THE RIOTERS." None of these names appear in the recorder's court docket for 1863, which indicates that none of them stood trial: Edward Allen, Isaac Baker, Calvin Barnes, D. Craig, James Cunningham, Patrick Gleason, John Hanford, Daniel Hickey, William Hickey, T.B. Hughes, Thomas Kilfoil, John Lawrence, B. McCra, William Mulholland, James Rood, Michael Ryan, George Ross, H.W. Shurtliff, John Stevenson, T. Warwick, Isaac Williams, Robert Wiston. Private Calvin Barnes was a soldier in the Company A of the provost guards. On March 10, 1863, the *Free Press* responded to the rival paper's mistaken assumption with a brief item titled "NO RIOTERS ARRESTED." The *Free Press* article describes the twenty-two as "stragglers" and notes that they were released the following morning.

Chapter 9

1. *Detroit Free Press*, March 10, 1863.
2. According to the prison register, Faulkner was 5'5", forty-two years old, and a native of North Carolina. (Michigan) State Prison Register, vol. 23, p. 20, Record Group 64-50, Archives of Michigan, Lansing. The register is the only known record documenting Faulkner's time in the state prison.
3. *Advertiser and Tribune*, March 7, 1863.
4. *Advertiser and Tribune*, March 9, 1863.
5. The fire marshal's report appeared in the March 31, 1863, afternoon edition of the *Advertiser and Tribune* and the April 1, 1863, edition of the *Free Press*.
6. *Advertiser and Tribune*, March 10, 1863. McCain's letter is a reiteration of a comment that appeared a few days earlier, in the March 7, 1863, edition: "Our Fire Department had arduous services to perform, and never was the value of the steamers more fully demonstrated. But the services of the hand engines should not be forgotten. Number nine, Peter Smith, Foreman, did noble service in preventing the spread of the fires across Brush street, between East Fort and Congress. Had it not been for the vigilance and hard work of this company the whole block on the South side of East Fort street between Brush and Beaubien, would have been destroyed." The newspaper emphasized that the Peter Smith from "number nine" was not the accused rioter. The geographic distribution of fire engines detailed in *Johnston's Detroit City Directory and Advertising Gazetteer of Michigan*, 1861 (Detroit: James Dale Johnston & Company, 1861), p. 245.
7. *Advertiser and Tribune*, March 10, 1863.
8. *Advertiser and Tribune*, March 9, 1863.
9. *Detroit Free Press*, March 8, 1863.
10. *Advertiser and Tribune*, March 9, 1863.
11. *Advertiser and Tribune*, March 9, 1863.
12. A four-man committee formed to gather donations for relief of the "sufferers by the riot." The *Advertiser and Tribune* of March 28, 1863 (afternoon edition), listed the donors: "Friends in Troy, Oakland County, $32.00; James F. Joy, $25; Mrs. Eliza E. Steward, $25; John Owen, $20; David Cooper, $20; Duncan Steward, $15; Chas. I Walker, $10; Walker &

Kent, $10; H. Hallock, $5; D.S. Walbridge, $5; Buhl & Ducharme, $5; F. Wetmore, $5; James & Son, $5; David Carter, $5; W.W. Hart, $5; Col. Joshua Howard, $5; Thos. W. Lockwood, $5; A.S. Fuller, $5; Mr. Austin, $3; C.P. Woodruff, $3; G.H. Shear, $2; Mr. Barns, $2; the Rev. J.M. Arnold, $1; A. McKay, $1; S.R. Mumbord, $1; F.M. Sumner, $1; A Friend, $140; Previously acknowledged, $290.25; Making [i]n all, $512.65."

13. *Advertiser and Tribune*, March 12, 1863 (afternoon edition).

14. The *Advertiser and Tribune* first addressed the rumor in the March 19, 1863, afternoon edition. The writer apparently repeated street gossip: "It has been hinted that these articles [bread and bacon] were not of the most palatable and wholesome character." The article ended with a caveat: "It is possible that injustice has been done to the acting Mayor in this matter, and if so, we shall take great pleasure in correcting any misapprehension that may have gone abroad." Phelps' letter to the *Free Press* was reprinted the next day, in the March 20, 1863, afternoon edition:

> Soon after the late riot, I gave notice that at my store I would distribute a quantity of bread and meat among the sufferers calling upon me for relief. In the interval above five barrels of meat and over a thousand pounds of bread have done to feed the hungry here and in Canada, and so far as I am aware expressions of kindness and gratitude have followed each donation.
>
> From rumor only, I learn that prejudiced parties are endeavoring to depreciate the quality of the subsistence furnished, and I therefore invite such of the public as are disposed to credit malicious representations, to call and examine what of the little stock is remaining uncalled for.
>
> Without money and without price I gave the mite I had to bestow, and only hope that all in proportion to their ability have already given or will contribute to relieve the necessities of the unfortunate ones, who in that unexpected moment became homeless, and dependent upon the cold charities of the world.
>
> Yours, respectfully,
> FRANCIS B. PHELPS

15. *Advertiser and Tribune*, March 7, 1863 (afternoon edition), and March 9, 1863.

16. Bloss worked for the American Seed Store and Nurseries, a Detroit-based agricultural wholesaler located at 24 Woodward Avenue. The company's advertisement in Johnston's Detroit City Directory of 1861 names Bloss the firm's "Genl Agent." Bloss was also the secretary of the Detroit City Temperance Society. *Johnston's Detroit City Directory and Advertising Gazetteer of Michigan*, 1861 (Detroit: James Dale Johnston & Company, 1861), pp. 42, 202 (advertisement).

17. *Advertiser and Tribune*, March 10, 1863.

18. Quoted in the *Advertiser and Tribune*, March 12, 1863.

19. *Detroit Free Press*, March 8, 1863.

20. *Detroit Free Press*, March 10, 1863.

21. *Detroit Free Press*, March 24, 1863. The incident took place on Sunday, March 8, and Bowers' trial on Monday, March 23.

22. *Advertiser and Tribune*, March 11, 1863. *Detroit Free Press*, March 11, 1863.

23. The report of the special police force was published in the March 10 edition of the *Advertiser and Tribune*. Two incidents in particular bear noting: "Officer Peter Smith reported that negroes on Kentucky street, about eight or twelve, are said to be armed with muskets. A file of soldiers were sent up by the Mayor to prevent any disturbance or outbreak." "Officer Lockwood reported that he saw a number of negroes on Indiana or Kentucky street, some 30 or 40 in all,—a majority of them armed with knives, shot guns, muskets, &c.—counseled them to keep within doors and not create any disturbance."

24. *Advertiser and Tribune*, March 13, 1863.

25. Quoted in the *Advertiser and Tribune*, March 9, 1863.

26. *Detroit Free Press*, March 7, 1863.

27. *Advertiser and Tribune*, March 9, 1863.

28. *Detroit Free Press*, March 8, 1863.

29. *Detroit Free Press*, March 8, 1863.

30. *Detroit Free Press*, March 8, 1863.

31. *Detroit Daily Post*, January 1, 1870; also, the *The Colored People of Detroit*, p. 15.

Chapter 10

1. The Rev. Hunting's sermon is excerpted in *A Thrilling Narrative* on p.

17 with attribution given to the *Advertiser and Tribune*. A later item published in the March 19, 1863, afternoon edition under the headline "The Protection for All Is the Only Security for Any" contains the verbatim text of a sermon Hunting gave a week later, on Sunday, March 15. This text was republished on pp. 21–25 of *A Thrilling Narrative* but without attribution to Hunting.

2. The *Advertiser and Tribune* of March 10, 1863, ran a short piece summarizing Hunting's sermon.

3. The *Free Press* article names him "Benjamin Franklin Huckley," but according to the 1870 Census, his surname was "Hawkley." 1870 U.S. Census, Wayne County, Michigan, population schedule, Fourth Ward in the City of Detroit, p. 42, dwelling 292, family 326, NARA microfilm publication M593, Roll 712.

4. *Detroit Free Press*, March 24, 1863.

5. *Advertiser and Tribune*, March 10, 1863.

6. *Advertiser and Tribune*, March 13, 1863. The committee voted to have the resolution published in the *Advertiser and Tribune*, which obliged by placing the story on the front page of the March 13, 1863, edition. The *Free Press* did not report on the meeting.

Chapter 11

1. The coroner's inquest into the death of Charles Langer covered in the *Advertiser and Tribune*, March 11–17, 1863, and the *Detroit Free Press*, March 9–16, 1863.

2. The *Detroit Free Press*, March 11, 1863; *Advertiser and Tribune*, March 12, 1863.

3. The Boyd inquest covered in the *Advertiser and Tribune*, March 14, 1863, as well as *A Thrilling Narrative*, pp. 19–20. The account presented in *A Thrilling Narrative* is a verbatim republication of the *Advertiser and Tribune* piece from March 14.

4. Quoted in *A Thrilling Narrative*, p. 7.

5. Quoted in the *Advertiser and Tribune*, March 12, 1863; also *A Thrilling Narrative*, p. 20.

6. Verdict quoted in the *Detroit Free Press*, March 24, 1863.

7. Articles in the *Advertiser and Tribune* about both inquests included a plea for people with pertinent information to come forward and testify. At least one of the witnesses in the Langer inquest (Henry Lewen, a German immigrant) had responded to the plea. "Witness saw notice in the *Michigan Journal* requesting all persons who knew of the affair to call and testify, that was the reason he offered himself," noted an *Advertiser and Tribune* correspondent. *Advertiser and Tribune*, March 17, 1863.

8. *Advertiser and Tribune*, March 13, 1863.

9. "Intemperance, while on duty, is hereby declared sufficient cause for dismissal, and this provision of the regulations will be rigidly enforced." The appointment was marked "Approved March 12, 1863." Quoted in the *Detroit Free Press*, March 13, 1863.

10. *Advertiser and Tribune*, March 17, 1863.

Chapter 12

1. *Advertiser and Tribune*, March 11, 1863.

2. *Detroit Free Press*, March 23, 1863.

3. Testimony of William Sullivan and John Venn, *The People vs. Edward Crosby, William Naylor, Peter Doran, Charles Hall, Con Dwyer, John H. Davis, Antoine Downer, William Carlow, Andrew Manning, William Krueger, John Dollar, Timothy Drummond, Conrad Kalb, and William Crosby*. Also quoted in *The Detroit Free Press*, March 23, 1863.

4. Testimony of Edwin Jerome and Edwin Jerome, Jr., *The People vs. Edward Crosby, William Naylor, Peter Doran, Charles Hall, Con Dwyer, John H. Davis, Antoine Downer, William Carlow, Andrew Manning, William Krueger, John Dollar, Timothy Drummond, Conrad Kalb, and William Crosby*. Also quoted in *The Detroit Free Press*, March 23, 1863. The wording of Jerome's statement as published in the *Free Press* is very similar to the statement recorded in the trial transcript.

5. Testimony of William M. Lyon, *The People vs. Edward Crosby, William Naylor, Peter Doran, Charles Hall, Con Dwyer, John H. Davis, Antoine Downer, William Carlow, Andrew Manning, William Krueger,

John Dollar, Timothy Drummond, Conrad Kalb, and William Crosby.

6. Testimony of Mary Jones, *The People vs. Edward Crosby, William Naylor, Peter Doran, Charles Hall, Con Dwyer, John H. Davis, Antoine Downer, William Carlow, Andrew Manning, William Krueger, John Dollar, Timothy Drummond, Conrad Kalb, and William Crosby.*

7. Testimony of Lorena Lang, *The People vs. Edward Crosby, William Naylor, Peter Doran, Charles Hall, Con Dwyer, John H. Davis, Antoine Downer, William Carlow, Andrew Manning, William Krueger, John Dollar, Timothy Drummond, Conrad Kalb, and William Crosby.*

8. Testimony of Robert Bennette, *The People vs. Edward Crosby, William Naylor, Peter Doran, Charles Hall, Con Dwyer, John H. Davis, Antoine Downer, William Carlow, Andrew Manning, William Krueger, John Dollar, Timothy Drummond, Conrad Kalb, and William Crosby.*

9. Testimony of Lewis Pierce, *The People vs. Edward Crosby, William Naylor, Peter Doran, Charles Hall, Con Dwyer, John H. Davis, Antoine Downer, William Carlow, Andrew Manning, William Krueger, John Dollar, Timothy Drummond, Conrad Kalb, and William Crosby.*

10. These details from the examination of the "rioters" appeared in the *Detroit Free Press*, March 24, 1863, and March 25, 1863. No official files or testimony of the examination are known to exist, however the testimony included in recorder's court case files 450 and 452 appears to have come from this earlier hearing. Some of the statements carry dates from late March, and a few contain notations such as "examination adjd to 21st inst at 9 am" and "examination resumed this morning, March 21st/63 at 10-35." If these statements are from the police court examinations, then there are no extent trial transcripts.

11. Testimony of Thomas Skillman, *The People vs. Edward Crosby, William Naylor, Peter Doran, Charles Hall, Con Dwyer, John H. Davis, Antoine Downer, William Carlow, Andrew Manning, William Krueger, John Dollar, Timothy Drummond, Conrad Kalb, and William Crosby.*

12. An item in the March 25, 1863, afternoon edition of the *Advertiser and Tribune* depicted Hanifan as more of a victim than a perpetrator. "Mr. Jeremiah Hannifan, who was arrested on a charge of participating in the riot, has been honorably discharged, no testimony appearing against him. Mr. H. is a working Republican and was a mere looker-on at the time of the riot. The only witness against him was a person of questionable reputation, who failed to identify him." The "only witness" was Lorena Long.

13. There are conflicting news reports about this incident. According to the *Free Press* of March 26, 1863, Groghan waived his right to an examination, was released on his own recognizance, and left the city. "Bernard Groghan," the writer noted, "also waived his right, and left on his own recognizance, without even consulting the court as to propriety of the proceeding." A follow-up piece about the examinations, published on March 27, states that Groghan "escaped by mingling in the crowd on Tuesday last, and, in a very unmannerly way, left without even bidding the Court adieu." Since Groghan stood accused of a violent offense, it is not likely that the court allowed him to simply leave.

14. *Detroit Free Press*, March 27, 1863.

15. Criminal cases that occurred within the city of Detroit were tried in recorder's court. Those from outside the city limits were tried in circuit court.

16. *Detroit Free Press*, March 28, 1863.

17. *Advertiser and Tribune*, March 30, 1863 (afternoon edition).

18. *Advertiser and Tribune*, March 19, 1863 (afternoon edition); *Detroit Free Press*, March 19, 1863.

Chapter 13

1. *Advertiser and Tribune*, March 9, 1863.

2. This comment was a direct reference to the February 27, 1863, article about the alleged crime. The article ran with the headline "A Serious Charge—a Negro Commits an Outrage upon a Little White Girl."

3. *Advertiser and Tribune*, March 7, 1863 (afternoon edition); the article was reprinted in the March 9, 1863, morning edition.

4. VINDEX claims that J. Logan Chipman was an editor of the *Free Press*, which put the lawyer in a strange position.

Chipman's politics were aligned with those of the *Free Press* editors, but whereas the newspaper condemned Faulkner, Chipman championed his innocence before, during and after the trial. It is interesting to note that the lawyer's father Henry operated an early Detroit newspaper, the *Herald*, which ran from 1824 to 1829. For a brief history of early Detroit newspapers, see Clarence Burton, *Early Detroit: A Sketch of Some of the Interesting Affairs of the Olden Time* (Detroit: Speaker-Hines Press, 1909), p. 49. VINDEX letter from *Advertiser and Tribune*, March 20, 1863.

5. The similarities in content and wording indicates that the VINDEX and UNION letters may have inked by the same pen, one conceivably owned by an *Advertiser and Tribune* editor, who used the letters as a gambit to disguise editorial. *Advertiser and Tribune*, March 28, 1863 (afternoon edition).

6. *Detroit Free Press*, March 10, 1863.

7. *Advertiser and Tribune*, March 11, 1863. The "elopement of a negro with a white woman" is a reference to an affair between a Black barber and the married wife of a soldier discussed in a page-one article in the February 21, 1863, edition of the *Free Press*.

8. *A Thrilling Narrative*, p. 2.

9. *Jackson Citizen Patriot*, March 11, 1863.

10. (Michigan) State Prison Register, vol. 23, p. 20, Record Group 64–50, Archives of Michigan, Lansing; "Thomas Faulkner" in the 1870 U.S. Census, Wayne County, Michigan, population schedule, 3rd Ward, City of Detroit, p. 18 [handwritten], dwelling 58, family 71, NARA microfilm publication M593, Roll 712; *Advertiser and Tribune*, June 7, 1877.

11. *Detroit Free Press*, March 19, 1863.

12. *Detroit Free Press*, March 14, 1863.

13. *Detroit Free Press*, May 8, 1863.

14. *Detroit Free Press*, August 25, 1863. "Mary Clark, white, James Shamburg, John Brown, Mary Jane Dorsey, Mary Brown, negroes, were each sent to the House of Corrections for a year."

15. *Advertiser and Tribune*, March 14, 1863 (afternoon edition).

16. *Advertiser and Tribune*, March 14, 1863 (afternoon edition).

17. Quoted in the *Advertiser and Tribune*, March 13, 1863 (afternoon edition).

Chapter 14

1. Women did not serve on juries until they obtained suffrage through the 19th Amendment in 1920. Even then, courts shied away from employing female jurors in cases (like murder) that would lead to lengthy court action and which would take them away from their domestic responsibilities for a protracted period of time. For a specific discussion of female jurors, see Tobin Buhk, *Wicked Women of Detroit* (Charleston, SC: The History Press, 2018).

2. *The People v. Francis Carr*, in the Recorder's Court in and for the City of Detroit, County of Wayne, April 9, 1863, case file 445, Box 2, Record Group 2011-37, Archives of Michigan, Lansing. *The People v. Michael Hider*, in the Recorder's Court in and for the City of Detroit, County of Wayne, April 9, 1863, case file 446, Box 2, Record Group 2011-37, Archives of Michigan, Lansing.

3. *Advertiser and Tribune*, March 28, 1863 (afternoon edition). The *Tribune* described Prusher's crime: "While the fires were raging in several parts of the city, she called small boys into a wretched looking saloon, which she kept, and hired them, for liquor, to purloin all the articles they could, and to incite others to engage in the same nefarious business."

4. *The People v. Catherine Prusher*, in the Recorder's Court in and for the City of Detroit, County of Wayne, April 9, 1863, case file 441, Box 2, Record Group 2011-37, Archives of Michigan, Lansing.

5. The trials occurred in the following sequence:

• Edward Crosby: Monday, April 13–Tuesday, April 14, 1863
• William Naylor, first trial: Tuesday, April 14–Wednesday, April 15, 1863.
• John H. Davis: Thursday, April 16, 1863.
• John "Conrad" Kalb: Thursday, April 16, 1863.
• William Naylor, second trial: Friday, April 17–Saturday, April 18, 1863.
• William Naylor, third trial: Monday, May 25–Tuesday, May 26, 1863.
• Charles Hall: Friday, October 9–Friday, October 10, 1863.

The details of these trials from *The People vs. Charles Hall, William Naylor,*

Edward Crosby and John H. Davis in the Recorder's Court in and for the City of Detroit, County of Wayne, case file 452, Box 2, Record Group 2011–37, Archives of Michigan, Lansing. Although the four defendants were tried separately, the files for all four trials are included in one folder: case file 452.

6. Testimony of Isaac W. Ingersoll, *The People vs. Charles Hall, William Naylor, Edward Crosby and John H. Davis.* The pages recording trial testimony are not presented in a question-and-answer format. Instead, they court recorder condensed the testimony into first-person narratives. Ingersoll's business advertisement in Johnston's Detroit city directory for 1861 locates his business at 66 and 68 Fort Street East. *Johnston's Detroit City Directory and Advertising Gazetteer for Michigan*, 1861 (Detroit: James Dale Johnston & Company, 1861), p. 170.

7. Testimony of Ada R. Smith, *The People vs. Charles Hall, William Naylor, Edward Crosby and John H. Davis.*

8. Testimony of Dennis K. Sullivan, *The People vs. Charles Hall, William Naylor, Edward Crosby and John H. Davis.*

9. Testimony of Thomas Skillman, *The People vs. Charles Hall, William Naylor, Edward Crosby and John H. Davis.*

10. Testimony of Margaret Skillman, *The People vs. Charles Hall, William Naylor, Edward Crosby and John H. Davis.*

11. Testimony of J.D. Weaver and David M. Freeman, *The People vs. Charles Hall, William Naylor, Edward Crosby and John H. Davis.*

12. Contemporary news accounts as well as the trial record refer to Kalb as "Conrad," but he informed the court that his name was in fact "John" Kalb. *The People v. Conrad Kalb*, in the Recorder's Court in and for the City of Detroit, County of Wayne, April 16, 1863, case file 453, Box 2, Record Group 2011–37, Archives of Michigan, Lansing.

13. *The People v. Conrad Kalb*, in the Recorder's Court in and for the City of Detroit, County of Wayne, April 16, 1863, case file 453, Box 2, Record Group 2011–37, Archives of Michigan, Lansing.

14. Quoted in the *Detroit Free Press*, May 7, 1863. "Brian Grogan" served in the 10th U.S. Infantry Regiment. When he wrote the letter (April 29, 1863), his regiment was stationed near Chancellorsville, Virginia.

15. Testimony of Ebenezer W. Cutler, *The People vs. Edward Crosby, William Naylor, Peter Doran, Charles Hall, Con Dwyer, John H. Davis, Antoine Downer, William Carlow, Andrew Manning, William Krueger, John Dollar, Timothy Drummond, Conrad Kalb, and William Crosby.*

16. Testimony of Dennis K. Sullivan, *The People vs. Edward Crosby, William Naylor, Peter Doran, Charles Hall, Con Dwyer, John H. Davis, Antoine Downer, William Carlow, Andrew Manning, William Krueger, John Dollar, Timothy Drummond, Conrad Kalb, and William Crosby.*

17. In the 1850 Federal Census, under the block titled "Whether deaf, dumb, blind, insane, idiotic, pauper, or convict," Timothy Drummond is given the notation "D & Dumb." Sometime between 1850 and 1860, the family relocated to Ypsilanti. 1850 U.S. Census, Wayne County, Michigan, population schedule, city of Detroit, p. 145, dwelling 167, family 167, NARA microfilm publication M432, roll 365. 1860 U.S. Census, Washtenaw County, Michigan, population schedule, Fifth Ward in city of Ypsilanti, p. 196, dwelling 1343, family 1345, NARA microfilm publication M653, Roll 563. Also, Testimony of Dennis K. Sullivan, *The People vs. Edward Crosby, William Naylor, Peter Doran, Charles Hall, Con Dwyer, John H. Davis, Antoine Downer, William Carlow, Andrew Manning, William Krueger, John Dollar, Timothy Drummond, Conrad Kalb, and William Crosby.*

18. Testimony of John J. Bagley, *The People vs. Edward Crosby, William Naylor, Peter Doran, Charles Hall, Con Dwyer, John H. Davis, Antoine Downer, William Carlow, Andrew Manning, William Krueger, John Dollar, Timothy Drummond, Conrad Kalb, and William Crosby.*

19. Testimony of David M. Freeman and Thomas Skillman, *The People vs. Edward Crosby, William Naylor, Peter Doran, Charles Hall, Con Dwyer, John H. Davis, Antoine Downer, William Carlow, Andrew Manning, William Krueger, John Dollar, Timothy Drummond, Conrad Kalb, and William Crosby.* Chipman apparently wanted to avoid confusion regarding the two Freemans; during Chipman's cross, the boy identified his father as Bolivar Freeman.

20. Testimony of Robert Burley and Charles Allen, *The People vs. Edward Crosby, William Naylor, Peter Doran, Charles Hall, Con Dwyer, John H. Davis, Antoine Downer, William Carlow, Andrew Manning, William Krueger, John Dollar, Timothy Drummond, Conrad Kalb, and William Crosby.*

21. The 1850 census records indicate that the Hall family were neighbors to the Dollar family. Later, Charles Hall and John Dollar would be co-defendants at the trial of the "rioters." 1850 U.S. Census, Wayne County, Michigan, population schedule, 27th district, city of Detroit, p. 40, dwelling 383, family 461, NARA microfilm publication M432, roll 365.

Chapter 15

1. Some of the riot refugees may have had little choice but to return. According to an article in the *Advertiser and Tribune*, Canadian authorities were not as welcoming as hoped. "Some of them, learning that the citizens of Detroit had made temporary provision for them, have ventured to return, and it is not improbable that nearly all of them will be compelled to do so, since there is no very friendly feeling among the Canadians towards them. Indeed, our neighbors at Windsor are beginning to suffer some of the inconveniences of their sympathy for the secession element of this State—men who ran away to escape the draft, as well as from the sudden influx of negroes, and we learn they are about to establish a rigid police system, to guard against depredations which are becoming somewhat frequent of late." *Advertiser and Tribune*, March 10, 1863.

2. *The Statistics of the Population of the United States, Ninth Census (June 1, 1870): Volume 1* (Washington, D.C.: Government Printing Office, 1872), p. 39.

3. *Detroit Free Press*, November 24, 1869.

4. "In politics [Lane was] a democrat," noted the author of a brief, biographical blurb about Minot T. Lane in *Early History of Michigan. Early History of Michigan with Biographies of State Officers, Members of Congress, Judges and Legislators* (Lansing: Thorp & Godfrey, State Printers and Binders, 1888), p. 406.

5. *Detroit Free Press*, March 25, 1869.

6. *Detroit Free Press*, March 31, 1863.

7. A *Detroit Free Press* article about the raids identifies the people arrested in both houses: Christine Vannattee, Kate Shaw, Mary Giatt, Susan Smith, and "the landlady" in Thede's house, and Mary Murphy, Alice Hubbard, Alice's husband Henry Hubbard, and Catherine Nichols in "Irish Lib's" house. *Detroit Free Press*, March 31, 1863.

8. *Advertiser and Tribune*, April 1, 1863 (afternoon edition).

9. Recorder's court in and for the City of Detroit, County of Wayne, docket book, p. 235; *The People vs. Mary McKenzie and Terry Clowden* in the Recorder's Court in and for the City of Detroit, County of Wayne, case file 464, Box 2, Record Group 2011-37, Archives of Michigan, Lansing; *The People vs. Christina Thede* in the Recorder's Court in and for the City of Detroit, County of Wayne, case file 465, Box 2, Record Group 2011-37, Archives of Michigan, Lansing. *Detroit Free Press*, December 29, 1863. The *Free Press* article detailing Thede's capture identifies Dennis K. Sullivan as the arresting officer.

10. Recorder's court in and for the City of Detroit, County of Wayne, docket book, p. 239; *The People vs. Adolphia Fields* in the Recorder's Court in and for the City of Detroit, County of Wayne, case file 473, Box 2, Record Group 2011-37, Archives of Michigan, Lansing; Recorder's court in and for the City of Detroit, County of Wayne, docket book, p. 236; *The People vs. Elisabeth Boyd* in the Recorder's Court in and for the City of Detroit, County of Wayne, case file 466, Box 2, Record Group 2011-37, Archives of Michigan, Lansing.

11. *Detroit Free Press*, February 25, 1863.

12. *Detroit Free Press*, March 31, 1863; recorder's court in and for the City of Detroit, County of Wayne, docket book, pg. 234; *The People vs. Martin Blank and Catherine Blank* in the Recorder's Court in and for the City of Detroit, County of Wayne, case file 462, Box 2, Record Group 2011-37, Archives of Michigan, Lansing. The Blank Dance House was raided in late February 1863. During the raid, a number of people in the establishment fled. Dennis K. Sullivan ran them to ground, prompting a short item in the February

24, afternoon edition of the *Advertiser and Tribune*. The arrestees were described as "disorderly persons" and "hard looking pets [who] deserve a little rough handling."

13. Her story is told on the front page of the June 4, 1863, edition of the *Detroit Free Press*.

14. 1860 U.S. Census, Wayne County, Michigan, population schedule, Sixth Ward in city of Detroit, p. 106, dwelling 777, family 836, NARA microfilm publication M653, Roll 653.

15. Testimony of Julia Davis, John Esser, James Love, and Catherine Fontaine, *The People vs. Mary Shepard* in the Recorder's Court in and for the City of Detroit, County of Wayne, case file 474, Box 2, Record Group 2011-37, Archives of Michigan, Lansing.

16. Clarence M. Burton, ed., *The City of Detroit Michigan, 1701-1922, Volume 1* (Detroit: S.J. Clarke, 1922), p. 406. Silas Farmer, *The History of Detroit and Michigan, or the Metropolis Illustrated* (Detroit, Silas Farmer & Co., 1884), pp. 204, 207. For a detailed history of law enforcement in Detroit, see Burton, pp. 405-410, or Farmer pp. 201-209.

17. Farmer, p. 207.

18. Burton, pp. 406-407.

19. Farmer, p. 207.

20. *Detroit Free Press*, March 14, 1863. "It will be recollected that, in the testimony of the girls Mary Brown and Harriet Hoover, in the case of Faulkner..." The 1860 U.S. Census gives her name as Ellen Hoover, the youngest child of Dennis Hoover, a barber who resided in Detroit's Third Ward. The "H" and the first "o" in the entry were run together, so the name appears to have been spelled "Hover." According to the census record, Ellen was seven years old on July 31, 1860, which made her about ten years old in March 1863 (with a birthdate in 1853). She was given an "m" designation for "mulatto." 1860 U.S. Census, Wayne County, Michigan, population schedule, Third Ward in city of Detroit, p. 158, dwelling 951, family 1034, NARA microfilm publication M653, Roll 563. In Johnston's city directory, Dennis Hoover is listed as a "colored" barber residing at 153 Beaubien. *Johnston's Detroit City Directory and Advertising Gazetteer of Michigan*, 1861 (Detroit: James Dale Johnston & Company, 1861), p. 190. Her death record from November 1874 gives her age as twenty-three, which would put her birth year sometime in 1851 (making her eleven or twelve in 1863). This is consistent with at least one newspaper article about the "Faulkner Outrage" (*Detroit Free Press*, March 4, 1863), which describes her as "a colored girl named Ellen Hoover, twelve years of age." Ellen Helmer, Entry 418, p. 219. Return of Deaths in the County of Wayne, 1874, Department of Vital Records, Lansing.

21. *Detroit Free Press*, March 19, 1863.

22. According to the prison register, the pair were admitted on May 21, 1863. Both were capable of reading and writing and given a "good" designation for health. They served their full sentence and were discharged on August 18, 1863. Detroit House of Correction, Inmate Register 1861-1870, p. 50, entries for May 21, 1863, Burton Historical Collection, Detroit Public Library.

23. *Detroit Free Press*, May 22, 1863.

24. *Detroit Free Press*, May 22, 1863.

25. *Detroit Free Press*, March 6, 1863.

26. *Detroit Free Press*, June 8, 1869.

27. According to the prison register, Mary Brown was fifteen years old upon admission on June 7, 1869. She served the entire sentence of three months and was discharged on September 7, 1869. Once again, she was classified as in "good" health. Detroit House of Correction, Inmate Register 1861-1870, p. 159, entry for June 7, 1869, Burton Historical Collection, Detroit Public Library.

28. *Detroit Free Press*, August 25, 1863.

29. 1860 U.S. Census, Wayne County, Michigan, population schedule, Fourth Ward in city of Detroit, p. 89, dwelling 598, family 726, NARA microfilm publication M653, Roll 563.

30. *Detroit Daily Post*, February 7, 1870. The *Post* ran two articles, one published on January 1, 1870, and chronicling incidents of racial unrest before 1863; the other, published on February 7, 1870, presenting an overview of the Faulkner case and the 1863 riot. These articles, which were probably inspired by Faulkner's December 1869 pardon, were later republished in a sixteen-page pamphlet titled *The Colored People of Detroit: Their Trials, Persecutions and Escapes* and distributed by the

Rev. William Douglas of the Independent Methodist Episcopal Church. The preface explains the purpose of the reprints: "The Narratives herein compiled appeared as original articles in THE DETROIT DAILY POST, of January 1 and February 7, 1870, respectively, and excited so much interest among all classes that their preservation in other form seemed desirable, especially to the race more immediately concerned, not only for the instruction of readers, but in 'vindication of the truth of history.'"

31. Testimony of Catherine Cramer, *The People vs. Mary Brown* in the Recorder's Court in and for the City of Detroit, County of Wayne, case file 1295. Record Group 2011-37, Archives of Michigan, Lansing. A brief item in the *Detroit Free Press* of December 9, 1869, notes that "the Jury failed to agree" in the trial of "Mary Brown, a young girl a who is accused of pickpocketing." There was a different Mary Brown who ended up in police court in November 1869—a Black woman caught up in a raid and sentenced to the House of Correction. See *Detroit Free Press* of November 24, 1869, for details.

32. *Detroit Free Press*, December 1, 1869. "AGAIN IN CUSTODY.—Mary Brown, the indirect cause of the negro riot in this city, was arrested yesterday on complaint of a lady named Kremer, who accuses her of picking her pocket at St. Mary's Church, last Saturday evening. The prisoner was committed to jail for examination on Saturday." This short news item positively establishes Brown as the defendant in recorder's court case 1295.

33. Testimony of Elizabeth Siegle, *The People vs. Mary Brown* in the Recorder's Court in and for the City of Detroit, County of Wayne, case file 1297, Record Group 2011-37, Archives of Michigan, Lansing.

34. *Detroit Free Press*, December 8, 1869.

35. The register records Mary Brown's height at four feet and weight at 80 pounds, which contradicts the description of her in the *Detroit Post*. Detroit Metropolitan Police, Register of Arrests, Volume 2 (1869-1875), p. 2, entry for December 28, 1869, Burton Historical Collection, Detroit Public Library.

36. In August 1870, eight months after Mary Brown's conviction, census takers visited the Detroit House of Correction and catalogued the "residents." Brown is listed as "Maria Brown" and described as a fifteen-year-old white female. 1870 U.S. Census, Wayne County, Michigan, population schedule, the 2nd Department, 6th Ward, City of Detroit, p. 180 [handwritten], entry 6, NARA microfilm publication M593, Roll 713. The prison register records the entrance of fifteen-year-old Mary Brown on December 28, 1869. Sentenced to two years and six months, she was discharged six months early for "Good Time," leaving the House of Correction for a third time February 21, 1872. Detroit House of Correction, Inmate Register 1861-1870, p. 182, entries for December 28, 1869, Burton Historical Collection, Detroit Public Library.

37. *Muskegon Chronicle*, January 5, 1870.

38. The marriage was witnessed by George W. Hoover and J. Washington. Marriage of Ellen Hoover to Fletcher Chase, November 8, 1865, vol. 11-12, p. 208, Marriage Records from the Archives of Wayne County, Michigan (12 volumes). Vital Records Project, 1936. Ellen Helmer, Entry 418, p. 219. Return of Deaths in the County of Wayne, 1874, Department of Vital Records, Lansing.

39. *The Detroit Daily Post*, January 1, 1870; also, *The Colored People of Detroit*, p. 15.

40. *Detroit Free Press*, August 9, 1908.

41. *Muskegon Chronicle*, January 5, 1870.

42. *Detroit Daily Post*, January 1, 1870. Also, *The Colored People of Detroit*, p. 13.

43. *Detroit Daily Post*, January 1, 1870. Also, *The Colored People of Detroit*, p. 12.

44. *Detroit Daily Post*, January 1, 1870. Also, *The Colored People of Detroit*, p. 13.

45. According to an article in the *Detroit Daily Post* published just after Faulkner's release, Governor Baldwin was moved by a letter from "a leading Democratic politician and lawyer in the western part of the State, who had been present at the conviction of Faulkner, and who referred incidentally to the case with similar strong expressions of confidence in his innocence." The article did not identify this individual by name. *Detroit Daily Post*, January 1, 1870; also, *The Colored People of Detroit*, p. 15.

46. The article ends with an allusion to the powerful allies from Detroit who lobbied for his release: "and those who aided

in his conviction, now that the passions of the hour are dead, sought his release." The unnamed journalist refers to him simply as "Faulkner" and does not mention a first name. *Jackson Citizen Patriot*, January 4, 1870. The *Detroit Advertiser and Tribune*, in a piece about Faulkner's release, names him "William." *Detroit Advertiser and Tribune*, January 6, 1870. Another piece about the riot, published seven years later, names him "Thomas."

47. The marriage record describes Thomas as a forty-five-year-old "African." Record for Thomas Faulkner and Arneta Thomas, no. 2834, November 24, 1870, Return of marriages in the County of Wayne, p. 365. Secretary of State, Department of Vital Records, Lansing; FHL microfilm 4208211.

48. *Detroit Free Press*, March 21, 1871.

49. *Detroit Advertiser and Tribune*, June 7, 1877; *Detroit Free Press*, June 3, 1877. Faulkner served just under seven years of his life sentence, not eight as the article erroneously stated.

50. The *Free Press* obituary stated Faulkner's age as forty-nine, but other documents (see note 10) support an earlier birth date of 1825. The prison register lists Faulkner's age as forty-two (in March 1863), which puts his birthdate even earlier, at 1821. (Michigan) State Prison Register, vol. 23, p. 20, Record Group 64–50, Archives of Michigan, Lansing.

Chapter 16

1. *Advertiser and Tribune*, March 12, 1863 (afternoon edition).
2. *Advertiser and Tribune*, March 7, 1863 (afternoon edition).
3. *Advertiser and Tribune*, March 7, 1863 (afternoon edition).
4. *Advertiser and Tribune*, March 7, 1863 (afternoon edition).
5. *Advertiser and Tribune*, March 10, 1863.
6. *Detroit Free Press*, March 10, 1863.
7. *Advertiser and Tribune*, March 12, 1863.
8. *Advertiser and Tribune*, March 7, 1863 (afternoon edition).
9. *Advertiser and Tribune*, March 10, 1863.
10. The new draft law set the minimum age of service at twenty, which caused one *Tribune* journalist to comment, "Establishing the age of those liable to service at 20, instead of 18, as in our old military laws, is considered a mistake in the new Conscription act. It will diminish very materially the number to be drafted from." *Advertiser and Tribune*, March 12, 1863 (afternoon edition).

11. *Advertiser and Tribune*, March 28, 1863 (afternoon edition).

12. *Advertiser and Tribune*, March 28, 1863 (afternoon edition); *Detroit Free Press*, April 10, 1863; *The People v. Catherine Prusher*; *The People v. Michael Hider*; *The People v. Francis Carr*.

13. The report noted that "Morris Horan, blacksmith, who keeps shop on the corner of Larned and Wayne, was shot from the inside of a house occupied by negroes, next to the cooper shop, on Beaubien street, near East Fort." *Advertiser and Tribune*, March 7, 1867.

14. *Advertiser and Tribune*, March 7, 1863 (afternoon edition).

15. *Advertiser and Tribune*, March 11, 1863 (afternoon edition).

16. *Advertiser and Tribune*, March 9, 1863.

17. *Advertiser and Tribune*, March 10, 1863.

18. *Advertiser and Tribune*, March 14, 1863.

19. *Detroit Free Press*, August 10, 1911.

Epilogue

1. A brief item in the November 13, 1874, edition of the *Detroit Free Press* carried news of Sullivan's appointment.

2. *Detroit Free Press*, January 16, 1883.

3. Sullivan's obituary appeared in *Detroit Free Press* on January 16, 1883. His death notice in the January 17 edition notes "heart disease" as Sullivan's cause of death; the 1884 "Return of Deaths" records his cause of death as "asthma." "Dennis K. Freeman," record no. 531, page 231, Wayne County Return of Deaths, August 30, 1884, Michigan Deaths, 1867–1897, Department of Vital Records, Lansing, Michigan.

4. *Detroit Free Press*, December 6, 1892. "David M. Freeman," record no. 1518, page 355, Wayne County Return of Deaths,

Michigan Deaths, 1867–1897, Department of Vital Records, Lansing, Michigan.

5. *Detroit Free Press*, July 28, 1867.

6. The *Detroit Free Press* of June 27, 1867, featured a lengthy obituary that included a biographical sketch.

7. *Detroit Free Press*, June 29, 1867.

8. *Detroit Free Press*, July 23, 1865. A biographical sketch can also be found in Robert B. Ross, *Early Bench and Bar of Detroit: From 1805 to the End of 1850* (Detroit: Winn and Hammond, 1907), pp. 69–70.

9. *Detroit Free Press*, August 17, 1893. Only the court of Justice Shellenberger remained open, the *Free Press* writer noted, because he "had a case on hand which would admit of no delay."

10. *Detroit Free Press*, September 1, 1891.

11. Lane's obituary appeared in the *Detroit Free Press*, February 24, 1875.

12. *Detroit Free Press*, July 7, 1866.

13. *Detroit Free Press*, December 24, 1867.

14. Section C, Lot 13, Grave 6.

15. William J. Simmons and Henry McNeal Turner, *Men of Mark: Eminent, Progressive, and Rising* (Cleveland: G.M. Rewell and Company, 1887), pp. 685–689.

16. A story about the incident appeared on the front page of the December 27, 1873, edition of the *Detroit Free Press*. Brief items documenting Drummond's trouble with the law in the *Free Press* of November 7, 1865; June 22, 1866; October 27, 1867; May 24, 1870; June 19, 1870; and November 26, 1870.

17. The [Detroit] *Evening News*, December 27, 1873.

18. Utley's obituaries did not mention his first career as a journalist. *Detroit Times*, February 16, 1917; *Detroit Free Press*, February 17, 1917.

19. *Detroit Free Press*, July 22, 1871.

Appendix 1

1. Sen. B. Clark, *The Past, Present, and Future in Prose and Poetry* (Toronto: Adams, Stevenson & Co., 1867). The book begins with "Autobiography" in which Clark discusses his background, followed by a series of short essays and a collection of poems.

2. Curiously, Clark misspells Faulkner's name.

Appendix 2

1. Detroit House of Correction, Inmate Register 1861–1870, Burton Historical Collection, Detroit Public Library, pp. 17–28, 50.

2. Quoted in Richard A. Bolt, "Juvenile Offenders in the City of Detroit," *Publications of the Michigan Political Science Association*, vol. 5, no. 1 (September 1902): 42.

3. Detroit House of Correction, Inmate Register 1861–1870, Burton Historical Collection, Detroit Public Library, p. 50, entry for May 21, 1863.

4. Detroit House of Correction, Inmate Register 1861–1870, Burton Historical Collection, Detroit Public Library, p. 18, entry for February 12, 1863.

5. Detroit House of Correction, Prisoner Records, 1871–1876, Burton Historical Collection, Detroit Public Library, p. 3, entry for "Ray Reuben" and "Mary Rose."

Bibliography

Newspapers

Detroit Advertiser and Tribune
Detroit Daily Post
Detroit Free Press
Detroit Sunday News-Tribune
Elmira [New York] *Star Gazette*
Jackson Citizen Patriot
Muskegon Chronicle

Documents

Detroit House of Correction, Index to Inmate Register 1861–1876, Burton Historical Collection, Detroit Public Library.
Detroit House of Correction, Inmate Register 1861–1870, Burton Historical Collection, Detroit Public Library.
Detroit House of Correction, Prisoner Records, 1871–1876, Burton Historical Collection, Detroit Public Library.
Detroit Metropolitan Police, Register of Arrests, Volume 1 (1866–1869), Burton Historical Collection, Detroit Public Library.
Detroit Metropolitan Police, Register of Arrests, Volume 2 (1869–1875), Burton Historical Collection, Detroit Public Library.
Federal Census, 1850, 1860, and 1870.
Index to Criminal Calendar, Recorder's Court in and for the City of Detroit, County of Wayne, Volume 1, Record Group 2011–37, Archives of Michigan, Lansing.
(Michigan) State Prison Register, vol. 23, p. 20, Record Group 64–50, Archives of Michigan, Lansing.
The People v. Catherine Prusher in the Recorder's Court in and for the City of Detroit, County of Wayne, April 9, 1863, case file 441, Box 2, Record Group 2011–37, Archives of Michigan, Lansing.
The People vs. Charles Hall, William Naylor, Edward Crosby and John H. Davis in the Recorder's Court in and for the City of Detroit, County of Wayne, case file 452, Box 2, Record Group 2011–37, Archives of Michigan, Lansing.
The People vs. Christina Thede in the Recorder's Court in and for the City of Detroit, County of Wayne, case file 465, Box 2, Record Group 2011–37, Archives of Michigan, Lansing.
The People v. Conrad Kalb in the Recorder's Court in and for the City of Detroit, County of Wayne, April 16, 1863, case file 453, Box 2, Record Group 2011–37, Archives of Michigan, Lansing.
The People vs. Edward Crosby, William Naylor, Peter Doran, Charles Hall, Con Dwyer, John H. Davis, Antoine Downer, William Carlow, Andrew Manning, William Krueger, John Dollar, Timothy Drummond, Conrad Kalb, and William Crosby in the Recorder's Court in and for the City of Detroit, County of Wayne, case file 450, Box 2, Record Group 2011–37, Archives of Michigan, Lansing.
The People v. Francis Carr in the Recorder's Court in and for the City of Detroit, County of Wayne, April 9, 1863, case file 445, Box 2, Record Group 2011–37, Archives of Michigan, Lansing.
The People v. John Schoff in the Recorder's Court in and for the City of Detroit, County of Wayne, case file 417, Box 2, Record Group 2011–37, Archives of Michigan, Lansing.

The People v. Joshua Coon in the Recorder's Court in and for the City of Detroit, County of Wayne, case file 421, Box 2, Record Group 2011-37, Archives of Michigan, Lansing.

The People vs. Mary Brown in the Recorder's Court in and for the City of Detroit, County of Wayne, case file 1295. Record Group 2011-37, Archives of Michigan, Lansing.

The People vs. Mary McKenzie and Terry Clowden in the Recorder's Court in and for the City of Detroit, County of Wayne, case file 464, Box 2, Record Group 2011-37, Archives of Michigan, Lansing.

The People v. Michael Hider in the Recorder's Court in and for the City of Detroit, County of Wayne, April 9, 1863, case file 446, Box 2, Record Group 2011-37, Archives of Michigan, Lansing.

The Statistics of the Population of the United States, Ninth Census (June 1, 1870): Volume 1. Washington, D.C.: Government Printing Office, 1872, p. 39.

A Thrilling Narrative from the Lips of the Sufferers of the Late Detroit Riot, March 6, 1863, with the Hair Breadth Escapes of Men, Women and Children, and Destruction of Colored Men's Property, Not Less Than $15,000. Detroit: Published by the Author, 1863.

Books and Articles

Anti-Negro Riots in the North, 1863. New York: Arno Press, 1969. (Note: This slim volume of 72 pages is divided into two portions. The first portion, which is dedicated to the Detroit riot of 1863, consists of a reprint of *A Thrilling Narrative*.)

Burton, Clarence M., ed. *The City of Detroit Michigan, 1701-1922, Volume 1.* Detroit: S.J. Clarke, 1922.

Catlin, George B. *The Story of Detroit.* Detroit: Detroit News, 1923.

Clark, Sen. B., *The Past, Present, and Future in Prose and Poetry.* Toronto: Adams, Stevenson & Co., 1867.

Clark, Charles F. *Charles F. Clark's Annual Directory of the Inhabitants, Incorporated Companies, Business Firms, Etc., in the City of Detroit for 1862-'63.* Detroit: Charles F. Clark, 1862.

Clark, Charles F. *Charles F. Clark's Annual Directory of the Inhabitants, Incorporated Companies, Business Firms, Etc., of the City of Detroit for 1863-'4.* Detroit: C.F. Clark, 1863.

The Colored People of Detroit: Their Trials, Persecutions and Escapes, Containing Sketches of the Riots of 1833, 1839, 1850 and 1863, with a Full Account of the Loss of Life and Burning of Negro Tenements in the Latter Year, and the Conviction, Imprisonment and Release of William Faulkner, Together with Some Information Concerning the Concoction of the John Brown Raid. Detroit: The Detroit Daily Post, 1870.

Compendium of History and Biography of the City of Detroit and Wayne County, Michigan. Chicago: Henry Taylor & Co., 1908.

Early History of Michigan with Biographies of State Officers, Members of Congress, Judges and Legislators. Lansing: Thorp & Godfrey, State Printers and Binders, 1888.

Farmer, Silas. *The History of Detroit and Michigan, or the Metropolis Illustrated.* Detroit: Silas Farmer & Co., 1884.

Johnston's Detroit City Directory and Advertising Gazetteer of Michigan, 1861. Detroit: James Dale Johnston & Company, 1861.

Kundiger, Matthew. "Racial Rhetoric: The Detroit Free Press and Its Part in the Detroit Race Riot of 1863." *Michigan Journal of History* (Winter 2006): 1–29.

Parkins, A.E. *The Historical Geography of Detroit.* Lansing: Michigan Historical Commission, 1918.

Ross, Robert B. *Early Bench and Bar of Detroit: from 1805 to the End of 1850.* Detroit: Richard P. Joy and Clarence M. Burton, 1907.

Schneider, John C. *Detroit and the Problem of Order, 1830–1880: A Geography of Crime, Riot, and Policing.* Lincoln: University of Nebraska Press, 1980.

Simmons, William J., and Henry McNeal Turner. *Men of Mark: Eminent, Progressive, and Rising.* Cleveland: G.M. Rewell, 1887.

Valentine, L.L. "Sue Mundy of Kentucky." *The Register of the Kentucky Historical Society*, vol. 62, no. 3 (July 1964): 175–205.

Index

Numbers in ***bold italics*** indicate pages with illustrations

Adler, L. 23
African Methodist Episcopal Church (A.M.E.) 106, 120, ***121***, 140, 145, 146, 148, 194, 225
Alder, John 153
Allen, Charles 96, 185
Anderson, Dewitt C. 57, 192, 240n31
Ann Arbor (Michigan) 127
Archives of Michigan 6
Atwater Street (Detroit) 20, 22, 36, 49
Auberry, Frank 100, 152

Babbitt, John E. 96, 98–99, 154
Backus, Charles Kellogg 27–28
Bagley, John J. 156–157, 184, 194
Baker, H.E. 27
Baldwin, Henry P., Michigan Governor 12, 202
Ball, William 51
Barns, Henry 26–27, 29, 134, 222, 224
Barns, Jacob 28–29, 134, 238n16
Barrett, Dr. Charles H. 71, 76–78, 87, 214
Bates, George C. 27
Beaubien Street (Detroit) 22, 24, 25, 31, 36, 39, 45, 49, 62, 86, 91, 93, 97–102, 103, 104, 113, 115, 118, 119, ***121***, 122, 123, 128, 129, 130, 152. 155, 156, 162, 175, 178, 179, 183, 185, 193
Beauties of Amalgamation 35
Beeson's store 147
Bell, C.M. 49
Bell, Flora 49–51
Belle Isle (Detroit) 218, 221
Bennette, Robert 104–105, 145–146, 150, 163, 209
Biddle House 145, 148; *see also* Taber, Augustus B.; Taber, Job
Bingham, Henry H. 202
Bingham, Kinsley S. 27

Bird, Charles 40, 42–43, 239n6
"Black Bottom" 217
Blackburn, Rutha 15–18
Blackburn, Thornton 15–18
Blank, Catherine 192
Blank, Martin 192
Blodget, Julius 36, ***38***
Bloss, J.B. 107, 109, 130, 137, 147–148, 162, 165–166
Bonn, Louisa 10, 103–104, 106–108, ***110***, 116–117, 122, 246n21
Bonn, Parker 10, 103, 106–107, 117
Bowers, John 140
Boyd, Elizabeth 192
Boyd, Joshua 10, 11, 86, 93, 104, 108–110, 115, 130, 143, 145, 150, 162, 183–184, 210; inquest into the death of 155–158
Bradley, Cordelia 34–35
Briggs, Kitty 32, 56
Brockway, Elizabeth 45
Brockway, Zebulon Reed 44, 51, ***54***
Bromley, William 90
Brown, Flora 50
Brown, Henson 114, 118
Brown, Mary 9, 12, 170–171, 200, 228, 231, 241n6, 241n8, 254n27, 255n31, 255n32, 255n36; crimes after Faulkner trial 195–199; "Faulkner Outrage" 62–67, 70–73, 212–216; Faulkner trial 76–77, 84–85, 87–90
Brown, Mary (from the Fourth Ward) 198
Brown, Rosa 9, 62, 65–66, 71, 76–78, 198, 214, 241n7
"Brudder Green" 52
Brundage, Flora 50
Brundage, Frank 50
Brush Street (Detroit) 25, ***121***, 123, 129, 130, 193

261

262 Index

Buckner, Thomas 10, 98, 101, 102–103, *121*, 245*n*12
Buffalo [New York] *Express* 175
Burke, Edmund 236
Burke, Mag 32
Burley, Robert 119, 185
Burns, John 115, 118
Burton, Clarence 194
"The Bush" 31, 33

Calhoun, Dr. 107
Calhoun Street (Detroit) 203
Camp Hall, Virginia 181
(Joseph) Campau Avenue (Detroit) 91, 95
Campbell, Sarah 53, 231
Campus Martius *22*
Carey, Robert 9, 102, 161–162, 164
Carleton, William M. 27
Carlow, John 185
Carlow, William 9, 119, 161, 163, 183, 185–186
Carr, Francis 9, 11, 12, 161, 164, 176–177, 207
Catherine Street (Detroit) 57, 58, 192
Catlin, George 27
Central Market (Detroit) 203
Champ, William, Fire Marshal 8, 11, 37, 85, 91, 111, 118, *121*, 131–132, 147, 160, 209–210, 219
Champagne, Margaret 53, 231
Chandler, Zachariah 27, 30
Chase, Supply Pastor 200
Chicago Tribune 175
Chipman, Henry 48
Chipman, John Logan 8, 11, 47–48, *49*, 67, 70, 76–78, 84–87, 89–90, 161, 169, 178, 201, 220
Cicotte, Francis X. (Wayne County, Michigan, sheriff) 2, 8, 44, 76, 84–85, 87–89, 95–96, 169, 203, 220
Cincinnati Commercial 211
Clapp, Mary 40
Clark, Ann 116–117
Clark, Benjamin Cutler, Sr. 4, 15, 61, 75, 95, 102, 113, 127, 145, 150, 160, 167, 171, 176, 189, 204, 225, 240*n*32; *see also* "The Riot"
Clark, Charles 48
Clark, Fr. Ephraim ("The Prophet") 10, 23, 105, 111, 114–115, 120, 143, 145, 183
Clark, Michael 116
Clark, Phoebe 48
Clinton Street (Detroit) 22, *24*, 39, 53, 55, 91, 95, 97–100, 152, 153, 154
Close, William 96, 98–100, 152, 243*n*5

Colored Vigilance Committee of Detroit 18
Condon, George 118
Congress Street (Detroit) 20, 123, 128, 130, 195
Conover, James F. 27
Conrad, Joe 223
Conscription Act 1, 2, 80, *82*, 83, 207, 242*n*5, 256*n*10; *see also* 1863 Enrollment Act
Coon, Joshua 36, 49–52
Copperheads 1, 85, 169, 175
Coquilliard, Thomas 15, 17
Cornwell, Van Cleve & Barnes 67
Cox, Thomas 23
Cramer, Catherine 198
Croghan, Street (Detroit) 19, 62, 93, 98, 116, *121*, 128, 140, 156, 173
Crosby, Edward 9, 11, 12, 105, 109, 156, 161, 163, 178–180, 183–184, 186, 208, 244*n*9, 244–245*n*11
Crosby, William 9, 164, 183, 244*n*9
Cutler, Ebenezer 93, 112, 182–183

Dale, David 86
Dale, Marcus 10, 86, 104–105, 112, 117, 209, 222, 224
Dale, Mary 104, 106, 108
Dale, Synthia 86
Daly, J.W. (coroner) 150, 158
Darrow, Clarence 217
Davis, Jefferson 172
Davis, John H. 9, 11, 104–105, 119, 161, 163, 178, 180, 183, 209–210
Davis, Julia 24, 193–194
De Baptiste, George 174
[Detroit] *Democratic Free Press and Daily Intelligencer* 28
Democratic Party 28, 144, 171, 190
Dequindre Street (Detroit) 37
Detroit Advertiser 27
Detroit Advertiser and Tribune 5, 7, 25, 26–29, 31, 34, 37, 39, 51, 57, 58, 66, 70, 73, 75, 104, 128, 134–135, 147, 158–159, 160, 165, 174–175, 177, 191, 200, 201, 203–209, 216, 221, 224, 233; Conscription Act 82–83; coverage of riot 105, *110*, 114, 122, 124, 130, 136–137, 143; death of Joshua Boyd 155; Detroit Fire Department 131–132; "Faulkner Outrage" 213, 215; Faulkner trial 80, 90, 213; *Free Press* coverage of the riot 141–143, 211–212; William Faulkner's race 168–172
Detroit & Milwaukee Railway 20, 21, 49
Detroit Anti-Slavery Society 18
Detroit Central Police Station 223

Index

Detroit City Hall 77, 80, 91, 134, 140
Detroit City Provost Guard 91
Detroit Daily Post 17, 61–62, 144, 198, 200, 201–202, 254n30
Detroit Democratic Association 76
Detroit Evening Post 15
Detroit Free Democrat 27
Detroit Free Press 5, 7, 19, 20, 25, *26*, 27–29, 39, 40, 43, 47, 48, 49, 51, 52, 53, 56, 58, 100, 127–128, 135, 146, 158, 161, 164, 174–175, 181, 192, 200, 202, 203–204, 206, 219, 220, 223, 224; *Advertiser and Tribune*'s coverage of the riot 143; "amalgamation dens" 31–35; Conscription Act 80–82; death of Joshua Boyd 155; Detroit Fire Department 130–132; 1863 riot *110*, 111–112, 113, 122, 129, 140, 142; "Faulkner Outrage" 62–66, 70–73, 167, 201, 212–217; Faulkner trial 75–79, 82, 87–88, 136, 139; Mary Brown's reputation 195–199; racially inflammatory reporting 29–31, 137, 139, 148, 189–191; Republican Party 138; Schaaf seduction case 69; William Faulkner's race 167–169, 172–173; Wineman rape case 70
Detroit House of Correction 12, 24, 36, *44*, 45, 46, *54*, 56, 174, 177, 181, 186, 196, 197, 198, 199, 208, 219, 223; juvenile inmates 228–232
Detroit Metropolitan Police *38*, 194
Detroit River 16, 21, 37, 191
Detroit Times 28
Detroit Tribune 27
Division Street (Detroit) 97
Dollar, John 116, 183
Doran, Peter 9, 91, 97, 161, 163, 179, 183, 185–186, 207, 228
Dorsey, Mary J. 56
Douglass, Frederick 31
Downer, Antoine 9, 109, 112, 161, 163, 182–183
Drummond, Abigail 184
Drummond, Timothy 9, 102, 109, 161–162, 183–185, 223–224
Duffield, the Rev. George D.D. 134
Dwyer, Cornelius (Con) 9, 102, 161–162, 182

1863 Enrollment Act *82*, 83; see *also* Conscription Act
8th Michigan Cavalry 95, 154
Emancipation Proclamation 28, 138
Engels, Mary 223
Esser, John 2, 79, 193
Evans, Richard 122, 177
Evening News (Detroit) 224

Farmer, Silas *22*, 26, *92*, 133, 194; *see also Guide Map to the City of Detroit*)
Faulkner, Charles James 169, *170*
Faulkner, William 1–2, 9, 11, 12, 15, 19, 83, 92–93, 97, 99–101, 127–128, 133, 142, 147, 153–154, 162, 182, 196, 197–199, 211, 216, 221, 222, 240n5, 242n10, 247n2; "Faulkner Outrage" 2, 6, 61–67, 70–73, 95, 195, 201, 213–215; trial 75–80, 84–90, 139; uncertainty about his race 167–172
Fenn, John 2, 79
Fields, Adolpha 192
Fifth Ward (Detroit) 37
Fire Department (Detroit) 131, 136
firefighters 130
1st Michigan Infantry 1
1st US Colored Infantry 222, 224
First Ward (Detroit) 62, 124, 142
Flanigan, Mark 39
Fletcher, Charles 119, 143, 145, 150
Fontaine, Catherine 193
Fontaine, Louis 193
Ford, Henry 217
Fort Street (Detroit) 93, 103, 113, 119, *121*, 122, 123, 129, 130, 156, 175, 179
Fort Wayne military barracks (Detroit) 25, 80, 89, 93, 101
14th Michigan Infantry 221
4th Michigan Infantry 153
Fourth Ward (Detroit) 19, 23, 80, 96, 124, 140, 161, 191, 198
Fox, Josephine 33
Fox, Col. Dorus M. 124
Fox, William (pseudonym for William Faulkner) 66–67
Fralick, Mary 39, 43
Fralick, Peter (Wayne County, Michigan, sheriff) 8, 36, 39, 43, 46, *54*, 55, 85, 140, 202–203, 220
Franklin, Benjamin 129, 236
Franklin Street (Detroit) 20, 178, 191
Fredericksburg 1
Freeman, Bolivar 185
Freeman, David M. 8, 36, 85, 110, 124, 156–157, 179, 182, 185, 219
Freeman, David M. (son of Bolivar) 185
Freesee, Henry 103
French, Caroline 16
French, George 16
French, Julia Ann 172–173
Friend, Earnest 180
Frost, Milton 114
Fugitive Slave Act 18

Gallipolis, Ohio 86
Gavin, James Knox 9, 11, 47–49, 51,

67, 70–71, 76–78, 85, 88, 132, 134, 161, 164, 177, 179, 183–184, 194, 202–203, 209–210, 220
German Congregational Church 79
Gibson, William 103
Gies, Frederick 123, 130, 163
Gies Alley 93, *121*, 129
Gies wood yard, 185
Goodell, Lemuel 16–17
Gorten, Dr. John C. 62, 157, 162
Graham, Sophia 57
Grand River Street (Detroit) 86, 141
Gratiot Street (Detroit) 22, 37, 39, 45, 52, 86, 91, 97–98, 130
Greeley, Horace 172
Gries, Mary Ann 69–70
Griffin, Ellen 32
Griswold Street (Detroit) 90, 129
Groghan, Brian (Bernard) 10, 11, 96, 101, 123, 161, 163–164, 181–183, 222–223, 246n23, 250n13
Guide Map to the City of Detroit 22, 25, 92, 133; *see also* Farmer, Silas
Gunning, James 36, *38*
Gunning and Blodget Detroit General Detective Police & Collections Agency 36, *38*

Hall, Charles 10, 11, 12, 119, 161, 163, 178–180, 183, 186
"Hamtramck" 47
Hanifan, Jerry 10, 161, 163–164, 250n12
Harberd, Edward 117
Harper's Weekly 111
Hastings Street (Detroit) 31–32, 52, 94, 123, 129
Hawkley, Benjamin Franklin 146
Hebden, George 153
Henry (fugitive slave from St. Louis) 18
Henssler, Augustus W. 76, 87, 220–221
Hepburn, James 2, 50, 79
Herald, Matilda *54*
Hider (Heider), Michael 10, 11, 12, 161, 164, 176–177, 207–208
Higgins, Sarah 24, 192
Hill, Louis 34
Hoffman, Kate 49–51
Holton, Thomas 119, *121*
Hommel, Jacob 98
Hommel, Jane 98, 152–153
Hoover, Dennis 62
Hoover, Ellen 9, 12, 62–63, 66, 71–73, 76, 78, 84, 87–89, 195–199, 241n8, 246n15, 254n20
Hoover, Whiney 86–87
Horan, Morris 105, 208–209

House of Corrections for Juvenile Offenders (Lansing, Michigan) 228
House of Shelter (Detroit) 229
Houston, Louis 10, 86, 104, 109–110, 115–116, 145, 150, 156
Houston, Sally 222
Houston, Solomon 10, 86, 104, 108–109, 114, 150, 175, 180–181, 210, 222
Hughes, Francis 184
Hunting, the Rev. Sylan S. 106, 145–146; sermon of March 15, 1863 233–235

Independent Order of Odd Fellows 221
Ingersoll, Isaac 108, 113, 114, 178
Ingersoll, Lydia 114

Jackson, Thomas "Stonewall" 169
Jackson Citizen Patriot 172, 202, 205
Jacob, Moses 190
Jefferson Avenue (Detroit) 20, *38*, 146
Jenney, J.A. *196*
Jerome, Edwin 101, 162
Jerome, Edwin, Jr. 101, 162
John R. Street (Detroit) 93, 123, 129, 142
Johnson, Lucretia 56
Jones, James 74
Jones, Mary 122
Jones, William 104, 108, 113–114
Jones, William (city scavenger) 116
Joy, James F. 134
Judson, Sarah 35
"JUSTICE" 130

Kalb, John "Conrad" 10, 11, 109, 161, 164, 180–182, 210, 252n12
Kendall, David 147
Kentucky 106
Kentucky Street (Detroit) 141
King, John L. 98–99, 152
Knights of the Golden Circle 1
Krueger, William 93, 96, 101, 109–110, 115, 161–162, 183–184

L. Black & Co. *44*, 45
"Lafayette" Steam Fire Engine No. 1 *133*
Lafayette Street (Detroit) 93, 103, 109, 114–116, 118, *121*, 122, 123, 129, 148, 179, 185
Lafayette Street Unitarian Church 106, 145, 183
Lane, George 221
Lane, Justice Minot T. 9, 12, 45, 52, 56, 63, 70–72, 103, 161, 164, 173, 181, 190–191, 195, 197, 213, 221, 231
Lang, Lorena 76
Langer, Charles 11, 91, 93, 99–100; inquest 150–154, 157–158

Index

Larned Street (Detroit) 94, 123, 129, **133**, 135
Lawrence, Charles 19–20
Lee, Valentine 51
Lefevre, Alexander 10, 104–105, 161, 163–164
Lefevre, Peter Paul Bishop 115, 155
Leslie's Illustrated **151**
Levy, Leopold 118
Lewis, Rube 190
Light Guard 124
Lightfoot, Madison 16
Lightfoot, Tabitha 16
Lincoln, Abraham 27–28, 30
Lodi Academy 47
Louisville, Kentucky 17
Louisville [Kentucky] *Daily Journal* 25
Love, James 193
Lyon, William M. 162

Macomb County (Michigan) 46
Macomb Street (Detroit) 53, 55, 192
Manning, Andrew 10, 106, 161–162, 182
Mathews, Charles **121**, 122
Mathews, Mary **121**, 122
McCain, Hiram 130
McCarthy, Justice Timothy 150, 153, 158, 221
McGuire, Jim 223–224
McHugh, Andrew 118
McKenzie, Mary 191–192
McMillan, James **54**
Mechanic's Hall 45
Methodist Episcopal Church 222
Metropolitan Police Act of 1865 12, 194
Metropolitan Police Register of Arrests 199
Miami Avenue (Detroit) 93, 123, 129, 142
Michigan Avenue (Detroit) 61–62, 90
Michigan Central Depot 89
Michigan State Legislature 12
Michigan State Prison at Jackson 2, 89, 127
Miller, Catherine 49
Miller, J.B. **38**
Miller, John 10, 161, 163
Miller, Kate 51
"Milwaukee Exchange" 36, 49–51
Mix, Elisha 96
Monroe, Andrew 153
Monroe Avenue (Detroit) 79, 91, 97
Montreal Mining Company 48
Moore, Mary 62
Morton, Romulus 118, **121**
Mullet Street (Detroit) 117
Mundy, Sue 25

Naggs, Bridget 37
Naylor (Nailor), William 10, 11, 12, 105, 119, 161, 178–180, 183
Neil, Sabrina 45
New York Draft Riot **151**
New York Illustrated News **110**
New York State Reformatory 44
New York Tribune 172
"Nigger Joe" 35
19th Michigan Infantry 93
Ninth Army Corps 181
North Carolina 86, 221–222
Nutting, Prof. Rufus 47

Oakland County (Michigan) 86
Oakley, Thomas 123
Oberlin College 86
"An Observer" 131
Ohio (steamship) 16
O'Keefe, John 243*n*4
Orleans Street (Detroit) 20

Palmer, John 154
Past, Present, and Future in Prose and Poetry 225
Paton Alley (Paton Street, Detroit) **24**, 25, **26**, 93, 118, 189
Pennell, Alson 51
People (of the State of Michigan) *v. William Faulkner* 2, 6, 87
Perkins, John W. 91, 97
Phelps, Francis B. 95, 100–101, 124, 128, 135, 137, 141–142, 206, 220, 242, 242*n*1, 244*n*14, 248*n*14
The Pictorial War Record **110**
Pierce, Lewis 10, 86, 104, 110, 114–116, 150, 156, 163, 209–210
Police Court (Detroit) **24**, 25, 161, 174, 192, 198
Pontiac (Michigan) 33, 35
"Potomac" 224
Prentice, George 25
Preston Union School 185
Prusher, Catherine 164, 176–177, 207–208, 251*n*3

Quinby, William E. 28

Randolph Street (Detroit) 22, 91, 97, **121**, 129
Rankin, John 153
Recorder's Court (Detroit) 6, 46, 62, 191, 214–216, 219
Republican (Grand Old) Party 27, 137, 144, 170–171
Reuben, Ray 232

Index

Reynolds, Sarah 10, 104, 106–107
Reynolds, Whitney 10, 86, 93, 103, 116–118, 148, 175, 178, 221; cooper shop 103–100, *110*, 121, 128–129, 150, 162–163, 178, 180, 185, 222; residence 103–110, *110*, 112, 113, 115, *121*, 128–129, 133, 183, 208, 210
Richardson, Col. John H. 124
"The Riot" (poem by Benjamin Cutler Clark, Sr.) 15, 61, 75, 95, 102, 113, 127, 145, 150, 160, 167, 171, 176, 189, 204, 225–227
Rivard Street (Detroit) 37, 94, 123, 129
Roberts, Charles 114
Robinson, Capt. Erastus D. 95–96, 101, 157
Robinson, James 10, 161, 163–164
Romney, George (Michigan governor) 218
Rose, Mary 229, 231–232
Ross, Robert Budd 48
Rush, Henry 23
Russell House 100, 152
Russell Street (Detroit) 193

St. Antoine Street (Detroit) 23, 25, 39, 53, 93, 115–116, 118, 119, *121*, 123, 128, 129, 130, 192
St. Aubin Street (Detroit) 20
St. Louis (Missouri) 18
St. Mary's Canal 21
St. Mary's Church 198
St. Mary's Hospital 115, 150, 155, 157
Santayana, George 236
Schaaf, Catherine 69
Schaaf, John 67–69, 76, 241n15
Schaaf, Margaret 69
Scopes, John 217
Scott, Joseph V. 152
Scott Guard 124
Scripps, James E. 26, 238n16
2nd Baptist Church (Detroit) 200
Second Battle of Bull Run 1
2nd Michigan Infantry 153
Second Ward (Detroit) 22, 124
Seventh Ward (Detroit) 19, 20, 37, 80
Shaw, William 154
Shelby Street (Detroit) 129
Shepard, Mary 25, 192–194
Shermerhorn, James 28
Shiler, Gilbert 103
Shiloh, battle of 1
Siegle, Elizabeth 199
Singleton, Benjamin 119, *121*, 177–178, 210, 246n15
"Sixteen String Jack" 40
Sixth Ward (Detroit) 19, 44, 124
Skean, Edward 161, 163–164
Skillman, Margaret 179

Skillman, Thomas 163, 179
Sleaker, Louis 115
Sleker, Cyrus 10, 104–105, 161, 163–164
Smith, Ada 105, 178, 180
Smith, Dr. John C. 154
Smith, Lt. Col. Joseph Rowe (J.R.) 95–96, 100–101
Smith, Mary 67–68
Smith, Peter 10, 161–162, 164
South Carolina 106
Sprege, August 163, 210
Springfield [Massachusetts] *Republican* 175
Stadler, Chris 140
Stadler, John 140
Stadt Theater (Detroit) 199
Starkweather, John 51
State Reform School (Lansing, Michigan) 185
Steamboat Hotel 16
Stevens, Nellie 229
Steward, Eliza 134
Stewart, Dr. Morse 116, 150, 156
Stoll, Julius Justice 198
Sullivan, Dennis K. 9, 36, 37, 63, 72, 85, 93, 96, 102, 141, 158–159, 162, 164–166, 177, 179, 182–184, 191–192, 194, 204, 214, 219, 223; actions during riot 106, 109–111, 114–115, 120, *121*, 124, 130–131, 148; inquest into the cause of death of Joshua Boyd 155–156; "Milwaukee Exchange" raid 50–5
Sullivan, William 162
Swan, J.G. 147
Sweet, Henry 217
Sweet, Dr. Ossian 217–218

Taber, Augustus. B. 148; *see also* Biddle House
Taber, Job 148; *see also* Biddle House
"Tax Payer" 206
Taylor, C.H. 28
Tenth Ward (Detroit) 19, 20, 21, 82
Thayer, Lansing 109, 114
Thede, Christine 25, 31, 50, 191–192
Third Ward (Detroit) 19, 21–23, 53, 56, 57, 62, 75, 80, 85, 93, 96, 100, 104, 111, 118, *121*, 123, 124, 130, 132, 133, 140, 144, 146, 161, 163, 169, 189, 191, 194, 204, 206–209, 219, 221
Thomas, Arneta 203
Thompson Street (Detroit) 86
A Thrilling Narrative 4, 61, 98, 104, 108, 111–112, 119, 170–171, 225, 233
Timm, William 99, 151
Tippecanoe, battle of 106

Index

Tisler, Elizabeth "Lizzy" 67–68
Tisler, John 68
Toronto, Ontario (Canada) 17
Turner, William 20
27th Michigan Volunteer Infantry 93, 124, 140, 146

Underground Railroad 18, 21
Utley, Henry Munson 28, 64, 113, 200, 212–213, 215, 224

Van Stan, John 9, 20, 36, 91, 93, 96–100, 139, 221; shooting of Charles Langer 151–155, 157
Venn, John 162
VINDEX 168–169
Virginia 146, 155, 170, 172
Vitiger, Mary Ann 33

Walker, Edward C. 27, 133–134, 136, 139, 167–168
Walker, Hiram 27–28
Walker, Mary 32
War of 1812 106
Ward, Eber B. 27
Ward, Philip 74
Warren, the Rev. John A. 148
Warmsley, Robert 99, 151–152
Washington, Martin 52–53, 56, 57, 231
Washington, Mary 53, 57, 231

Wayne County (Michigan) Circuit Court 47
Wayne County (Michigan) Jail 22, *23*, 24, 87, 161, 182
Wayne Street (Detroit) *133*
Weaver, J.D. 179–180
Whiting, George L. 123
Whitney 74
Williams, Austin 57
Williams, Mary L. 86
Wilson, Frederick 103, 118, *121*
Wilson, John M. (Wayne County, Michigan, sheriff) 16–17
Wilson, Samuel 100, 151
Windsor, Ontario (Canada) 18, 35, 52, 143, 253n1
Wineman, Henry 69, 76, 212
Witherell, Benjamin Franklin Hawkins 2, 7, 9, 11, 12, 47, 49, 76, 78, 84, 86–89, 176–177, 180, 191, 201–203, 214, 219, 220
Witherell, Cassandra 47, 220
Woodmere Cemetery (Detroit) 203, 221
Woods, Kate "Pussy" 49–50
Woodward Avenue (Detroit) 37, 91, 93

Young, Fletcher 200
Ypsilanti (Michigan) 69, 184

Zion Baptist Church (Detroit) 203

www.ingramcontent.com/pod-product-compliance
Ingram Content Group UK Ltd.
Pitfield, Milton Keynes, MK11 3LW, UK
UKHW041931140426
5217IPUK00014B/422